**ideas and activities
for teachers and children**

creative
sciencing

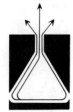 **ideas and activities for**

little, brown and company ◻ boston, toronto

creative sciencing

teachers and children

second edition

ALFRED DeVITO □ purdue university

GERALD H. KROCKOVER □ purdue university

COPYRIGHT © 1980 BY ALFRED DE VITO AND GERALD H. KROCKOVER

COPYRIGHT © 1976 BY SCOTT, FORESMAN AND COMPANY

LIBRARY OF CONGRESS CATALOG CARD NO. 79-89763

ISBN 0-673-39149-3

10

MV

PRINTED IN THE UNITED STATES OF AMERICA

Instructors using *Creative Sciencing* are encouraged to reproduce, for classroom use only, limited quantities of those pages bearing a copyright notice.

Creative Sciencing: Ideas and Activities for Teachers and Children, Second Edition, is a resource book for both preservice and in-service teachers. It is a valuable learning tool for the elementary science methods course, and it is a comprehensive source of ideas and activities for use in the elementary school classroom.

The organization of this book is based on several premises. One is that teachers want and need new, exciting science activities for their science programs. A variety of fresh, field-tested science ideas has been furnished. On pages *xiii–xvi* these activities are cross-referenced according to the processes of science and the content area covered. More importantly, each activity is written to evoke ideas from the reader, thus enabling each activity to serve as a springboard for further activities. This is the creative sciencing process.

Another premise is that teachers often have difficulty acquiring materials for successfully implementing science. The "Shoestring Sciencing" section of this book deals with doing more science for less money. Still another premise is that sciencing is action. Hence, a segment of this book, "Science Skills and Techniques," will help you master specific skills to do science in a safe, efficient manner. "Creative Science Recipes" includes useful recipes and projects that you can make with children.

Significant changes in the second edition include:

1. A thirty percent increase in the number of "Brainstorming in Science" (bis) activities.
2. An expansion of the "more" activities in the bis section.
3. Nearly doubling the number of "Shoestring Sciencing" (ss) activities from eighteen to thirty-four.
4. The addition of twenty "Creative Sciencing Recipes" (csr) following the "Science Skills and Techniques" (sst) section. These recipes feature simple, inexpensive ways to make clays, paints, gases, and other materials for the classroom.
5. The three appendixes have been updated and expanded. Appendix A is a table that classifies the bis activities according to related subjects such as reading, language arts, mathematics, social studies, art, and music. Appendix B presents a Celsius-Fahrenheit Conversion Table, a Metric System Table, and a Metric-Imperial Equivalents Table. Appendix C, Sources for More Ideas and Activities, has been expanded by forty percent to allow for newly published materials.
6. The alternative "Contents by Skills and Subject Area" has been retained and expanded.
7. An index of key words has also been developed, allowing easy access to the idea or activity desired.

Coupled with our companion text, *Creative Sciencing: A Practical Approach,* Second Edition, a complete methods course flexible enough to meet the needs of most science methods instructors is now available.

We would like to thank the more than sixty instructors of college and university elementary science methods who previously used our book and who, when surveyed, responded with helpful comments. We would also like to thank the three reviewers whose constructive comments also guided us: Dr. Lowell Bethel, University of Texas at Austin; Dr. Shirley Brehm, Michigan State University; and Dr. Aime W. Strawn, University of Illinois at Chicago Circle.

A special thank you goes to Barbara De Vito for typing the manuscript and to Sharon Krockover for proofreading the manuscript.

Alfred De Vito

Gerald H. Krockover

brainstorming
in science □ bis
page 1

A SNEAK PREVIEW   *page 2*

CONTENTS

shoestring
sciencing □ ss
page 233

MORE FOR LESS   *page 234*

science skills
and techniques □ sst
page 303

creative sciencing
recipes □ csr
page 341

This topical table of contents is designed to help you organize your science program around specific subjects and find ideas on how to reinforce general science skills your students need to practice. If you want to follow up on activities your students enjoyed, consult the list of related activities at the end of each activity in the text. These related activities may carry you from one subject area into another, but then science is open-ended!

science skills

subject areas

ideas and activities
for teachers and children

creative
sciencing

brainstorming in science □ bis

a sneak preview

Some of the hundred sciencing activities in this section are confined to science. Many transgress into other areas: social studies, mathematics, reading, language arts, art, and music, which can encourage students to utilize science as a part of life as a whole, not a separate entity.

Each investigation is introduced as a unit independent of the others. When the material warrants precautions because of the age of the children involved, they are included as a

warning

Very few activities in science apply specifically to only one grade level. You must tailor the science investigation to your needs and the children's. A good example is the time-honored one called "Why does a burning candle go out?" This could be used as a first-grade problem or it could be restructured into a suitable third, fifth, eighth, twelfth, or college-level investigation. What separates these instructional levels? In a first-grade class the teacher ignites the candle, puts a glass jar over it, and waits. The children describe their observations. They may make several inferences. They may even propose tentative explanations. If you were instructing this activity at a higher level you would probably need to extend it. How does one extend an activity? That is what brainstorming is all about.

First, think of as many ways of manipulating the material on hand as you can. You have a candle, a match, a glass jar, some available air, and a surface on which the glass jar rests. Which variable could be changed? You could change the candle. How many kinds of candles do you have? There are birthday candles, food-warmer candles, short fat candles, tall skinny candles, colored candles, and many other types. Do all burn alike when placed under the glass jar? What do candles contain? They are made of wicks and wax, and have definite shapes. Do any of these properties give you ideas for carrying the activity forward? What about the glass jar? Does its volume and corresponding shape give you a clue for extending the activity? Exchange this container with one that has the same volume but a different shape. Does this change the candle's burning time? Does it change any other observations? Would changing the match lead you anywhere?

When brainstorming, don't cast out any idea as foolish until you have had a chance to examine it. Brainstorming can produce a gentle trickle of ideas or an avalanche. Accept it either way; an idea is an idea. If you don't like it, you can always discard it later, but for the moment keep it. Who knows, it may germinate and flower into a useful idea.

When you are brainstorming along, what could you do to involve students and extend the lesson even further? Brainstorming is a self-quizzing procedure. It invites you to ask many questions:

What if you used jars of three sizes, each doubling the volume of the next smaller one? What kind of a time record would you get? Could you infer this? Try it!

What if you changed the seal? The glass jar resting on the counter surface may be an ineffective seal, leaking gases in and out. Try another substance, such as grease or Vaseline, as a surface seal between the jar and the counter. Does this change your observations?

What if you used water as a seal? Water, like air, is mobile. Place the candle in the bottom of a basin. Add water to the basin. The water should be about 1 cm deep. Will this provide new observations? Try it. This approach should open all kinds of new vistas.

What do you know about the air in the glass? You know it contains a gas that supports combustion. When the candle goes out, does it mean that all the gas to support combustion is used up? The candle gives off something as it burns, a gas called carbon dioxide. It will not support combustion and it is a heavier gas than the one supporting combustion (oxygen). Does the candle go out because it has used up all the combustible gas or is it drowning in its own carbon dioxide? How can you gather information to support or refute this idea? Would elevating the candle provide useful information? You could use three jars and three candles, each object the same size. Position the three candles (a soda straw anchored in clay with a birthday candle on top will do). Put one at the lowest level in a jar; one at the midpoint height in the second jar; and one near the top of the third jar. Which candle do you predict will burn the shortest time? The longest? Or, do you think they will all go out at the same time? Try it.

What if you placed all three candles in one large jar but set them at three elevations? Which would go out first, second, and last? Or, would they all go out at once? Again, try it.

What if you covered a burning candle with an opaque container? What evidence could you use to find out if and when the candle went out?

Most science activities can quickly be tailored for greater challenge by insisting on more rigor in the observing and quantifying that evolve from the activity. The amount of difficulty in the questions you ask is also important. Specific pieces of equipment and the mathematical, language, and reading requirements that you impose on a learning situation can move a lesson from simplicity into sophistication. A ball rolling down an inclined plane may be a third-grade observation activity. But introducing thermometers, timers, balances, protractors, and metric rulers where appropriate, requiring different degrees of accuracy, and appropriate reading and language arts activities to go with it, can make this into a very challenging activity that can be used with older students.

There really is no end to the scope and directions in which creative sciencing can lead you, if you are curious and willing to engage yourself and your students in this kind of thinking. This great range of applications makes it unnecessary to provide performance objectives and stated grade levels for individual activities in this book. You make the decisions about who, what, when, where, and how to teach. From these decisions, you alone put together the why.

observing—the first
stepping stone in science

Have you observed yourself lately? Without further observations, how many of these questions can you answer?

Do you know if your eyes are above, below, or in line with your ears?

Do you know if your toenails grow faster than your fingernails?

When you fold your hands, interlocking your fingers, do you know which thumb of which hand ends up on top? Is it always the same one?

Do all your fingers have the same number of bones?

When you wrinkle your brow, how many major horizontal lines are formed?

What proportion of your overall body length is your head length?

Without looking, could you reproduce the basic line pattern of your left (or right) palm?

Are the shapes of your earlobes alike?

Do the moons on your fingernails match the moons on your toenails?

Which protrudes farther, your bottom lip or your top lip?

How well did you score? If you got better than five out of ten, you did extremely well.

Why do we see all those parts of our bodies without remembering them? Many people see but not all are good observers. Observing is using several or all of the senses — sight, touch, hearing, taste, and smell. When you observe, you look for the characteristics that make something what it is — its properties. Remember also that observations should include a reference to some standard unit of size, weight, temperature, or the like if one is applicable. Make your observations quantitative. "Short," "tall," "heavy," or "light" are meaningless or at least useless compared to observations that specify "ninety-six cm tall" or "a mass of four g."

You can extend this unit by observing objects common to the children. Select any one of the objects and assemble a set of questions that challenge the students to observe.

Adapted from Alfred De Vito, "Observing," *Science Activities,* vol. 8, no. 1 (September 1972), pp. 24–25. By permission.

How many finger recesses has a telephone dial? What letters appear in the first recess? Or, on which finger recess is the letter Q?

What are the properties of a Ping-Pong ball, a penny, a mealworm, a pool of water, a burning match, a parakeet?

Related activities include bis 13–17, 21, 28, 32, 81, 91, 120; and ss 12.

☐

the tumbler garden has it all

Science activities can be one-idea, one-shot propositions. Not so with the tumbler garden; it can go on forever. It doesn't necessarily have to, but it could. It is a good science activity because it runs the gamut from observation through experimentation. It is timely in that it can be a short-run study of seeds imbibing and roots growing, or it can extend to a study of how light, heat, color, moisture, soil variations, nutrients, air, and sound affect plants. Some tumbler-garden plants will reach maturity, flower, bear seeds, and even reproduce. The tumbler garden seems to have it all.

You'll need drinking glasses (baby food jars work well). Any jar that has straight, not tapered, sides will do. You will need seeds, paper toweling, and water. A Magic Marker is helpful in marking the exterior of the glass with the type of seeds used, date, and experimenter's name. The seed choice depends a lot on the grade level you are working with. Remember that

some seeds are poisonous

and children should be cautioned against eating or tasting them. The younger the child, the more impatient he or she will be. Children want instant growth. They want to plant today and rush in tomorrow to see a six-foot plant. For them, mung beans work well. They won't be six feet tall, but they'll show growth. Corn takes longer to germinate. Lima beans are always good, and the size of the seed allows for a noticeable root system.

Wash the bottles or tumblers thoroughly. Dry them. To plant the tumbler garden, take a paper towel and roll it into a cylinder. Place it in the tumbler so that it hugs the walls. A tapered tumbler does not work as well because the cylinder cannot hug the container's walls. If you are using a vertical-walled drinking glass your problems are minimal, but finding twenty or thirty drinking glasses can be a problem. Mayonnaise jars or baby food jars are easier to get, though those too are not perfect. The mouths are smaller than the bases, keeping the paper cylinder from hugging the sides of the bottle. Resolve this problem by shortening the cylinder so that its height is below the point where the bottle begins to constrict.

With the cylinder in place, stuff cotton (or crumpled paper toweling) inside the paper cylinder to force it against the wall of the container. The cotton will retain moisture for the seeds and later the plant.

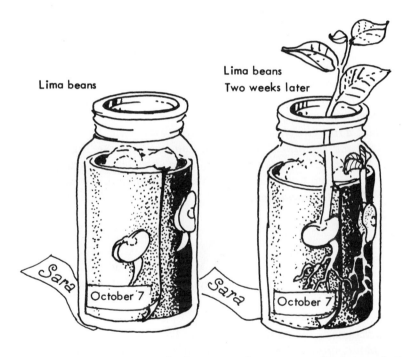

Lima beans

Lima beans
Two weeks later

Sara
October 7

Sara
October 7

Now, insert your seeds between the paper cylinder and the glass. This will let you observe the growth of the seeds. Water the cotton and paper towel, but not so much that you can see the water. Water as needed.

Activities before planting the tumbler garden:

Observe the seeds. How are they alike? Unlike? Measure the seeds. What is their mass and volume, and what are their overall dimensions?

Devise a system for classifying the seeds: color, size, shape, weight. Infer which seeds will grow best.

Infer which seeds will grow tallest. Does the largest seed of a variety always grow to be the tallest plant?

Where is the best location for a seed inside the tumbler? Should it be on the bottom? Halfway up? Near the top? Or buried in the middle of the cotton?

Is there a right or wrong position in which to plant a seed?

What are the advantages of planting all one variety of seed instead of a broad variety in one tumbler jar?

Where should you place the tumbler garden after planting the seeds? In darkness? Shade? Sunlight?

How will temperature affect the growth? How will humidity affect the growth? How will air currents affect growth?

Will the seeds grow better if you put them in sawdust, coffee grounds, or vermiculite instead of cotton?

After planting, try these procedures:

Record the date and the amount of water when watering the tumbler garden. Record the temperature daily.

Measure the amount of light in the area of the tumbler garden. Use a light meter. Measure growth in various parts of the plant over specific periods of time.

Collect data. Graph your results. One axis could be "amount of water" and the other "height," or you could choose "light" versus "height." Or, make a bar graph to show which varieties grow tallest when light, water, and time are constant. Compare your graph with graphs made by other students involved in similar activities.

more...

Which part of the leaf grows most?
Which part of the plant's stem grows fastest?
Do plants grow better under lights of one color or another?
How do plants react to rotation during their growth?
What does mold growing on seeds do to the plant's growth?
How can you keep mold from growing on the seeds? Try using a bleach solution to wash the seeds before planting, but

observe the precautions on the label!

Do plants react to human emotions? Or music? Do plants have feelings?

more...

Find out how deep seeds should be planted by filling a large glass with about one inch of soil. Pack the soil down and then place a few seeds next to the glass wall on the inside. Use large seeds such as garden beans or peas. When planting seeds, consider the size of the container: if all seeds took root and grew, would they choke each other and die? Don't overplant.

Place one more inch of soil in the glass and pack it down. Plant a few more seeds next to the glass. Repeat until you have three distinct layers of seeds and soil. Moisten the soil with water and place the glass in a warm, dark location. Which layer of seeds sprouted the best?

Wet a big sponge and squeeze out most of the moisture. Sprinkle it with rye, clover, cress, or mustard seeds. Pierce the sponge with a nail attached to a string, and hang the sponge in a sunny window. Keep the sponge moist and watch the sponge green up!

Place a piece of wood about 3 inches long and ¾ inch across in a flowerpot and plant a seedling such as a young marigold about a ½ inch above it. Place the wood in firmly so that it will make a barrier as the roots go down. After a few days, brush aside enough soil so that you can observe the roots beginning to find their way around the wood. Replace the soil and check again in a few more days.

Fill a small bottle or plastic vial with pea or bean seeds. Fill the bottle with water. Stopper the bottle with a cork or piece of plastic held by a rubber band. As the seeds begin to swell, observe what happens after 6 to 8 hours.

Do roots orient themselves and grow downward? Fill a baby food jar or some other container with wet cotton. Slip some lima or kidney bean seeds between the cotton and the sides of the jar. After a few days you can observe the roots growing downward from the bean. Cap the jar with a stiff piece of cardboard. Invert the jar. In a few days, again observe the seed roots. What happened to them? This action is called *geotropism*. The force of the earth's gravity attracts the roots downward.

In addition to geotropism, plants also respond to the location of water, and this response can be in conflict with geotropism. Plant some lima or kidney bean seeds in a large, shallow tin filled with sawdust in the center of which a porous pot of water is sunk. The plant's roots will grow in the direction of the water seepage from the pot. This root movement toward water is called *hydro-tropism*.

Related activities include bis 26, 31, 55, 111, 115; ss 12; sst 10 and 12.

□

mimicry, or kopy kat

An unfortunate hobo trying hard to go unnoticed would not wear his normal regalia attending the opening night at the opera. He would be too obvious. Some animals, by their shape, construction, or the color of their bodies, can avoid being conspicuous providing they stay in their special environment. This outward likeness of an animal to parts of plants is called *mimicry*. *Diapheromera femorata*, commonly called walking stick, is a prime example.

Rearing insects to portray this characteristic may not always be feasible. Good activities to introduce mimicry, strengthen powers of observation, and apply some quantification skills are possible, nevertheless. Try these.

Purchase several boxes of inexpensive toothpicks. Keep one box of toothpicks in their natural color. Color with spray paint or soak in food coloring another box of toothpicks. A green or deep brown color should do fine. Let them dry. Count out the natural and colored toothpicks into bundles of 50 or 100. Divide the class in half (or involve another class). Send one group out to select several equal-sized plots of grass-covered ground. The plots should be uniform, something like 6 meters by 6 meters. Provide the group with one bundle of colored toothpicks plus a bundle of the natural-colored toothpicks. Have the students scatter them over the selected area. Have the second group collect as many of the different colored toothpicks as they can find. Record and plot this information on a graph using "number" for one axis and "color" for the other. Compare the results over several trials. Repeat this activity using bare ground. Compare the number of each color collected with the initial collection. How do the two totals compare? Does the color of the background affect which toothpicks are found easily?

This can also be done with uniform buttons or with buttons of mixed colors. What other objects could you use to get across the idea of mimicry?

Using a hole punch and paper of different colors, punch out ten small discs of each color. Stick a pin through each. When most of the students are out of the room, have the few remaining position these small pinned discs about the room in plain sight, protected by a background color. When the students return, have them find as many of the colored discs as they can. Keep a tally. Which were the hardest to find? The easiest?

more...

If you want to hide a cut, unmounted diamond, using your knowledge of mimicry, where would you hide it? Are there any dangers in this procedure?

Why would an animal want to be conspicuous? A plant? You?

What about such changes as light (day to night), seasons (summer and winter), and weather (wet and dry)? How might these conditions affect animals who mimic their environment?

Bring a chameleon to class. Show how changing its environment affects its color.

Prepare a terrarium with toads and insects. See how these animals blend with their surroundings. Change the color of the light entering the terrarium. What effect, if any, does this have?

Related activities include bis 12 and 32.

☐

growing crystals

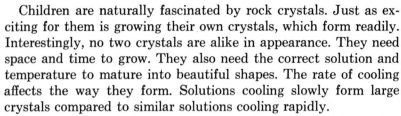

Children are naturally fascinated by rock crystals. Just as exciting for them is growing their own crystals, which form readily. Interestingly, no two crystals are alike in appearance. They need space and time to grow. They also need the correct solution and temperature to mature into beautiful shapes. The rate of cooling affects the way they form. Solutions cooling slowly form large crystals compared to similar solutions cooling rapidly.

Fill a glass jar with hot water. Add salt as long as it keeps dissolving. Have a piece of cardboard ready with a piece of string hanging from it. The string may be threaded through holes punched in the middle of the cardboard. Make the string just long enough to reach the bottom of the jar. Weight its end by tying to it a small piece of metal, a bolt, screw, or nail. Drop the string into the hot solution. Cover the jar with the cardboard and put the jar in a quiet, warm place where it can cool slowly. Observe the salt solution each day for several days. What do you observe? Compare your observations from day to day.

Boil 3/4 cup of water in a clean pan. While the water is boiling gently, stir in granulated sugar, little by little, until no more will dissolve. That will probably take about two cups of sugar. Pour the hot solution into a glass tumbler. Put a silver spoon in the tumbler while you pour the liquid and it will absorb enough heat to keep the glass from cracking. Remove the spoon. While the solution is still hot, lay across the tumbler a pencil to which you have tied a piece of clean cotton string. Again, weight the bottom of the string with a small, clean metal object. Hang the string in the solution. Set the tumbler in a quiet, warm place. The solution should form crystals that are commonly called rock candy. How do these sugar observations compare with those on your salt activity?

Dissolve about an ounce of table salt in a half pint of boiling water. Pour the solution into a shallow plate. Place a string in the solution and over the edge of the dish. Allow the solution to evaporate slowly for a day or two and then with a magnifying glass you can see the crystals of salt in the dish and along the string. How do these crystals differ from the ones formed in the two previous activities?

How has the rate of cooling affected the crystal growth?
How does limiting the space for formation affect the crystal growth?
How does the concentration of these materials in solution affect the size, shape, and other characteristics of the crystals?

How does altering the temperature of the solution affect the crystal growth?

more...

Try growing alum crystals, cobalt chloride crystals, sodium carbonate crystals. Construct three-dimensional cardboard models of your crystals (See sst 13).

Bring samples of crystals to class. Do they all look alike? How are they alike? How are they different?

Diamonds may be a girl's best friend, but are diamonds crystals? Although they may be found as crystals in nature, they are usually faceted ("cut") to show off their beauty.

Examine a mothball. Describe your observations.

Related activities include bis 26; ss 1, 6, 14; and sst 13.

many happy returns

Used greeting cards are excellent sources of ideas for observing and writing motivational activities for children. Children can use the printed messages as a beginning for a poetry activity.

Using the card on page 15, prepare verse to go with the card cover.

Next, using some of these opening lines, make up some card designs and verses of your own:

ON THIS SPECIAL DAY

THOUGHTS OF YOU

A SPEEDY RECOVERY

start collecting old greeting cards!

You will have many happy returns after you try this creative sciencing activity in your classroom.

Try everyday products and the commercials that go with them. Can you write new commercials?

Related activities include bis 6, 28, 33, 63, and 127.

returns happy many (in reverse)

Design a greeting card to go with the verse opposite. Use your creativity and imagination to the fullest.

or try this one —

It is so nice to know
someone as special as you —
Wishing you much happiness
may your wishes come true

or this one —

My greetings convey
to you today
All my friendship
warm and true
to let you know
I'm thinking of you!

or this one —

I'm bringing you a get-well wish
and may it come true
then very soon you will be
just as good as new!

Related activities include bis 5, 28, 33, 64, and 127.

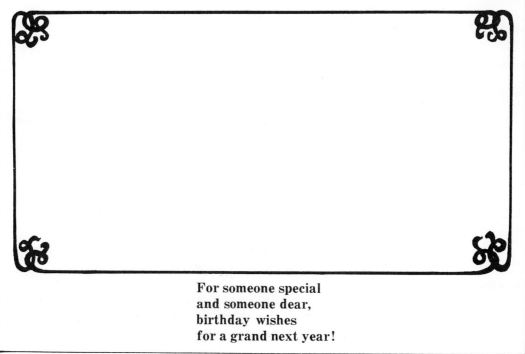

For someone special
and someone dear,
birthday wishes
for a grand next year!

temperature variations
and brine shrimp

Brine shrimp eggs are easily obtainable in powdered form at most pet stores or pet supply houses. Follow directions on the containers to be sure the eggs will hatch.

Students may want to explore the conditions necessary for successful shrimp hatching, including these variables:

1. Light
2. Amount of water
3. Salinity of the water
4. Type of salt (iodized table salt, noniodized table salt, rock salt used in water conditioning, kosher salt)
5. Amount of oxygen supplied (you could use a fish-tank bubbler and record the time left in the water)
6. Temperature of the water.

Once the eggs have hatched, these six variables could also be investigated first with the baby and then with the adult shrimp.

The temperature variable is easy to investigate. The following experiment, conducted in a fifth-grade class, could serve as a model.

Dry egg

Egg in
salt solution

First larval
form

Second larval form

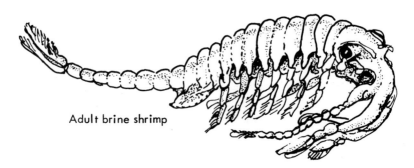

Adult brine shrimp

*Children found that brine shrimp were living and functioning
well at 24° Celsius. They put five shrimp into eight containers
of water, half of them at temperatures higher than that of the
original container (24° C), and half at lower temperatures.
The shrimp were observed at 0, 2, 5, 15, 27, 36, 45, and 47
degrees Celsius. At 47° C the shrimp died, but at zero (a decrease
in temperature comparable to the maximum increase), the shrimp
lived!*

*What inferences could you make from the reported results
of the experiment?*

The children in this experiment recorded the activity observed,
the appearance of the shrimp, the temperature, and whether or
not the animals survived.

Other questions that children may want to investigate:

What do brine shrimp eat?
What eats these shrimp?
*Do the shrimp react to light in the same way as they react to
changing temperatures?*
Do brine shrimp react to sound?

more...

*Vary the amount of salinity (the concentration of salt) in
the hatching tanks. Do all the eggs hatch? Do all the shrimp
survive? Why does an elevated temperature or a drastic increase
(or decrease) in salinity have harmful effects on the shrimp?*

*Are people affected by high temperatures? By lack of fresh
water? Which of the following can be considered least vital for
sustaining people in an artificial environment like that in a
spacecraft: temperature, light, water, food, oxygen?*

*With the knowledge you have gained from your experiment
with temperature variations and excess salinity in the brine
shrimp water, tell how changing an animal's environment can
affect it. Can changing conditions ever help an animal? Give some
examples.*

Related activities include bis 12 and 31.

□

the dissolving contest

Any commercial hard candy such as Lifesavers will do. Pass one candy to each student. On the signal from you, all put the candy in their mouths. Advise them to use only a whole one, not to chew it, and to record or signal when they have thoroughly dissolved the candy. Signal the start of the dissolving contest. Record the individual dissolving times, and have the class collect all the relevant data. Who won? Who placed second? And third? Who took longest? What was the average dissolving time? What was the range? Do girls dissolve the candy faster than boys? What factors influence the rate of dissolving?

Drop a candy into a glass of water. What affects the rate of dissolving? Can you relate the components of this activity to components of the dissolving contest? This analogy can be interesting. What part of the human body compares with the glass? What serves the same purpose as the water? Is temperature involved in both instances? Can motion affect the rate of dissolving? What human factors, which might either hasten or delay the rate of dissolving, would not be present in the glass of water activity?

In how many ways can you make a candy dissolve faster? Try temperature, stirring, exposed surface area, or the liquid used. The rate of dissolving is affected by many things. One important consideration is the exposed surface area. Compare the rate of dissolving to the time it takes for two halves to dissolve; four quarters; eight eighths; pulverized. What do you observe? Record the data and graph your results.

How would a flavored candy or one with another color affect your results? Try it!

more...

How many household items can you name that will dissolve? In separate glasses of water —

not in your mouth!

put an aspirin, a teaspoonful of soap powder, and a tablespoonful of salt. What else will dissolve? Try some pennies, a shoestring, or a handful of leaves. How long do you think it would take for these to dissolve? Can you think how you might get them to dissolve faster? Why don't you dissolve when you take a bath?

Does an ice cube dissolve or melt in a glass of water? In the air (on a plate, of course!)? Is there a difference between melting and dissolving? Can things dissolve in air?

Can you dissolve as much salt or sugar in a glass of water as you want to? What are the limits for each?

Compare the formulation of crystals with the process of dissolving.

Related activities include bis 42, 47, 71, and 93.

□

bubble trouble

Get a bubble-blowing solution and a bubble blower. Better yet, make your own solution from liquid soap (or synthetic detergent) and water, and use a soda straw as your bubble blower. Caution: make sure you blow *out* through the straw —

do not suck in!

Find out who can blow the smallest bubbles, the biggest bubbles, the most bubbles, the fewest bubbles. What observations can you make about the winner in each category? What techniques did he or she use to win?

Can you blow more bubbles with warm water than cold water?
Does the length of the straw or size of the opening make a difference?
Can you describe the shape of a bubble?
Does the type of soap make a difference?
Can you blow a square bubble?
Can you devise a way to blow bubbles within bubbles?
Can you devise a way to blow a composite bubble (that is, a bubble attached to another bubble)?
What do you observe when you look through a bubble at an object?

more...

Does the surface of the bubble move? If you prick a bubble with a pencil, what will happen? Can you hold a bubble in your hand? Do bubbles float? Why do bubbles fall to the ground? Are balloons bubbles? Can you make a bubble with bubble gum? What do you need to make bubbles? How many kinds of bubbles can you think of? Are eggs bubbles? Is a ball of ice cream a bubble? What about a soccer ball? A football? Have you ever blown bubbles under water? Can you blow out a candle with a bubble? Try it!

more...

Try changing your bubble solution. While two caps of dish-washing liquid in a glass of cold water work well, a bit more soap can improve the bubbles. Also, adding a teaspoon of sugar or glycerine can achieve some interesting results. Try it! Try using rainwater instead of tap water. With these new mixtures, use some new, creative bubble wands. Try a funnel. Try a wire loop. Or, try a soda straw which has one end split and folded back. It doesn't look great, but what a bubble maker!

Related activities include bis 27, 34, 59, and 107.

classifying with cookie bars

Obtain these ingredients:

1 box graham cracker crumbs
1 box white granulated sugar
1 3½ oz can coconut
1 pound butter or margarine
1 6 oz pkg unsweetened chocolate
  chips
1 6 oz pkg sweetened chocolate
  chips

1 6 oz pkg butterscotch chips
1 4 oz pkg slivered almonds
1 4 oz pkg walnuts
1 can sweetened condensed
  milk
1 9 x 13 inch pan
1 mixing bowl and spoon

Have the children observe the foods that have been purchased to make the cookie bars, using *all* their senses.

To make 54 cookie bars, use this recipe:

1½ cups graham cracker crumbs
1 stick butter or margarine
  (½ cup)
1 cup chocolate chips
  (½ sweetened and ½
  unsweetened)

1 cup butterscotch chips
3 tablespoons sugar
½ cup slivered almonds
½ cup walnuts
1⅓ cup coconut
1 can sweetened condensed milk

Directions

Melt the butter in the 9 x 13 inch pan. Mix the graham cracker crumbs and sugar in a bowl and then mix with melted butter. Pat firmly into bottom of pan. Sprinkle chocolate and butterscotch chips over this, then add the almonds, walnuts, and coconut. Pour one can of sweetened condensed milk over the top. Bake at 350°F for 25 minutes or until lightly browned around edges. When cool, cut into 1 x 2 inch bars. You should have 54 pieces.

don't eat the cookie bars yet!

Which original ingredients can be identified and classified in the cookie bar? Did you say that the graham cracker crumbs, sweet chocolate chips, unsweetened chocolate chips, butterscotch chips, slivered almonds, walnuts, and coconut could be identified and classified? Did you say that the sugar, butter, and condensed milk could not be identified and classified?

You can compare the taste of the combined ingredients with the taste of any ingredient by itself. Do they taste alike?

now you can eat the cookie bars!

more...

For additional activities in classification you might want to try other recipes and publish a Classification Cookbook. Other foods that are excellent for classifying activities include party mix, cereals, Granola, chocolate "samplers," raisin bread, fruit cake, bean salads, fruit salads, and canned or frozen mixed vegetables and fruit cocktail.

Related activities include bis 21, 106; ss 2 and 15.

the case of the
burning cheese puff

The words *heat* and *temperature* are often confusingly used interchangeably and incorrectly. Temperature is a measure of how hot or how cold an object is and it is measured in degrees Fahrenheit or Celsius. Heat, on the other hand, is a measure of what makes objects get hot and is measured in calories. These calories are similar to, but not exactly the same as, the calories you count when you're on a diet.

Try this experiment:

Obtain a bag of cheese puffs. Randomly select several samples from the bag.

Determine the mass of those cheese puffs. (Don't forget the units, such as grams.)

Obtain a small metal juice can (like a frozen orange juice can) and pour a measured amount (in milliliters) of water into it.

Record the initial temperature of the water in degrees Celsius.

Place three cheese puffs under the juice can of water, which is positioned on a wire square on a ring stand. Hold the cheese puffs in place with a bent paper clip stuck in a ball of clay for support. Strike a kitchen match and light the cheese puffs.

be careful not to burn yourself!

After the cheese puffs have burned completely, record the final temperature of the heated water.

Subtract the initial temperature from the final temperature; this is the temperature change.

The volume of water (in ml) times the temperature change (in degrees Celsius) is the number of calories of heat provided by the cheese puffs to heat the water. Now you can calculate the number of calories of heat given off by the cheese puffs to heat the water.

If you want to manipulate the units for this problem you need to know that the density of water is 1 gram per milliliter and the heat capacity of water is 1 calorie per gram degree. Figure out how your units cancel so that you end up with an answer in calories.

Check your final answer with a friend who has tried this investigation. Are your answers the same? Why or why not? What variables can you list that would account for any differences?

If you want to change your answer to kilocalories (diet calories) you will need to know that it takes 1000 calories (c) to make 1 kilocalorie (C). How many kilocalories of heat were given off by the burning cheese puffs?

Try substituting a burning peanut or marshmallow for the cheese puff.

Burn a cube of sugar (one teaspoonful) and determine how many kilocalories of heat were given off. Compare your figure (the mathematical one — not your waist) to the one in a diet book.

Using the Calorie chart in the diet book, add up how many kilocalories you consume in a day and in a week. How does your body use up the Calories you swallow? Why do people who get plenty of exercise stay thin?

Related activities include bis 7 and 47.

☐

pill-bug pedways, or isopod ideas

Next time you lift up that rock or observe all those little bugs scurrying across the sidewalk at night, collect them for creative sciencing activities. They're called pill bugs or sow bugs or isopods, and when disturbed (an inference) they curl up into a little ball or "pill."

Pill bugs can be used for:

1. Pill-bug observations.
2. Measuring pill bugs. How large is the largest? The smallest? Is the largest pill bug the oldest; is the smallest the youngest?
3. Experimenting with pill bugs. Do pill bugs prefer high or low temperatures? Do pill bugs prefer light or dark areas? Can pill bugs see? What do pill bugs like to eat? Can pill bugs swim? Can pill bugs differentiate between colors? Will a pill bug move backward; sideways? Can pill bugs hear? Can pill bugs smell? What do pill bugs prefer to eat? How do pill bugs communicate?

A good alternative to the pill bug is the mealworm, which will also work well and may be obtained in most pet stores. Earthworms work well too.

Related activities include bis 3, 7, and 18.

□

sensing your environment
by seeing

You will need an overhead projector or any similar light source, a clear glass mixing bowl with water, and blue, red, and yellow food coloring.

Place the bowl with water on the projector and swirl the water around a few times so that it is moving slightly. Add one or two drops of blue food coloring. What do you observe?

While the water is still slowly swirling, put a few drops of yellow near one side of the bowl and a few drops of red near the other side. What observations can you make now?

If the water stops moving, use the tip of a pen or pencil, barely breaking the water surface, to start new patterns and designs.

Try to predict what will happen if colors are added in a different sequence, such as beginning with red and then adding blue or yellow. Do you get the same results?

more...

As an appraisal, have the students illustrate poems that deal with color and seeing.

Related activities include bis 1, 14–17, and 81.

□

sensing your environment
by touching

Make a touch book out of laminated poster board and ring binders. To each page attach an object for the children to touch. Have a grease pencil at hand for writing on the laminated surface.

Have the children touch each object in the touch book and record below it a touch word, such as *hard*, *soft*, or *rough*, which

describes the object. Discover how many words can be used to indicate how an object feels by touching!

Where applicable, ask the children to try to describe their observations comparatively and then quantitatively. *How* hard? *How* rough?

Then have each child make his or her own touch book, using 5 x 8 inch index cards.

Related activities include bis 1, 13, 15–17, and 81.

□

sensing your environment
by smelling

Prepare five smelling containers, using any type of opaque container. Place five different objects, such as garlic, nutmeg, apple, coffee, and pepper, in each container and cover with cheesecloth.

Have children smell the containers and describe the smells coming from them. Let them guess what is in the container.

When you select your smells, try to include some objects with similar smells and some with dissimilar smells. Also, caution children about smelling everything in sight.

*things like ammonia and household lye
are extremely dangerous if inhaled!*

more...

Can you identify locations in your home or in the school by smelling? Try it!

Related activities include bis 1, 13, 14, 16, 17, 28, and 81.

□

sensing your environment
by tasting

Give every child a quarter of a piece of bread and ask the group to tell how we can make it taste sweet. Try their suggestions, such as adding sugar.

How can we make it salty? Sour or bitter (use lemon juice)?

Collect a group of fifteen or twenty foods, such as sugar, sweet chocolate, orange, grapefruit, lemon, cookies, pretzels, salted crackers, and potato chips. Have the children classify them. What properties were used for classifying them? Was taste one of them?

Next, have the children prepare their own cookbook arranged by the way foods taste. It will have a sweet section, sour section, and others. Maybe you'll end up with some recipes worth trying at home.

Don't forget to warn children about indiscriminately tasting any- and everything —

some things are poisonous

Related activities include bis 1, 10, 13–15, 17, 21, and 81.

☐

sensing your environment
by hearing

Behind a barrier, have three or four children put on a skit using words and sounds of their own choosing. They might take a trip to the supermarket, do mathematics, or go swimming. The children on the other side of the barrier must try to tell what the skit was about from the sounds they hear. The children should try to list the sounds heard and the order in which they were heard. What sounds helped identify what the skit was about?

Have children tell about the sounds they hear when a car, a truck, or a train passes.

What sounds do you hear on a camping trip? In the playground? In a quiet room?

Related activities include bis 1, 13–16, 70, 81, and 99.

☐

skulls and skins

When you take that next museum field trip and visit the skulls and stuffed animals, prepare a sheet of action-oriented questions the children can take along.

You can observe skulls, from which the children can infer the type of diet the animal follows and the use it makes of its different teeth; its size, estimated by observing its skull; and its age, also from observation.

Specific questions:

1. What do you infer is the function of the large hole at the base of the skull?
2. Has the skull any teeth that you would infer would have less functional value than others?
3. Has environmental pollution had any effect on these animals?
4. How do bones of birds and bones of land animals differ?

The children should then observe the stuffed animal and correlate the size of the animal, its age, and its diet to the corresponding skull. They can also infer the functions of the animal's toes, hair, nails, size, and coloring.

A box of assorted bones can be collected from farms, markets, and conservationists. Children can infer what type of animal the bone is from. Was the animal old or young? What is the structure and function of each bone? Where would these bones fit into the skeleton?

Having worked with skulls and skins, the children can observe the live animal. They can locate similar bones in the live animal

Can you match the bones with the animals?

Porcupine

Weasel

Deer

and make comparative observations. After constructing a chicken foot, they can observe an actual one in use.

This approach can turn the useless agony of memorizing bones into worthwhile sciencing activities, developing many skills.

Related activities include bis 38, 62; ss 7 and 11.

□

stone counts

Find some glacial till, which is unsorted, unstratified drift laid down directly by melting glacial ice. It is composed of rock fragments of all sizes, brought together randomly, ranging all the way from boulders weighing several tons to tiny clay particles. If you live in a glaciated region, your state geological survey or local conservation agent can tell you where the nearest till is so that you can get a sample.

Sift through the till and try to identify the rock fragments. You could prepare a small sample collection for comparison. If you live in the Midwest the seven most common rocks will probably be granite, sandstone, shale, limestone, basalt, chert, and coal. From a sample of a hundred rock fragments, have the children determine the percentage that are granite.

Using a bedrock map from your neighboring states (obtainable from your state geological survey or the United States Geological Survey) try to find possible sources for the rock fragments you have identified. How far away are these sources? How far might the glacier have traveled? Can you infer why the glacier would carry the rock fragments this far and then drop them?

Related activities include bis 22, 60, 90, and 95.

□

flying discs

Plastic flying discs can be purchased under many trade names at discount and sporting goods stores. Many ideas can be generated with these discs:

Whose disc can go the farthest distance? The shortest? What throwing technique is used for each task (overhand, underhand, above the chest, below the chest)?

Whose disc can fly most accurately toward a target, for example, a target at a distance of 15 meters?

Can you make the disc go out and return? Try it.

Tape various weights of clay (balancing them) to the disc. Design an experiment to investigate the relationship between mass and distance. Collect evidence. Prepare a graph of mass versus distance. As the mass increases, does the distance traveled increase?

Can you make your own disc? Try paper, cardboard, or aluminum foil discs, and nonbreakable plates. Can you design a disc that will go farther than the commercial ones?

more...

Are flying saucers fact or fiction? Collect evidence to support your stand.

Can you find pictures or drawings of UFO's or flying saucers?

Related activities include bis 30, 45, 80, 86, and 117.

□

a sensy fruit salad

Have each child bring in one of his favorite fruits (you will probably receive apples, oranges, bananas, tangerines; maybe grapes, pears, raisins, berries, lemons, grapefruit, peaches).

Each child can record observations (3 x 5 inch card) about each fruit, such as color, texture, shape, size, taste, and smell.

Have the children place fruits on a common table and exchange descriptions. Then they can try to match the description with the fruit. If they can't do it, maybe they need a more detailed description.

more...

Have them make a fruit salad with all the fruits brought into class. The components of the salad can then be classified according to observable properties. The highlight of the lesson will be eating it!

Related activities include bis 10, 54, 106; ss 15 and 18.

correlation by
insoluble residues

The word *correlation* is used in earth science to explain how two things (such as rock layers or fossils) match or go together. Insoluble residues can be used to illustrate geological correlation.

Within a radius of about 15 miles from your school, obtain samples of a carbonate rock, such as limestone, from several locations. To dissolve the rock you will need to use hydrochloric acid

Adapted from Gerald H. Krockover, "Correlation by Use of Insoluble Residues," *Journal of Geological Education* (January 1971), pp. 29–30. By permission.

(HCl) of 50% concentration (that is, dilute the concentrated acid with an equal amount of water).

*caution: remember, always add acid to water;
never the reverse!*

Use about 25 g of the rock in a 1000 ml beaker with about 150 ml of 50% hydrochloric acid added in small amounts to digest the rock. You will need to be careful not to let the material foam over the top, and you may need to experiment with the quantity of rock and acid used to obtain maximum digestion.

Once the rock has been digested, a material (the insoluble residue) will be deposited on the bottom of the beaker. Pour off the liquid that remains and filter the insoluble residue (a suction filter works best). Wash the residue with water several times to remove any remaining acid.

These residues can be weighed and their masses compared (you will need a balance that weighs to the nearest 0.01 g). The percentage of residue by mass can be calculated by dividing the sample mass by the residue mass and multiplying by 100.

Children can examine the residues with either microscopes or hand lenses and record their observations. They may be able to identify siliceous material, pyrite, hematite, silicified bryozoans, gypsum, or clay.

Children will then need to decide if their residues "correlate" with each other. Did they get similar results from the same location or from two nearby locations? What limitations on data and sources of error should be allowed? Is any additional information needed to obtain correlations, such as the color of the rocks collected, diagnostic fossils, bedding characteristics?

Maybe a geologist could be invited to the class to explain how insoluble residue analysis is used locally.

Related activities include bis 19, 60, 90, and 95.

□

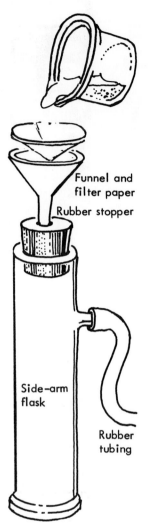

Funnel and
filter paper

Rubber stopper

Side–arm
flask

Rubber
tubing

inferring from pictures

Pictures, including snapshots, magazine illustrations, or slides, can help teach children to distinguish between observations (statements based on the five senses) and inferences (interpretations resulting from observations).

Let's use picture A. Our observations would include these:

1. There are nine lights in this hallway.
2. Two paintings are hanging on the wall at the end of the hall.
3. A clock is on the wall.
4. The clock reads 2:50.
5. No people are in the hallway.

Inferences would include:

1. It is 2:50 A.M.
2. It is 2:50 P.M.
3. This is the hallway of an art center.
4. The walls are made of brick.
5. The floors are linoleum.

Children should be able to present evidence to support their inferences, such as number 1: "It is 2:50 A.M., because I *observe* that the hall is empty." Or, number 2: "It is 2:50 P.M., because I *observe* that the hall is empty and *infer* that the building is closed."

At what time of day do you infer *that picture B was taken? What is your evidence?*

How many floors does this building have?

What do you infer *that the three small windows in the center of each floor signify? What is your evidence? What observations could you make to accept or reject this inference?*

Are all the rooms occupied? What is your evidence?

How many phones do you expect would be used in the part of the building shown?

Picture C should provoke much discussion.

Observe picture C. Record your observations.

Now state three inferences.

Did you observe the bird in the lower right-hand corner?

What new *inferences can you make with this additional evidence?*

Facts and guesses

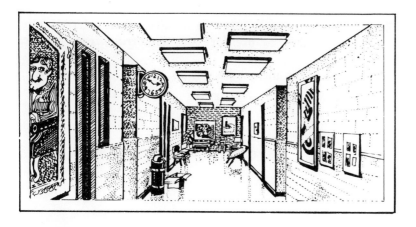

Observe the people in the background. Are these giants? Monsters?

The people are visiting a miniature city. What interesting pictures can you find to use for your "inferring from pictures" activity?

Related activities include bis 24, 32, 33, 46, 73, 85, and 96.

☐

more information, please

Observation is the basis of all science. Refining your observational skills is an ongoing process. At no time can we say, "Now I can observe without missing a thing." We become better and better observers as we practice, but there is always room for improvement. There is no *one* lesson or *one* set of lessons to teach children to become excellent observers. Astute observation is the result of practice continued throughout the grades. A good observer is a good observer, in science as well as in art, music, social studies, reading, and mathematics.

"More information, please" is a quest for more facts about a situation. It's a game. Place eight or ten (the number depends on the grade level) large pictures mounted on oak tagboard on the blackboard tray. With the students seated advantageously, say: "I am thinking of a picture. Which one is it?" Any response now would be a sheer guess. The students may and do ask for "more information, please." You must then narrow the number of pictures down by stating that (for instance) "a fence is visible in it." Four pictures may have fences in them, eliminating the other pictures. The students again ask, "More information, please." You must then provide them with another clue, carrying on until only one picture remains. This activity trains the children to scrutinize, compare observations, and think of similarities and differences. It also develops the habit of asking for "more information, please" when they feel they haven't enough facts on anything they are learning.

more...

Have students bring in their own pictures and challenge other students. What benefits will result from students assuming the instructor's role in the game of "more information, please"?

Related activities include bis 23, 32, 42, 46, and 85.

☐

nac uoy daer siht?

Codes and ciphers touch our lives in many ways. We use area codes, zip codes, key words, and abbreviations. This activity is designed to help children develop communication skills by sciencing.

Does the title of this activity make sense to you? Check the note at the bottom of this page.*

Try this one:

ep zpv lopx xibu uijt tbzt?

To understand this message, just change each letter to the one that comes before it in the alphabet.

The two messages are ciphers; you had to *de*cipher them to read and understand them. This system changes the order of letters or words, or substitutes the letters or words for other letters, words, numbers, or symbols. Try writing several cipher messages of your own.

---

* "Can you read this?" You could if you read each word backwards in the order listed.

Codes, on the other hand, usually substitute letters, words, numbers, sounds, signs, sights, or sentences for other words, sentences, or whole messages. George Washington used codes during the Revolution. The police and army also use codes. Here is a typical one:

For the word *car* use *white*.
For the word *stolen* use *green*.
For the word *armed* use *yellow*.
For the word *hostage* use *pink*.
For the word *wanted* use *black*.
For the word *men* use *purple*.

One code message might be *Black Two Purple Green White*, which translates as *Wanted: Two Men in Stolen Car*.

Try making code books and then use them for communication.

more...

Investigate other ciphers and codes, including hobo codes, the Morse code, intelligence codes, alphabet ciphers, backward ciphers, skytale ciphers, number-box ciphers, and dot, tine, zigzag, and triangle ciphers.

peek pu eht doog krow!

more...

DECIPHERING WEATHER CODES

Visit the Flight Service Station at the nearest airport to obtain surface aviation weather reports. Each surface aviation weather report contains some or all of the following elements in this order:

1. **Station Designator:** a three letter identifier such as INK (Wink, Texas), LAX (Los Angeles, California), LAF (Lafayette, Indiana).
2. **Type and Time of Report:** either an hourly observation or a special report (SP).
3. **Sky Condition and Ceiling:** height in hundreds of feet and a three-letter condition abbreviation — LAF 7 SCT 250 SCT means "Lafayette, Indiana, scattered clouds at 700 feet and 25,000 feet."

4. **Visibility:** the greatest distance objects can be seen and identified through at least 180° of the horizon; reported in statute miles and fractions — in LAF 7 SCT 250 SCT 6, 6 means visibility 6 miles.

5. **Weather and Obstructions to Vision:** includes all forms of precipitation, such as T (thunderstorm), R (rain), Tt (severe thunderstorm), H (hail), S (snow).

6. **Sea Level Pressure:** given in three digits to the nearest tenth millibar with the decimal point omitted; sea level pressure usually is greater than 960.0 millibars and less than 1050.0 millibars; the first 9 or 10 is omitted; to decipher, prefix a 9 or 10, whichever brings it closer to 1000.0 millibars; thus, LAX–129 means "Los Angeles–1012.9" and "INK–990" means Wink–999.0.

7. **Temperature and Dew Point:** these are reported in whole degrees Fahrenheit; they are separated from sea level pressure by a slash (/); temperature and dew point are separated also by a slash; thus, INK . . . 77/63 means temperature 77°F, dew point 63°F.

8. **Wind Direction, Speed, and Character:** wind follows dew point and is separated by a slash. The first two digits are the direction *from* which the wind is blowing. It is given in tens of degrees referenced to true North — 01 is 10°, 21 is 210°, 36 is 360° or North. The second two digits are speed in knots. A calm wind is reported as 0000. Thus, INK . . . 1112G18 means "wind 110 degrees at 12 knots with gusts at 18 knots."

9. **Altimeter Setting:** this follows Wind Direction, Speed, and Character, and is separated by a slash. The normal range of altimeter settings is from 28.00 inches to 31.00 inches of mercury. The last three digits are transmitted with the decimal point omitted. To decipher, prefix a 2 or 3 to the coded value, whichever brings it closer to 30.00 inches. Thus, 996 means 29.96 inches and 013 means 30.13 inches.

10. Remarks, if any, follow the altimeter setting and are separated from it by a slash.

Now let's put all the information together:

Station Designator	Sky Condition and Ceiling	Visibility Weather	Sea Level Pressure	Temperature and Dew Point	Wind Direction, Speed, and Character	Altimeter Setting
MKC	15 SCT 250 SCT	1RH	132	58/56	/18Ø7	/993
Kansas City	15,000 feet 25,000 feet scattered	1 mile rain-hail	1013.2	58°F 56°F	180° 7 knots	29.93

Try deciphering one on your own:

LAF 12Ø SCT 15 16Ø/61/53/19Ø4/ØØ3

You are now ready to pick up those aviation weather reports and work with them in your classroom.

Related activities include bis 44, 52, 92; and ss 16.

charcoal gardens

Charcoal gardens are an interesting and inexpensive way to start studying crystals. Place some coal or charcoal in a bowl. Mix ¼ cup of water, one tablespoon of household ammonia, ¼ cup of table salt, and ¼ cup of laundry bluing into a solution in a container. Pour this solution over the coal or charcoal, spreading the thick slurry of salt evenly over the coal. A little food coloring or dye placed here and there on the coals will add color to the growing crystals. The coals should be about half submerged in the solution.

Many factors affect the results of the charcoal garden. Try using porcelain or glass bowls, comparing the results in those and in aluminum trays. What could account for any differences you observe? Try charcoal, coal, brick, or sponge. Try deep jars or open-faced bowls.

You can get interesting artistic effects by inserting many wooden toothpicks, arranged in some kind of pattern or design, into your sponge. The solution will be drawn up into the toothpicks, and crystals will form on them beautifully. For added interest, you might soak your toothpicks in food coloring.

What effect does the room temperature have on your crystal garden's rate of growth? Try growing a garden in other places, such as the refrigerator, over the heater, in a closet, or in an oven.

How does the humidity of the air affect the rate of growth of your charcoal garden? You may want to use a wet and dry bulb thermometer to determine the relative humidity, then place gardens in places of different humidities.

more...

What would happen if you completely covered the lumps of coal or charcoal with the solution?

Could you use sugar instead of salt as a basic ingredient in your crystal garden? What other ingredients could be substituted?

Can you relate this activity to crystal growth in nature? How does it differ?

Related activities include bis 2, 4, 31, 55, 115; sst 9 and 12.

the mystery toothpicks

Materials needed for this activity are five toothpicks, an eyedropper (or soda straw), and water. The surface on which this activity is performed can be critical. A smooth counter top works well, but try other surfaces too.

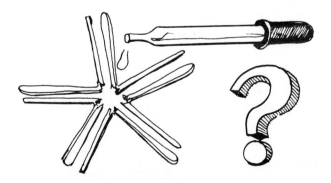

Bend the toothpicks in half so that they do not separate but are held together by fragments. Arrange them with the broken edges in the center of a circle. Using an eyedropper or soda straw, squeeze a drop of water in the center of them.

What do you observe? Did you predict that a star would appear? Can you infer what happens to dry wood when water is added to it?

Related activities include bis 32, 36, 42, 85, and 107.

☐

five-sense plays

Most observation activities seem relegated to the primary level, probably because primary children have not yet mastered the fundamental skills of reading, writing, and arithmetic, and observing seems to be within their ability. When they advance to the intermediate grades, there is less emphasis on observing and more on acquiring content and specific skills. Observing should be at the heart of all curricular areas, and should be propagated through all the grades.

It does not always have to be presented as an organized lesson. One daily mention or several reminders a day will alert the class to your purpose. Statements like "What is different in the classroom today? What is not in the same place as it was this morning?" This will mean some occasional rearranging or additions by you to the classroom. If the class has a visitor, a school nurse, principal, janitor, or parent, have children describe the visitor's size, weight, complexion, dress, and unique items such as rings or tie pins. If a second visitor comes to the room, repeat the procedure. This time, extend the involvement by requesting comparative observations. Who is taller? Who is heavier? Who is older? If the observed persons cooperate, you could end up with the actual figures for comparison.

Continually rewarding successful engagements with observational exercises will encourage children. Frequent classroom activities can sharpen one's ability to observe and heighten interest in science and other subjects. Who observes better than an artist? Is a scientist an artist?

Select an object. Have a student describe it to the class. The class will not have seen the object or be able to see it while it is being described. From the student's description the class tries to name the object. Your choice of the object can have much to do with the ease or difficulty in the activity. Usually the student describes the purpose of the object which can be a giveaway. Saying that some object is used to open doors tells too much too quickly. You may want to say that the object's use cannot be mentioned. In lower grades, you may want to show the students four or five objects. Without letting the class know, have a student select one of the four or five previously disclosed objects. This procedure provides a framework within which to operate. They are now familiar with the original items and can tie the description to one of those items. This approach allows for more success. The activity will be more difficult if you make the initial items more similar than dissimilar.

When you provide materials for instruction in observation, try to involve all the senses. Bring in three cans of food. Take off the labels. Have the students describe the contents of the cans by hefting and shaking. Then punch a small hole in each can. Allow them to smell each food item. Which foods smell alike but taste different?

Children enjoy fabricating five-sense plays. These are sequenced events in which the authors decide in what order to perform tasks to be detected by the class. They have the class put their heads down on their desk tops with eyes closed. The five-sense playwrights may remain stationary in specific areas of the room, or they can move about. A sequence of events is initiated. One child in one corner of the room may set a ticking clock in motion; a second in another corner may release a pine-scented odor from a spray can; a third child may be popping bubble gum somewhere else in the room; and a fourth in stocking feet may be quietly walking up and down aisles pulling a light string over the children's ears. The simplicity of it all masks the inherent science. These activities can be performed randomly or in a repeated sequence.

The sense most used in observation is sight, but involvement in five-sense plays makes the students aware of how important *all* the senses are.

more...

What can you think of to stimulate observation indoors? Outdoors? Who needs senses, anyway? Try eliminating one of your senses for a short time. Design an activity eliminating the sense of touch, or sight.

Related activities include bis 1, 13–17, 21, 81, and 127.

pressure, area, mass, and weight

On graph paper with centimeter divisions, trace the outline of your hand. Imagine that you have just completed a one-hand handstand. The traced-hand outline would enclose the area that would have supported your entire weight. Approximate the number of square centimeters enclosed within the traced-hand outline. Divide your weight by the number of square centimeters. This gives you the pounds per square centimeter of pressure you would have exerted on a surface if you had done that one-hand handstand.

Understanding weight and pressure isn't as hard as a one-hand handstand, but for some students it runs a close second.

Instruction in a pressure-area relationship can be extended to include exercises in volume, surface area, mass, weight, and density. Instead of handprints, use prepared wooden blocks whose dimensions are whole units. You may have to clarify some terms before starting instruction. Mass and weight cause much consternation for students as well as teachers. For most students and adults, weight is an observed value registered in response to an object placed on a scale. The weight is usually expressed in Imperial units, such as ounces or pounds. Consistent with the elementary national curriculum projects, at the intermediate level, we promote here a distinction between mass and weight and stress expression of these values utilizing the metric system.

WHAT IS WEIGHT?

Weight is the common name for the measurement assigned to the force of gravity on a specific mass. The weight of an object depends on two things: the quantity of matter (mass) it contains, and the strength of the earth's gravitational attraction at the location where the weighing is computed. This gravitational force (or gravity) is more precisely called acceleration of gravity. A spring balance is used to measure this gravitational attraction in newtons or ounces.

The earth is not a perfect sphere. It is slightly flattened at the poles and may be more accurately described as an oblate spheroid. The radius from the center of the earth to the pole is 27 miles shorter than the radius from the center of the earth to the equator. Therefore, the pull of gravity at the poles is stronger than at the equator because that region is closer to the center of the earth. The same object measured on a spring scale at two locations may reflect different weights. Would you, if placed on a spring scale,

Adapted from Alfred De Vito, "Understanding Pressure and Area," *Science Activities,* vol. 6, no. 4 (December 1971), pp. 28–30. By permission.

weigh more at the poles or the equator? Would the quantity of matter of which you are composed change? Would there be the same amount of you?

WHAT IS MASS?

How much would you weigh on the moon? An astronaut had a weight of 180 pounds recorded on a spring balance on earth; using the same apparatus on the moon, his weight would be recorded as 30 pounds (approximately 1/6 of that recorded on earth). This changed reading is in response to the differences in the power of the moon's and the earth's gravitational attraction. Would the quantity of matter of which the astronaut is composed have changed? Is the matter one-sixth of what it was on earth? Mass is the measure of the quantity of matter an object possesses. The mass of an object does not change.

Mass does not vary with location. All matter can be defined as that which has mass and occupies space. Location affects the measure of weight. To measure something that does not change, we must have some way to measure things that occupy the same amount of space regardless of the location. This would be the quantity of matter, or the mass.

Mass is usually determined by comparing the mass of an object with that of the mass of a known object using an equal-arm balance. Unfortunately this procedure is often referred to as weighing, even though it is mass and not weight that is being measured. If the mass of an unknown object is calculated at the equator, and then the entire apparatus is transported to the polar regions (or the moon), the known mass would still balance the unknown mass, and the mass would be the same in all locations.

The gram is the fundamental unit for measuring mass. The unit of mass is related to a fixed physical measure, a piece of material with a specified mass. A spring scale measures weight and an equal-arm balance determines mass.

Mass is also considered in response to motion. Mass is the name given to a property of matter that might be called, "the tendency not to move." Mass is a measure of inertia that can be described as that property of matter because of which a force must be applied to it in order to move it or accelerate it.

WHAT IS DENSITY?

Density is a measure of the amount of matter in a specific volume of space. It can be calculated by using the formula —

$$\text{Density} = \frac{\text{Mass}}{\text{Volume}}$$

Mass is expressed in grams in the metric system, and volume

is expressed in cubic centimeters. Thus, density is expressed in grams per cubic centimeter. Density is independent of size. A wooden sphere 6 cm in diameter has the same density as a wooden sphere 6 m in diameter. The mass of the two, however, is quite different.

ACTIVITIES WITH A BLOCK OF WOOD

The advantage of cutting the wooden blocks into dimensions that are whole units of length, width, and height is that computation of volume and pressure is easier. White pine wood works fine. Some questions to ask about the wooden block:

1. What is the length, width, and height (in cm) of the wooden block?

2. What is the volume (in cm³) of the block?

3. What is the surface area (in cm²) of each face?

4. What is the total surface area (in cm²) of the block?

5. Determine the weight (n) of the block. A newton (n) is equivalent to 0.224 lb.

6. Determine the mass (g) of the block.

7. What is the density of the wooden block? (The density of white pine is about 0.6 g/cm³.) If you cut the wooden block in half, would the mass change? Would the density change?

8. The pressure that an object exerts depends on the area on which the weight of the object rests. Does the weight of the wooden block change when we reposition the block in space? Weigh the wooden block in three orientations. The observed weight should be the same. Using graph paper ruled in square centimeters, trace the outline of the wooden block in three orientations. In each the same weight is distributed over a different area. What is the pressure per square centimeter for the block in each orientation? In which case is the pressure per square centimeter the greatest? The least?

more...

Have the students trace the outline of one heel of their shoes on square-centimeter graph paper. If they balance their weight on one heel, what will the pressure be as distributed over this area? If they traced a spike heel of a woman (again, balanced on one heel) who weighed 120 pounds, how might this explain why women occasionally leave heel marks in linoleum floors?

Related activities include bis 41, 104; and sst 11.

water rocketry

Many discount or toy stores sell water rockets in varied shapes and sizes. They are operated by filling the rockets with water and using hand pumps that are included to build pressure. These rockets are safe to use

providing they're not pointed at other children, teachers, or windows

These are some of the variables that can be investigated:

How does the number of pump strokes relate to the height reached by the rocket? How can you measure the height it reaches? Could you compare it with the known height of other objects? Time it. Calculate the speed of the rocket.

How does the temperature of the water relate to the height reached by the rocket?

How does the size of the rocket affect the height it attains? Does a two-stage rocket go higher than a single stage?

Describe how the wind direction affects the height the rocket reaches. What about temperature? Humidity? Do you predict that it will go higher in the winter than in the summer?

Can the rocket's color be a factor in the height reached? Explain.

more...

Make a rocket-propelled boat. You will need these materials: a small tooth powder or talcum powder container that can be punctured; a soap dish; a small candle; some pipe cleaners; and water in a large dishpan to make a lake on which the boat will be propelled. With a nail, punch a small hole near the top edge of

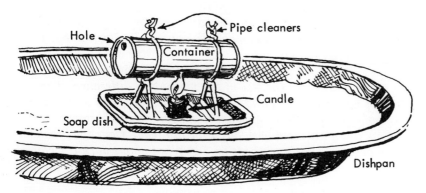

Hole · Pipe cleaners · Container · Candle · Soap dish · Dishpan

the container. Place some water in the container. Mount it so that it will stand horizontally in the soap dish; do this by twisting the pipe cleaner stems around the container in such a way that they will support it. Place the mounted container carefully over a lighted candle in the soap-dish boat. Place the soap-dish boat on the water in the dishpan. How does this experiment resemble the way a rocket lifts off from a launching pad?

Try using different fuels for your rocket or boat, such as vinegar and baking soda or carbonated water (soda pop). Remember these ingredients generate gases.

be sure all outlets for the expanded gases
are open and the expanded gases
are free to escape

Related activities include bis 20, 45, 63, 80, 86, 100, 117, 118; and ss 19.

☐

behold the mold

bis 31

Collect materials such as bread, fruit, and baby food jars. State the conditions that will enable you to grow the best mold with these materials.

caution: wash hands thoroughly after working with
this activity and do not inhale the mold spores!

Try capping a moist baby food jar that has been washed thoroughly. After several days, take off the cap and observe any mold that has grown. What factors can you identify that have contributed to the growth of this mold?

Who can grow the most mold? Which mold collection has the greatest variety of colors?

Does mold grow in a dry baby food jar? Does mold grow in all moist jars? Does the size of the jar make a difference? The type of jar? The type of lid? How much water needs to be added for mold growth? Will too much water retard mold growth?

Can you grow mold with any type of bread? Does rye bread grow better mold than wheat bread? What about dark rye com-

*pared to light rye? Does "fresh" bread grow more mold than
"old" bread?*

*How long does it take fruit to get moldy? Does it take longer
for peaches, apples, or bananas to mold? When does the mold
begin to form? Before or after the fruit dries out?*

*Describe the growth pattern of the mold. Does it get taller or
does it cover more of the object's surface?*

*Does the amount of light affect the growth of mold? What
about temperature?*

more...

*Expose slices of moist bread in several places or wipe each slice
on a different surface. Compare the mold growths. Examine the
molds with a magnifying glass. Is mold a plant?*

*Try growing mold in darkness. After a week or two, switch
the mold to bright light. What observations can you make?*

*Using what you have learned about mold, design an experi-
ment to stop mold from growing.*

*Try growing mildew (not mold) on different types of cloth.
Can you grow mildew on surfaces other than cloth?*

Related activities include bis 2, 26, 55, 115; and sst 12.

mystery pictures

Collect pictures or take pictures of the unobvious, such as a
close-up picture of a phonograph record, a close-up of a floor mat,
part of a plant or animal, or a picture from space.

Several sample pictures for you to cut out and use are included.
Usually a description of the picture is taped to the reverse side.
A child who feels ready for a further description turns the picture
over.

What observations can you make? What inferences? What do
you think each picture represents?

What do you see in the pictures?

Picture A

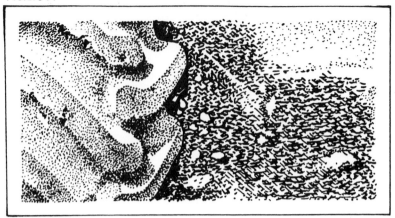

Picture B

Picture C

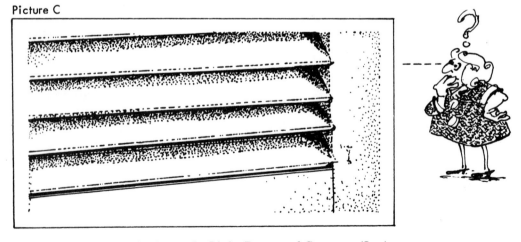

In reference to picture A: Did you observe that it had ridges and was horizontal? It's an old tractor tire being used as a sand-box.

Picture B: Did you observe a series of rectangles and a reverse arrangement across the top? You're correct; these are shingles from a roof. Did you observe a shadow across the shingles? It's not a tree; it's the photographer.

Picture C: Did you observe continuous lines? Notice that some are darker than others. Do you infer that this is house siding? You're close. This is a close-up of a shutter found attached to a house.

try mystery pictures today!

Related activities include bis 23, 27, 36, 42, 85, and 126.

□

pollution-picture problems

bis 33

Find some pictures and make up pollution-picture problem cards — P³ Cards — as illustrated in the example, which you can cut out or copy. Better yet, have your children make some. Six more ideas are provided below for you to use.

P³ Card 1

Find three pictures, each illustrating one of the scenes listed:

1. Soapsuds floating on top of some water.
2. A woman washing her clothes by hand in a wash tub.
3. A lake with sailboats in the background and dead fish in the foreground.

If pictures 1, 2, and 3 are all related, explain what caused the situation in picture 3. Be specific!

Which of these is
the BEFORE picture
and which is the
AFTER picture?

How did you decide
on your answer?
What were your
reasons?

P³ Card 2

Collect pictures showing these situations, and arrange them in no particular order:

1. A boy standing next to a sign that says, "Polluted — Unsafe for Swimming."
2. Raw sewage being dumped into a lake from a large industrial plant.
3. A beach with many dead fish and plants washed up on the shore.

Can you explain how what is happening in *one* of these pictures could cause what you see in the others?

P³ Card 3

Find two pictures showing these things happening:

1. A residential street, with a man burning a pile of leaves at the curb.
2. A residential street — with nice houses — but with one large hole between two of the houses.

Is there anything wrong in these pictures? Describe what you see, and explain what might happen.

P³ Card 4

Collect four pictures, each showing one of these scenes:

1. Two men standing in the middle of a city with gas masks on.
2. A brick wall with many empty cans piled up against it.
3. A man sitting on a dock with a fishing rod — his line is in the water, which is filled with floating, dead fish.
4. A smog-filled city street with one man, barely visible, trying to read a street sign.

Write down what you would consider an appropriate title for each of these pictures. Can you think of a title for all of them together?

P³ Card 5

Collect these three pictures:

1. An airplane flying very low over a house.
2. A man using a jackhammer to tear up a street.
3. A man cutting a beautifully cared-for lawn with a power mower.

Describe how you would feel if you lived in the house in picture 1 and this situation occurred about every six minutes. If you earned your living doing what the man in picture 2 is doing, how would this work affect your life? Your family? Your health? Although the man in picture 3 is on a beautiful lawn with lovely flowers and fresh air, how would you feel if you were standing next to him?

P³ Card 6

Explain how a visitor from another planet might describe the earth people's ways of life if these were the only things he happened to see on a brief visit here:

1. An old junk yard.
2. A football stadium after the game, with candy wrappers, hot dog papers, and popcorn containers littered all over the empty stands.
3. Overturned garbage cans in front of a brick wall, which has names scrawled all over it.
4. A view from the air of a densely populated housing project, with houses all crowded together.
5. Dead fish lying on a deserted beach.

Related activities include bis 56, 89; and ss 3.

□

carbon dioxide

Carbon dioxide and oxygen are probably the two most important gases for life on our earth. More is generally known about oxygen. It supports combustion. We need to breathe it to live. Carbon dioxide is often thought of only as something we exhale as part of the air.

Carbon dioxide in solid form is called Dry Ice. It is a fascinating substance, which you can get from frozen food plants or ice cream dealers. Several cautions must be stressed when working with Dry Ice.

never place Dry Ice in a closed container with an airtight top!

Enormous pressures can accumulate as the solid changes to a gas and expands. Anything under pressure is a potential danger, and carbon dioxide is no exception.

never touch Dry Ice

Carbon dioxide in a solid form (Dry Ice) is so cold that it may cause severe freezing of the skin. Use a stick, salad tongs, plastic utensils, or a piece of cardboard to handle it safely. Keeping aware of these necessary precautions for working with Dry Ice, let us investigate some of the fascinating activities that can be done with it.

Place a small piece of Dry Ice on a smooth, level table top. Give it a slight push. The fragment fairly glides along. It floats on a thin film of carbon dioxide gas, which it gives off and which separates it from the table top.

Make a small cavity in a piece of Dry Ice with a knife or a screwdriver. Put a drop of water in the cavity. Repeat this with a drop of oil, a drop of glycerine, and a drop of kerosene. What happens to these liquids?

Place several pieces of Dry Ice in a glass tumbler half full of rubbing alcohol. Place a grape, an olive, a small pickle, and a piece of banana in the tumbler. Allow them to remain in the tumbler for 10 to 15 minutes. Remove and drop these items to the floor. What do you observe?

Assemble an equal-arm balance from a meter stick. Suspend a paper bag from each arm of it. Into one paper bag drop a small piece of Dry Ice. Quickly balance the other arm of the equal-arm

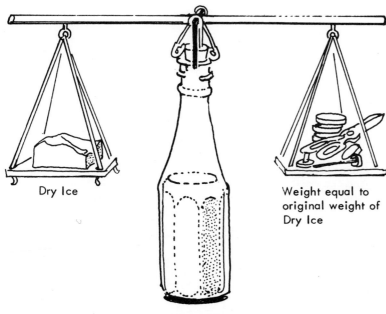

Dry Ice

Weight equal to original weight of Dry Ice

balance by adding clay or paper clips. Describe your observations over the next few minutes. What explanations do you have to explain what you see?

The "Dracula" drink is always an impressive sight. Put a piece of Dry Ice in a tumbler full of water. White "smoke" pours out. This is not carbon dioxide but a fog formed of tiny droplets of water that condense from the air as it is cooled by the Dry Ice.

Carbon dioxide, when dissolved in water, makes "carbonated" water and carbonated drinks. Is it a food?

This one's on me!

more...

Does Dry Ice melt? Does ice? List some properties of both. Does Dry Ice occur naturally? Would the results be different if plain ice were used instead of Dry Ice in the equal-arm balance experiment with two paper bags?

Related activities include bis 59 and 91.

bis 65

food chains

Find animal poems and have the children relate them to a food chain. Have them draw or paint their food chain.

Try this extract from Dr. Seuss's *Scrambled Eggs Super.**

I went for the kind that were mellow and sweet
And the world's sweetest eggs are the eggs of the Kweet
Which is due to those very sweet trout which they eat
And those trout ... Well, they're sweet 'cause they only eat Wogs
And Wogs, after all, are the world's sweetest frogs

* From *Scrambled Eggs Super*, by Dr. Seuss. Copyright 1953 by Dr. Seuss. Reprinted by permission of Random House, Inc., and Elaine Greene, Ltd. Also published in *The Dr. Seuss Story Book* by William Collins Sons and Co. Ltd.

And the reason they're sweet is whenever they lunch
It's always the world's sweetest bees that they munch
And the reason no bees can be sweeter than these . . .
They only eat blossoms off Beezlenut Trees
And these Beezlenut Blossoms are sweeter than sweet
And that's why I nabbed several eggs from the Kweet.

more...

What is a food chain? What happens if one link in the food chain is destroyed — what if the Beezlenut trees didn't blossom or a big fish ate up all the trout?

Make up another food chain that ends with human beings and begins with grass. And one that begins with sea horses. And one that begins with ants.

Do the numbers of the items in the food chain affect the chain? If there are more bees than the frogs can eat, how is the chain affected? If frogs eat other things as well as bees, how is the chain affected?

Related activities include bis 10 and 46.

☐

why does a
burning match curl up?

When we see in the common the uncommon, the rewards of observation are greatly increased. A burning wooden kitchen match is not an unusual sight, but it can be an interesting one — if we observe with our thought window open.

Take one wooden kitchen match. Strike it. Hold the match in a horizontal position. Do not rotate the match. Hold it steady so that it remains intact after burning. Observe it burning. How many of your senses did you involve in your observation? As the match burns near the end, blow it out. What do you notice? Wooden kitchen matches burned under these conditions should curl upward. You may want to repeat it several times to verify this statement. Exercising due caution, have each child burn a wooden match. How many matches curled upward?

This activity promotes observation. It also allows us to quantify how long a match burns, how many curl upward, and it also poses a problem. We need to do some thinking to reach some explanation of why a burning (wooden) match curls up.

Questions that may open up an idea:

Do all matches, including paper matches, curl up? If not, then perhaps wooden kitchen matches have something unique that causes the observed result.

What bearing does holding it horizontal and not rotating the match have on the result? Would the match curl sideways if it were held vertically? If it were rotated?

Does the fact that the match is made of wood have any bearing on the result? If so, do you know anything about wood that might lead you to an explanation? Wood burns. It is a cellular structure.

When the match burns, where is the hottest portion of it? The lower portion or the top portion? Which portion do you infer burns more completely?

What other objects bend or curl when light or heat is applied to them? Have you ever observed a plant bend toward the light? Have you ever observed a bimetallic strip react to heat? Can you use this information to offer a possible explanation of why a burning match curls up?

Related activities include bis 27, 41, 42, 102, and 108.

□

parquetry blocks

To help the children work well with spatial relationships, make a set of parquetry blocks or purchase a set from Playskool, Inc., Division of Milton Bradley Company, Chicago, Illinois, 60618.

Have the children match the patterns provided or those you make to go with your homemade set. Then have the children make their own patterns with the blocks.

Obtain sample floor tiles or carpet odds and ends and have the children make patterns with them.

Have them make pattern cards for the patterns created and see if other children can make the same pattern using the card.

Related activities include bis 81 and ss 6.

□

animal tracks

Where do you think you might find animal tracks near your school? Why? What animals might have formed the tracks?

When you find a footprint of an animal, put a cardboard collar around it (a half-pint milk container with both top and bottom cut out works well). Mix some plaster of paris with water so that it is thin enough to pour and fill the track to the top of the collar. Allow the plaster to harden. Have the children formulate hypotheses about the factors involved in the time it takes the plaster to harden.

don't pour the remaining plaster into the sink!

Hardening plaster of paris becomes warm. (Where does the heat come from?)

While waiting for the plaster to harden, can you decide in which direction the animal was going? Was it walking or running? What

| Milk carton | Footprint | Casting the footprint |

| Negative cast | Casting the negative | Positive cast |

observations support this notion? Was it an adult or baby? Was there more than one animal?

When the cast is completely set (hard and dry to the touch), brush it off and you will have a raised (negative) cast of the footprint. Why do you think it is called a negative cast? How do you make a positive cast?

To make a positive (indented) footprint, grease the negative cast with petroleum jelly, fit a collar around it, and fill with more plaster of paris. The positive cast will show the impression of the animal's foot just as it appeared in the mud or sand.

more...

Other tracks you might want to try are: tire tracks, airplane tracks, people tracks, plant tracks, and rock tracks. You can probably think of other types of tracks and questions to ask about them.

Next, try measuring raindrop tracks by filling a shallow box half-full of flour. Let several raindrops hit the surface. Take the box inside and let the flour dry for about one hour. Search carefully just under the surface, and you should find hard pellets of flour which are perfect casts of the raindrops. Remove them and measure their diameter. How does the mass of the various raindrops compare? Are they all the same?

Make tracks or fossils out of clay molds. Also, try using plasticene or Play Dough. Roll out the clay so that it is flat like a cookie. Place petroleum jelly on the object to be cast (such as a shell). Make the imprint into the clay by pushing down on the shell.

Carefully melt some paraffin in a double boiler over a heat source. This should be done only by the teacher. Add one crayon for color.

caution: molten paraffin is highly flammable and can inflict severe burns!

Carefully pour the wax into the clay mold. Do not disturb until it cools (about 30 minutes). Holding it under cold water helps to hasten the cooling process. When cool, carefully peel off the clay and you have a fossil. Use a paper clip to clean off any excess clay.

You are now ready to make your own track or fossil collection!

Related activities include bis 18, 62; ss 7 and 11.

☐

fun with mirrors

bis 69

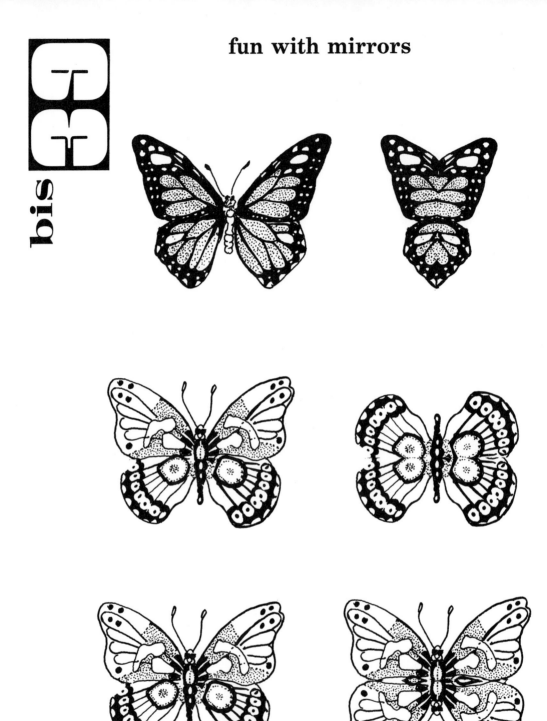

Now make your own from stamps or stick-on seals, words or drawings, flowers, pictures, and puzzles.

more...

Place an arrow on a sheet of paper against a mirror. Which way does the mirror image point? Hold a typewritten sentence before a mirror. Can you read the sentence reflected in the mirror? Take a second mirror and with it look at the sentence reflected in the first mirror. Now can you read it? Why?

With two or more mirrors, make a periscope. Can you make one that goes around a corner?

What other things reflect images? Why do windows reflect images at night? Does water act like a mirror sometimes? Can people act as mirrors? Have a friend stand in front of you and act like a mirror, reflecting your movements.

Related activities include bis 85, 126; ss 5; and sst 13.

□

pinto-bean radioactive decay

From a bag of pinto beans select a hundred at random and put them in a shoe box. Mark one inside wall of the shoe box with a dot. Assume that each pinto bean represents one atom of the radioactive element called *bean*. With the lid on, shake the box for a specified time interval, such as 10 seconds, which could represent a span of time in years. After the first interval remove all the beans that have their black spot pointing in the direction of the dot. These beans represent atoms of the element *bean* that have decayed. *Record* the number of active atoms that remain in the box.

Shake the box again, removing the beans that have their black spot pointing toward the dot. Record the new number of active atoms.

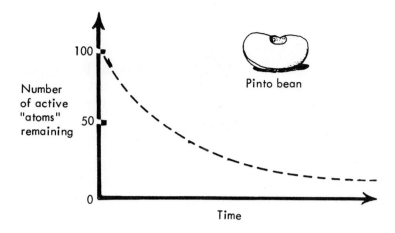

Pinto bean

Number of active "atoms" remaining

100

50

0

Time

Continue this procedure until all the beans have been removed from the box.

Construct a graph of your data showing the rates of radioactive decay for *bean*. From the graph, determine the half-life (when fifty are left) of the element *bean*.

more...

What other objects could you use? Safety matches, pennies, stamps, paper clips, thumbtacks? Can you think of others?

Try these and compare their half-lives. How does the half-life using pennies with a head-or-tail possibility differ from using pinto beans and their orientation toward the dot?

Because of their sensitivity and ease of culture, pinto beans make a convenient start at qualitative air pollution analysis. They are particularly sensitive to sulfur dioxide and show it with bleached spots on the leaves between the veins. The eleventh day after emergence is their peak of sensitivity. Plant your pinto beans in a pot and, when they emerge from the soil, transport them to the site you intend to test (a heavily trafficked corner, down-wind of a factory, for instance). Observe your plant daily for 14 days, checking for sclerotic spotting, and record your findings. To make sure you are obtaining true results, plant a control in the same type of pot and soil, but grow it in a "clean" environment.

Related activities include bis 43, 82, and 87.

the Cartesian diver

For instilling observational and inferential skills, this activity has to be rated as one of the best. When students can manipulate something and see a direct response, they become thoroughly engrossed. Some even become mesmerized.

You will need a clear wine or catsup bottle, an eyedropper, water, and a cork that fits your bottle.

Fill the clear bottle to the very top with water. Fill a drinking glass with water to determine the upright floatability of the eyedropper. Put the eyedropper in the water glass. Take up some water into the dropper. Too much water will cause the dropper to sink to the bottom; too little water will make the dropper difficult to submerge. The dropper should have enough water to barely float. When this condition is reached, put the dropper in your filled water bottle. Place the cork in the bottle and press down slowly. Stand back: excess water may squirt out.

With enough pressure the dropper dives to the bottom. When the pressure is released, it rises to the top. This action can be repeated almost endlessly.

Test of water level in dropper   No pressure   Pressure applied with cork

An explanation for this action and reaction can be obtained by observing the water level inside the dropper as it changes position in the bottle.

Which is heavier, air or water?
In which position is the air inside the dropper compressed most?
When the air is compressed does the dropper contain more water, less water, or the same amount?
In which position do the dropper and its contents weigh most?
Why does the dropper come back up when the pressure is released?

When participants in the activity arrive at an explanation that satisfies them, have them try this:

more...

Take a small wooden safety match. Cut off a small segment (7 to 8 mm), including the head and a small portion of the wood behind the head. You may need to experiment a little with the length because matches vary from manufacturer to manufacturer. Put this small portion of the wooden match into your water bottle. Press firmly on the cork. The small section of wooden match reacts to the pressure in the same way as the dropper.

Is the explanation for this behavior and that of the dropper the same? Are the same components involved? What is the structure of wood? When the match is at the bottom, is it heavier than it was when at the top of the bottle? How does it get heavier? Question yourself; you'll pry out an explanation.
How many variations of the Cartesian diver can you construct?

Related activities include bis 29, 48, 102, 104, 108; and sst 11.

bis 42

where did the water go?

Using two test tubes, rubber stoppers, and glass tubes as shown in the illustrations, try this experiment:

Fill the tubes so that they have *identical* warm water levels. Add rock salt to tube B and, using the rubber stopper (push the stopper in or out), adjust the water levels so that they are still identical. Ask the children to predict what will happen. Usually three conditions will be anticipated:

1. The water level will *rise* because the rock salt melts.
2. The water level will *fall* because the rock salt melts.
3. The water level will *not change* because the rock salt will not melt.

In our experience, most children will choose the first prediction. After approximately one hour, they will observe that the water level has gone down. Where did the water go? Children may now formulate hypotheses about that.

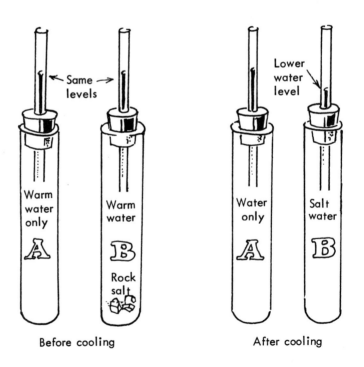

Adapted from Gerald H. Krockover, "Where Did the Water Go?" *Science Activities* (January 1973), pp. 38–39. By permission.

Did the water level go down because a gas was produced? Or did the water evaporate? Did the salt absorb the water? Did the water absorb the salt? See if you can design experiments to find out where the water went.

more...

Further investigations might include trying table salt or sugar instead of rock salt. Do you get the same results? What if you used two liquids, such as rubbing alcohol and water? Are the volumes of any two liquids additive?

Related activities include bis 23, 24, 47, 96, 102, and 104.

normal variation

Data become more meaningful and convenient only when they are tallied and graphed. Because experimental data often are "normally" distributed, it is important to understand what the normal distribution means and the relationship it reveals.

Normal distribution occurs when several measurements are made on one variable. The variable can be height, weight, speed, temperature, or time, among others. Normal distributions also appear when we measure characteristics within a species. With humans we can measure heart rate, finger length, pulse rate, blood pressure, and other characteristics. Normal variation is the range of any one of these measures. For example, if you measure the height of the students in your class you probably would find ten per cent are exceptionally short, ten per cent are exceptionally tall, and the rest fall within a range that might be called normal height. Repeated measurements of subsequent classes over ten years would allow you to verify the height of students at your grade level and enable you to predict with some validity approximately how many exceptionally short and tall students you might expect next year.

The data collected when we measure a characteristic in a population will be normally distributed, tracing a bell-shaped or normal curve.

Using ten dry lima beans and a metric ruler, measure the longest plane of the ten beans tó the nearest millimeter. To collect more data quickly, have the students exchange data. Forty or fifty measures should be sufficient. Tally all the data. In millimeters, arrange the data from smallest to the largest measure and record how often each measure occurs. Plot this information on a graph. How does your curve from the lima bean measurements differ from an ideal normal-shaped bell curve?

How many beans that might be called extremely small *did you have? How many* extremely large *ones did you have? How do these two figures compare? How many so-called normal lima beans were counted?*

more...

If you elected to measure another characteristic of the lima bean, would these categories remain about the same?

What other objects could you use? Try plotting length or width of leaves taken from a large plant; scallop or clam shells also work well.

Related activities include bis 40, 82, 87, and 123.

what's in a name?

bis 71

Hot / Cold
Up / Down
Long / Short
Fast / Slow
Conductor / Nonconductor
Noodle / Macaroni
Child / Adult
Baby / Child

When is hot hot or cold cold? Is a candle flame hot when compared to a blowtorch flame? Is a glass of tap water cold when compared to an ice cube?

When is long long or short short? Is a jump rope long when compared to a clothesline?

Teachers and children need practice in developing operational definitions for words so that they will mean more than just names.

Children can fill several containers with water of varying temperatures and decide which is hot and which is cold. They may decide to prepare a scale arranging the containers from hot to cold, or they may want to order the containers by their temperatures, with any temperature greater than 50° C classified as hot and any lower as cold.

Cold		Hot
0° C	50° C	100° C

This is an operational definition of hot and cold. Where would you place lukewarm?

Another definition might be conductor or nonconductor. Using a battery, wire, and light bulb, explain how you could test several objects for conductivity, such as: coins, scissors, chair legs, rings, pens, staplers. If the light bulb lights, the object is a conductor.

You can see that this idea has no limit.

When is a child a child and an adult an adult? A noodle a noodle or a macaroni a macaroni?

Have you thought about honest vs. dishonest, the truth vs. a lie?

Related activities include bis 52, 57, and 69.

inclined-ramp rollers

A rolling stone doesn't gather much moss, but it attracts a lot of attention. A basic law of the jungle is that anything that moves merits looking at; survival depends on that. It is only natural that inclined runway (or inclined plane) activities are interesting as well as creative sciencing activities.

Use any board (wood, Masonite, cardboard V-shaped trough), steel ball bearings, table tennis balls, marbles, a metric ruler, a timer, a balance, a protractor, graph paper, and carbon paper.

Mark measures on your inclined plane so that distances may be observed and recorded. Extend the measurements beyond the inclined plane. Roll an object down the inclined plane. Record the time the object takes to move through a specific distance. Calculate the speed (speed equals the distance divided by the time it takes to travel this distance).

Extend the activity by varying the objects rolled down the inclined plane. Keep the size constant and vary the mass. Keep mass constant and vary the size. Does this change the speed?

who uses safety belts?

Instead of using spherical objects, use a small plastic or metal car and add weights to it. Record and graph speed as the weight is increased. What happens when you change the height of the inclined plane? Place a loose object in the toy car. Roll the car down the inclined plane. Place a heavy brick or several heavy books in the path of the car. What happens to the loose objects? What opportunities to measure do these activities provide students?

COLLISIONS

Roll spherical objects down the inclined plane. Place lighter, heavier, or same-size spherical objects in the path of the oncoming sphere. Let them collide. On impact, record distance and direction traveled by both objects. What happens when a heavier object hits a lighter object, or vice versa? Does changing the speed of the oncoming ball alter things? How does this collision relate to a rushing fullback and a waiting stationary linebacker? Change the elevation of the inclined plane. What happens to your results?

If the spherical objects are heavy enough, pressure-sensitive carbon paper placed under light paper will record the track left by the balls as they react to the collision, giving a permanent record and allowing for more accurate measurement of angles.

page 72

Vary the surface of the inclined board. Use the plain surface, wax the surface, use different materials such as corduroy, silk, or cotton to cover the inclined plane, for surfaces with different textures. How does this affect the speed? You can also get some interesting results by varying the object's texture. Roll the sphere in oil, or wax it. Place glue on the wheels of the plastic or metal car, roll it in sand, let it dry, and then run it down the inclined plane.

more...

Next, move the inclined plane activity outdoors. A playground slide or a seesaw makes a very good inclined plane with a long runway.

Related activities include bis 20, 30, 51, 86, 114, 117, 118; ss 4 and 19.

what happens next?

Tiger, the gray-striped alley cat, discovers a fishbowl with one big fish in it. With his whiskers twitching and his nose to the glass, Tiger's eyeballs slide back and forth, following the fish swimming around and around in the bowl. Unknown to the tomcat, the fish is a meat-eating piranha. *What happens next?*

Alice and Dotty are in the supermarket shopping for watermelons. They both arrive at the watermelon bin at the same instant. Only one watermelon is sitting in the bin. *What happens next?*

The Kentucky Derby horses are in position at the starting line. A truck backfires. *What happens next?*

Mother sets the sack of groceries on the radiator and runs to answer the telephone. A carton of ice cream is in the sack. *What happens next?*

A moth is fluttering around the dining room ceiling while the Smiths are eating mushroom soup. *What happens next?*

An express train is rolling rapidly along the tracks as a red heifer cow lumbers up onto the rails. *What happens next?*

Sam Simple turns his jalopy onto a one-way street — in the wrong direction. *What happens next?*

Ann and Melissa are carrying their dishes on trays in the lunchroom line. Ann stops abruptly. *What happens next?*

more...

Children can draw pictures of each situation and then a picture of what they think happens next. Or, they can prepare short stories or tapes on what they think happens next.

Children can use their own ideas or magazine pictures for their own "What Happens Next?" activities and exchange them with one another. Or, one "What Happens Next?" activity can be given to all the children and the variety of pictures and responses can be used for discussion.

what happens next?

Related activities include bis 23, 24, 42, and 53.

☐

which antacid? or
the morning after the night before

Which antacid may be best for you? You may feel as if your life depends on it. Many commercial antacid products are readily available at drugstores with lots of trade names. They can provide an interesting science activity. The problem is, Which product generates most gas?

You will need materials for a gas-collecting system, plus a little courage and some practice. Get a simple, shallow aluminum pan, plus a closed container (flask or bottle) fitted with a stopper that has a piece of glass tubing through it (a soda straw through a cork, with the area around the straw sealed with wax or clay, will do). Also, find a connecting hose to siphon off the gas, and an inverted, closed container (the glass) filled with water that allows the water to be displaced by the incoming gas. Attach a piece of tape to the side of the container and mark off units for measuring the volume of the gas. The drawing illustrates the procedure. To invert a full glass of water, first place in the shallow pan two flat objects (rubber erasers will do). These will keep the inverted glass jar resting off the bottom. Once the reaction starts, the hose leading from the flask collecting the gas must be placed under the inverted glass filled with water. Put enough water in the shallow pan to cover the objects holding the glass off the bottom. This water level will hold the water inside the jar when it is put in place.

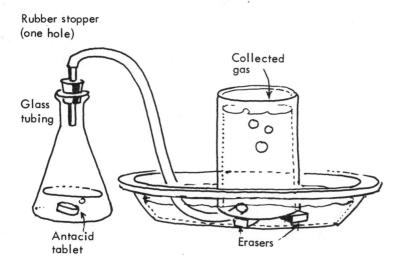

Rubber stopper
(one hole)

Glass
tubing

Collected
gas

Antacid
tablet

Erasers

How do you get the inverted glass of water into position? Fill a glass with water up to the brim. Place a 3 x 5 inch card over the mouth of the glass. With the flat of one hand over the card, press firmly against the glass and invert it. Do this over a sink — at least for the practice runs. You should be able to feel the card adhering to the inverted glass of water. There is a slight suction. Gingerly move it over to the shallow pan. Remove your hand. Lower it into place. When the glass is under the water in the pan and over the erasers, slip out the card and lower the glass.

Position the hose under the inverted glass. Put a little water in the flask. Drop in 1/4 tablet of your favorite antacid. Notice the reaction in the flask, how the gas bubbles within the inverted glass, and how the water is displaced by the gas. Collect data to measure the amount of gas given off by an antacid.

more...

Can you measure the amount of gas collected? How does the amount of gas collected vary with increased amounts of an antacid? Graph the results using 1/8, 1/4, 3/8, and 1/2 of a tablet.

be careful! remember any gas built up in a closed system is a potential danger — keep the lead hose clear!

Time your results as well as measuring the amounts of the gas. Does changing the temperature or amount of the water in the flask affect the results? Try hot, cold, or lukewarm water.

Does the variety of water affect the results? Try tap water, distilled water, salt water.

Compare equal amounts of different antacids. Which appears to be the best generator of gas? Which is the best antacid?

Was any gas lost? Does the gas combine with the water? How would you find out?

Related activities include bis 57 and 71.

comparing densities
with a hydrometer

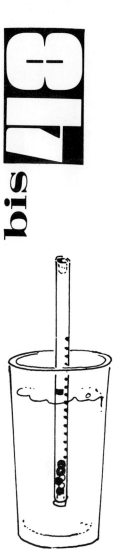

You need a base or reference in order to compare things. Water often is used for this purpose. It has a density of 1.0 g/cm³, or 1. Either things are less dense than 1 g/cm³ and float, more dense than 1 g/cm³ and sink, or they are equal in density, barely submerge in water, and do not sink to the bottom.

A good device for comparing densities is a hydrometer, which is easy to make. Fill the end of a clear plastic straw with melted sealing wax. Sealing wax is waterproof and is more effective than other waxes. Using a metric ruler and a waterproof marker, mark the straw in centimeter and half-centimeter units. Place some BB's, plus sand if necessary, in the bottom of the clear plastic straw. Put the straw in a large graduated cylinder or clear bottle filled close to the top with water. Put the weighted straw in the water. Adjust the BB's and sand so that the straw floats upright in the liquid. Mark the level of the water on the straw, labeling it 1. This will be the density reference point for water. What does it mean if "1" is clearly visible above the liquid level when the straw is floating in a liquid other than water? When the number 1 is below the surface of another liquid?

Using other containers filled with liquids such as syrup, alcohol, turpentine, and olive oil, check the level of the hydrometer compared to the reference point when in water. Can you infer which liquid would float on water? Sink below water? Try each example to prove your inferences.

more...

Try salt water, distilled water. Compare warm water with ice-cold water. Do they all have the same densities?

Try a density cocktail. Put in a jar some motor oil, popcorn oil, and water; almost any amount of each will do. Also add one piece of cardboard, two pieces of paraffin from a candle, and a small rock. Shake this mixture and let it stand. Can you predict the sequence of liquids as they settle out? Which will be on top? On the bottom?

Place an ice cube in cooking oil. Can you infer what will happen? Describe your observations. How can this be related to the movement of ocean currents?

Leave your hydrometer in salt water for a day or two. Does the density change?

Related activities include bis 65 and sst 11.

□

pop-bottle pouring

Measuring the volume of liquids with pop bottles can be fun and interesting.

Obtain fifteen or twenty jars of assorted sizes. Arrange them from smallest to largest and number them from 1 to 20.

Then, using a pop bottle as a standard unit of liquid measure, you can check the jars by pouring water from a pop bottle into the jar and recording the volume of the jar in pop-bottle units (pbu's) for each container.

The jars can now be ranked by the number of pbu's each will hold.

Did you get the same order for the jars ranked by number of pbu's held as you did when you initially arranged them by size? If not, why not? What were your sources of error?

Can you relate the pbu's to the metric volume measure (liters), or to the Imperial volume measure (quarts)?

What other measures could you use instead of pop bottles? Try medicine cups, paper cups, Styrofoam cups, medicine vials, and dropping bottles.

Related activities include bis 54, 69; and ss 24.

□

keysort classifying

Before doing this activity you will need to prepare a keysort classifying card. Cut this card out and tape or glue it to a piece of cardboard or manila folder of the same size. You will need many copies of this card; feel free to duplicate it.

On this card are forty punched holes, which will allow you to select up to forty characteristics of an object such as a mineral, bird, or leaf. Add more holes if you need more categories.

Using a paper punch, punch out holes near the edge of the card, as in the drawing. Be careful *not* to punch through the edge of the card or through the numbers!

Let's use a mineral classification key as our example, but you can use almost any subject or topic. Your only limits are your creativity and imagination.

Children can decide the mineral properties that could be used to classify them. Properties such as color, streak, luster, hardness, taste, texture, and magnetic or nonmagnetic.

We can divide color into numbered categories for our card:

1. White
2. Not white

Similar card categories might be established like this:

3. Salty taste
4. No salty taste
5. Magnetic
6. Not magnetic
7. Scratches your fingernail
8. Your fingernail scratches it
9. Feels greasy
10. Not greasy
11. Glassy
12. Dull
13. Streak
14. No streak

Halite

1 2 3 4 5 6 7 8 9 10 11 12 13 14 15 16
17
18
19
20
21
40
39
38 37 36 35 34 33 32 31 30 29 28 27 26 25 24 23 22

You can get as specific as you wish, using Mohs' hardness scale and specific gravities, or both.

Prepare one card for each mineral you include in your classification.

Let's use the mineral halite. Card numbers that would need to be punched out through the margin for halite would be 1, 3, 6, 8, 10, 11, and 13. This is shown in the sketch.

Make additional cards for any other minerals you want to include in your set. Make sure that you write the name of each mineral on the appropriate card.

When your card set is as complete as you wish, you are ready to try to classify an unknown mineral. Using a knitting needle or anything like it that will fit through all the holes in any stack of cards, you are ready to classify your unknown mineral.

If the mineral is not white, put the needle through hole 2 on the card and all the not white minerals will drop out. Discard the cards on the needle and use the drop out cards to continue classifying. (If only one card drops out, that is your mineral.)

If the unknown mineral is magnetic, put the needle through hole 5 and all magnetic minerals will drop out.

Continue this until only one card drops out. This is your mineral.

Questions to consider:

1. If one card drops out, can you be positive that it is the unknown mineral?
2. What would you do if your classification task ended with two cards?
3. What would you do if your classification task ended with no card dropping out?

Remember: A classification scheme is only as good as the properties used to make up the scheme and is valid only for the objects in the scheme.

What other uses could you make of classification cards in reading, language arts, mathematics, and social studies? How do computers use classification cards?

Related activities include bis 89 and ss 2.

□

the pendulum, or
the man on the flying trapeze

The man on the flying trapeze is a wonderful sight. Pendulums are not quite as captivating, but they involve much of the same physics. Pendulums can be elaborate or simple. Either way the principle is the same. A hanging bob is at rest, or it is in motion, and it will come to rest unless acted on by some other force. From a cup hook screwed into a meter stick suspended across two chair backs, hang a weighted object from a string. Set the weighted bob in motion. How long does the bob continue to swing?

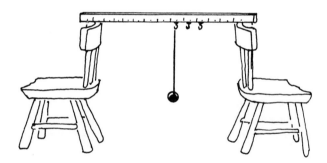

Investigate what happens when you change the length of the string. If the shape remains the same and the mass is altered, how does the mass of the weighted bob influence your results?

If the shape and mass are kept constant and the type of material is altered, how would the new material of the weighted bob influence your results?

Does the distance you pull the weighted bob out from the center influence your results? Try it.

Allow two similar bobs to hang (on same lengths of string) from the crossbar. Let one remain at rest, swing the other into an arc of approximately 30°, and predict what will happen to the stationary ball when one moving ball collides with the stationary ball.

What happens when we raise both similar bobs and release them simultaneously? Keep the angle of incidence small so the balls hit each other head-on.

This could be expanded to additional changes: change the weight of one bob. What do you think would happen in such cases? Try it.

What will happen here? Try it.

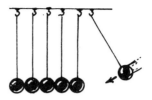

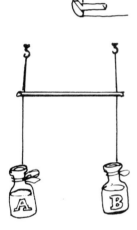

Present this situation to the students. Suspend two bottles filled with colored water or sand. Place a piece of dowel between them. Suspend it by cutting a notch in each end of the wood, as shown. Start container A swinging and watch what happens to both A and B. Have the students describe their observations. What explanation can they offer for the observed behavior?

more...

With a coil spring and a weighted object like a plastic bird attached to one end, design an experiment to investigate the effect of the bird's size on the number of oscillations, when the starting length is kept constant; and the effect of changing the size of the coil spring on the number of oscillations, keeping the starting length and bird size constant.

Graph the size of the coil against the number of oscillations and make several predictions. Test your predictions.

more...

Set up a simple pendulum and observe the effect on its period of altering amplitude, mass, and length. Then measure the corresponding values of length and periodic time. Suitable graphs should be plotted and the required length predicted.

Related activities include bis 94; ss 4 and 20.

what does it say? or
you don't need to know the language

This is an exercise in organization, observing, classifying, inferring, and predicting.

Using acceptable English, reconstruct sentence number 1 so that it can be read as you think it was intended. (Assume that Dekro is the trade name of a watch.)

1. *IMPORTANT*

Dekro, valid, be, be, sold, who, the, the, by, dated, and, in, guarantee, filled, jeweler, correctly, to, must, watch, this.

Analyze sentences 2 through 6. What words can you group together permitting you to infer that perhaps they have the same meaning in the various languages?

2. *IMPORTANT*

Pour être valable, la présente garantie doit être correctement remplie et datée par le concessionnaire Dekro qui a vendu la montre.

3. *WICHTIG*

Dieser Garantieschein ist nur gültig, wenn er vom Dekro-Uhrmacher, der die Ihr verkaufte, ordnungsgemäss ausgefüllt und datiert worden ist.

4. *IMPORTANTE*

Per essere valida, la presente garanzia deve essere correttamente compilate e datata dal concessionario Dekro che ha effettuato la vendita.

5. *IMPORTANTE*

Para ser válida, la presente garantía debe estar correctamente rellena y fechada por el concesionario Dekro que ha vendido el reloj.

6. *IMPORTANTE*

Para ser valida, a presente garantia deve ser preenchida correctamente e datada pelo agante Dekro que vendeu o relogio.

7.

What might you infer sentence number 7 says?
Related activities include bis 44 and 57.

☐

situational science activities

Science is, among other things, a search for answers. Answers are preceded by questions. To resolve some questions in science we must get physically involved because we have to manipulate concrete objects, such as fruit flies, reagents, test tubes, flasks, and beakers. This is not necessarily true of all problem situations. Some are altogether intellectual experiences in which ideas are the only things manipulated.

Children, as participants in this enterprise called science, assess, organize, and interpret data. This is sometimes reflected in long, scientific investigations, like a study comparing the path of the sun across the sky during all seasons of the year. Other science investigations may last as little as several days, a week, or several weeks before culminating. This culmination may or may not result in an answer to the problem.

Along with long and short investigations in science, children need daily experiences with the same procedures, such as assessing, organizing, and interpreting data. These daily thinking excursions can be provided for by situational science activities. These activities do not replace the "normal" science program; they augment it. These situations are brief confrontations with real or fictitious situations supplied by the instructor in the form of duplicated handouts for reading. Challenged to solve the problems, the students may map out strategies, raise appropriate questions, and consider differing explanations.

Each student can contribute to this exercise because no previous knowledge is usually required. Involvement in these activities supports the creative venture that science is. The situations do not have any "right" answers; some have no answers at all. This baffles the students who have come to think, erroneously, that all answers to problems are to be found between the covers of books. Situations that do not have apparent answers can be utilized in the sense that you can ask, What questions, if you had the answers, would help refine the explanation? You may furnish additional facts to maneuver the discussion to a conclusion or simply end it by asking:

Do we have enough information? What possibilities do we now know of? What more do we need to know?

Some examples:

WHO OR WHAT BELONGS WHERE?

The unlabeled floor plan of a school building may be used as a situational science activity.

Have the children examine the floor plan. You may wish to have them label specific areas in which typical schoolroom assignments go on. Or you may choose to leave areas unlabeled. You provide as much or little information as necessary to involve your students in as much sophistication as you think suitable. You, as the arbitrator, may assume one or more of these roles: principal, secretary of the board of education, chairman of the board of education, architect, taxpayer. Each allows you to move the interaction forward or slow it down, as you see fit.

Depending on the grade level, one or more of these questions (better yet, conjure up some new ones) may be asked of your students:

Where would you locate your classroom?
What factors influenced this decision?
What room assignments would you make for classrooms housing children in grades 1 to 6?
Where should the principal's office be located?
How should the location of the principal's office be related to other areas?
Where would you put the nurse's office? Where would you place the music room? The art room?
Should the large area on the right be a gymnasium or a cafeteria?
If the large room on the right is a gymnasium (or a cafeteria), in which direction would you add on an additional room for a cafeteria (or a gymnasium)?
What additional information would be useful in making a better decision?
How many uses can you think of for the open grass area?

From Alfred De Vito, "Who or What Belongs Where?" *Science and Children*, vol. 12, no. 4 (January 1975), p. 31. By permission.

Who or what belongs where?

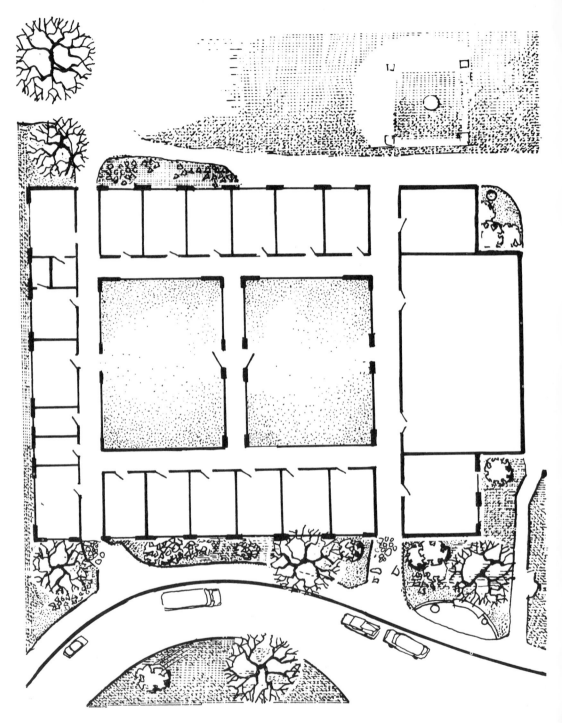

The students' responses should always be accompanied by a suitable reason. You as the moderator (in your different roles) challenge or accept each response as you promote thinking with the problem of "who or what belongs where?"

HARRIET'S HOLIDAY

Nila and Donna are two sisters who lived in an apartment building. One of their neighbors was a retired schoolteacher named Harriet. Among their other neighbors was a young couple whose parents wanted to visit them for a month. The parents of the young couple lived in Hawaii. The young couple looked for an apartment for their parents but could not find one for just a month. They happened to mention this to the schoolteacher, who suggested that she and the visiting parents swap apartments. She would live in their home in Hawaii for one month and they could live in her apartment for one month. The arrangements were made. Harriet left for Hawaii. The next day the young couple's parents arrived. They lived in Harriet's apartment and drove Harriet's car. They stayed exactly one month. Nila and Donna expected Harriet home the day after the parents left. For two weeks they waited and still Harriet did not return, or at least it appeared that she had not returned.

Here are some facts:

Harriet's car remained in front of her apartment.
Harriet's daughter lived in the same town.
Occasionally the daughter was seen entering the apartment and from time to time she would start the car and allow it to run.
It was football season. Harriet was a real football fan. She always attended the college games in town. If she had returned on time, she could have attended two of the remaining games.
The town was in the Midwest. Harriet had no relative other than her daughter who lived in town.

Nila and Donna began to wonder what had happened to Harriet. For what reasons might Harriet not have returned?

ENGINEERING NOAH'S ARK

God commanded Noah to build an ark. It was to be 300 cubits (492 feet) long, 50 cubits (82 feet) wide, and 30 cubits (49 feet) high. The ark was to have a door on its side, a skylight, and three decks, each deck divided into many rooms.

From Alfred De Vito, "Engineering Noah's Ark," *Science and Children,* vol. 11, no. 5 (January/February 1974), pp. 32–33. By permission.

Noah was warned of a forthcoming flood of waters upon the earth. It was to rain upon the earth forty days and forty nights. He was told that the flood would destroy every living thing. Noah was commanded to gather together at least two of every living creature (a male and female of each). These were to be placed on the ark along with Noah and his family of sons and their wives. All were to be kept safe on the ark until the flood waters passed away. All this Noah did.

It is thought that the capacity of the ark was approximately 5500 tons, enough for at least 1000 pairs of animals. Also it is believed that Noah's ark had no sails, no oars, and no engine. It is further believed that the ark could not be steered, for it had no rudder.

Suppose you were Noah and you agreed to design and build the ark, to assemble the animals of the earth, and to feed and care for all these living creatures, how would you do it?

Design an ark using the measurements and requirements provided. Do you think Noah's ark looked like a typical boat? What would your ark look like? Make a sketch or build a model of your ark.

Noah's ark was to have three decks. Which animals would you put on the lowest level, the middle level, and the top level? What reasons can you give for placing the animals where you did?

An ark 30 cubits (49 feet) high is a tall ark. How would you get the animals of the earth up and into the ark? Once you got them up there, how would you get them to the level you wanted them at?

In your design of the ark, you must provide for storing food for the animals as well as the people on the ark. How will the appetites of the living creatures of the earth affect their distance from the food storage area?

Where on Noah's ark would be the best place to locate yourself and your family?

Some 4000 to 5000 years later (in 1955), Fernand Navarra, a French businessman and amateur explorer, found on Mt. Ararat in eastern Turkey an estimated 50 tons of wood buried in a glacial ice pack. Samples of this wood have been identified as hand-tooled oak, treated with a pitchlike substance. It is a mystery how so much wood got to this spot, at an elevation of 14,000 feet. It is several thousand feet above the treeline and more than 300 miles from the nearest trees of any size. Airplane pilots flying over Mt. Ararat have repeatedly reported a ship-like shadow in the ice. Mr. Navarra believes that this wood is the original material of the biblical ark of Noah. What do you think?

page 88

SAILOR BEWARE

Off the coast of the continental United States lies a mysterious area of ocean. An imaginary line connecting Bermuda, Florida, and Puerto Rico forms the boundary of this so-called Bermuda Triangle, which covers about 440,000 square miles of open sea. Some lovers of hair-raising sea mysteries have called it the Deadly Triangle or the Twilight Zone.

These reports are strange but true:

1. Columbus sailed through the triangle in 1492. He recorded seeing a strange bolt of fire fall into the sea. Several days later his men were terrified by a baffling disturbance of the ship's compass.
2. Between the years 1781 and 1812, four American naval vessels disappeared without explanation.
3. In 1918, the U.S.S. *Cyclops* sailed northward into the triangle — and disappeared. Not one clue was ever found.
4. Since 1946, some twenty other ships and airplanes have disappeared completely. One strange reported case involved five Navy torpedo bombers. Inside the deadly triangle, the patrol leader radioed, "Strange things are happening. We can't be sure of any direction. Even the sea doesn't look as it should." Then all was silent. A rescue seaplane was sent out. In twenty minutes it too vanished without a trace.
5. In 1963, a merchant ship, a fishing boat, and two Air Force tanker jets disappeared.

Though many ships and planes travel this triangle each day, an unusual number of craft have vanished without a trace. Neither wreckage nor victims were ever found.

What explanations can you suggest to account for these strange events?
How might you set out to support your explanations?
Would you travel through or over the Bermuda Triangle?
Is this rate of losses natural for every 440,000 square miles of open sea?
Is anything unusual about the position of this triangle on the earth's surface that might account for these strange events?

A PALEO-INDIAN KILL

Eight thousand five-hundred years ago a group of hunters on the Great Plains stampeded a herd of buffalo (bison) into a gulch and butchered them.

Adapted from Alfred De Vito, "Stop, Read, and Think — A Buffalo Stampede," *Science and Children,* vol. 12, no. 2 (October 1974), p. 30. By permission.

Here are some facts:

Bison are gregarious animals. They have keen smell but relatively poor vision. They move in herds of 50 to 300 animals.

The arroyo was approximately 200 ft long. Its narrow western end was only about 1½ ft deep and the same in width, but it grew progressively deeper and wider to the east. Halfway down the arroyo its width was 5 ft and its depth 6 ft; farther down it was 12 ft wide and 7 ft deep.

The arroyo contained the remains of 200 bison, whose bones were found in three distinct layers. The bottom layer held 13 complete skeletons; the hunters had not touched these animals. The second layer had essentially complete skeletons from which a leg or two, some ribs, or the skull were missing. These bison had been only partly butchered. The top layer contained single bones and segments. Sixteen calves (remains) were uncovered.

The geology of the surrounding area was composed of a reddish brown, friable (easily broken) rock.

The Paleo-Indians were very artistic.

During a feast a man could consume from 10 to 20 lb of fresh meat a day.

100 lb of fresh meat would provide 20 lb of dried meat.

About 75% of the bison were completely butchered, which would mean that the total weight of bison meat would have been 45,300 lb.

There was very little wood in the area.

A Plains Indian could completely butcher a bison in an hour.

10 lb of meat per person a day were eaten. The remainder was preserved. The preserved meat and fat, together with the hides, would have weighed about 7,350 lb.

Reconstruct the scene. What facts here will help solve these problems? Find:

1. *The month of the year in which the hunt took place.*
2. *The direction in which the wind blew on the day of the kill.*
3. *The direction of the hunters' drive.*
4. *The manner in which they butchered their quarry.*
5. *The choice of cuts to be eaten on the spot.*
6. *The probable number of hunters involved.*
7. *How long they remained at this location.*
8. *How much meat (weight) each member had to carry away.*

WHAT'S YOUR DECISION?

By some unusual circumstances, a small airplane crash-landed on a large ice floe in the upper North Atlantic Ocean. All in the small plane survived. The group consisted of the pilot, who was a world famous explorer; a movie star; a minister; a young child; a pregnant woman; an old man dying of a terminal illness; the Secretary-General of the United Nations; and a famous eye surgeon, who was on the brink of an important breakthrough in his research which might aid thousands of blind individuals to see.

The ice floe is drifting southward into warmer water and melting rapidly. It will melt completely before it reaches any major shipping lanes. Enough flotation equipment was salvaged from the airplane to construct a small raft for only one person. When the ice floe is completely melted, which individual should be allowed to use the raft? Or should no one use it? What is the basis for your decision?

WHAT'S GOOD FOR WHOM?

Much wildlife has been killed in recent years as a result of human technological developments. Many wild animals have fled into land not yet touched by people. Assume that in "Hidden Valley" in the Arctic Tundra, the last herd of "Malibar moose" has found a safe home. Once abundant in the cold regions of North America, the animals have been driven away or killed by advancing civilization. This is their last stand.

The Great Alabaster Oil Company has discovered an oil deposit in Hidden Valley and is taking steps to begin drilling.

Permit the students to raise their own questions and concerns in this complicated situation through role-playing a debate. Some questions you might pose to begin the debate are:

Do we have a problem?
Who will benefit from the oil deposit?
Who will not benefit by it?
What are some of the short- and long-term gains?
What are some of the short- and long-term losses?
How can we settle the problem?
Do we need additional information?

With these and additional questions that you and the children raise, let each child choose one of the following roles:

A local government conservation official
A driller for the Great Alabaster Oil Company
An elected leader of the local area
The person in charge of discovering new oil deposits for the oil
    company
The head of the "Save Our Wildlife" society
An Eskimo from a nearby village
A resident of a town located near Hidden Valley
A person from the antipollution committee
The secretary of commerce in the area

From Alfred De Vito, "What's Good for Whom?" *Science and Children,* vol. 10, no. 5 (January/February 1973), p. 32. Reproduced with permission. Copyright 1973, by the National Science Teachers Association, 1742 Connecticut Ave., N.W., Washington, D.C. 20009.

THE DELICATE DILEMMA

If the current quality of life on earth is to be maintained, it has been stated that zero population growth at the 7 billion level is required. With controls, by the turn of the century the world should reach a stable population of 7 billion people. Without controls, the population of the world by the year 2000 might reach close to 35 billion people.

With the recent major accomplishments in the space program, some people have suggested that a solution to the world's overpopulation is the colonization of space. It has been suggested that we simply prepare to move out to another planet in our own galaxy or another galaxy.

By contrast:
The United States space vehicle Eagle III *is to land on a nearby planet next summer. One of its assignments is to test soil samples on the spot for signs of life. Life would be indicated by the presence of such organic compounds as carbon dioxide and methane.*

If evidence of life is found, world biologists would be most anxious to compare life on this planet to earth life in the laboratory.

The problem:
Scientists are arguing whether to keep or kill living things a spacecraft eventually may bring back from other places in space.

Some thoughts:
Living things brought in from space may infect the earth and endanger all of us.

Some scientists believe living organisms from other places in space would be so affected by the earth's temperature, humidity, and oxygen content that they would be difficult to keep alive, even in a laboratory. Thus, they doubt that any living thing brought to earth would present a threat of infection.

Some scientists believe that what we might learn from living things brought from outer space would be so valuable, we should take the risk.

Other scientists believe that the threat from unknown danger is so great that no risk should be taken.

Are there solutions to these problems? Should we colonize space? If earth people invade space, might we infect the planets we land on? Should we permit living things from outer space to invade earth? What do you think?

Success with situational science activities depends on your accepting the value of reading and verbalizing about science. Also, a freewheeling questioning technique must be developed and used. Situational science activities can be a valuable adjunct to your sciencing in the classroom. It can also be an aid to your reading program.

You can learn to write your own situational science activities. Think of situations that arise around the house or school, and read the papers and periodicals for others. You should look for interesting, puzzling situations or those which provoke inquiry. Then write them up like an inquiry. It does take practice, but it is worth the results.

Related activities include bis 23, 24, 32, and 46.

□

licorice lengths

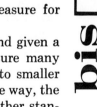

The task of dividing long pieces of licorice into equal lengths so that each member of the class will get the same measure is an excellent measurement activity.

Children can select their own standard units of measure for dividing the licorice into equal pieces.

Once standard units of licorice have been obtained and given a name (any name will do) they can be used to measure many objects. The standard unit may need to be divided into smaller units for measuring small objects accurately. In the same way, the standard unit may need to be combined with several other standard units to measure large distances, such as the length of the room.

Once these activities have been accomplished, the licorice standard units can be converted to either the metric or Imperial systems by comparison with an appropriate ruler.

more...

Why are standard units — in this case, units of measurement — important? How do they help make communication easier? Are large measurements easier to understand?

Who decides what units the United States use?

What units of length are used in America? Why do we have two systems? Which one do you like best? Where do they come from?

Measure some of the objects in the room in centimeters and inches. Do some come out in whole numbers, like 10 or 24? If a desk is 2 meters long, what does this tell you about the measurements used in its construction?

Related activities include bis 49, 69; and ss 24.

☐

sandwich-bag gardens

Fold a piece of paper toweling (any type of toweling will do) in half in one direction and then fold it in half in the opposite direction so that it will fit into about two-thirds of a sandwich bag (6¼ x 5½ inches).

Fold the paper towel again to make a tray about 3 cm in width for the seeds (see the figure). To observe the roots of the plants, make small holes (depending on the size of the seeds) in the bottom of the tray.

Open the tray, insert the seeds you want to use, and reclose the tray, taping the ends. Slide the folded towel into the sandwich bag and dampen the towel with a measured amount of water.

Questions to consider:

Where should I place (hang) my sandwich-bag garden for best growth?

How much water will it need? How many times a week should it be watered? Do different types of seeds need different amounts of water?

What types of seeds will grow best? How long does it take for your seeds to germinate?

 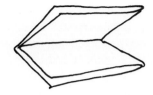

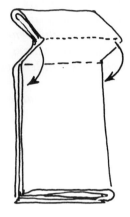 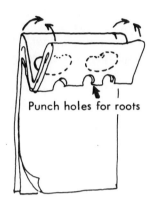

Punch holes for roots

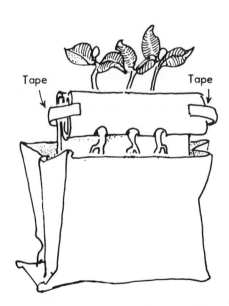

Tape   Tape

How many seeds should I use in each sandwich bag? Should all the seeds be of the same type?

Does the type of toweling make a difference? Try it and see.

Does the type of sandwich bag make a difference? Test it.

more...

Make a "living" bulletin board.

Test small quantities of fertilizer. Does fertilizer really make a difference? Graph stem and root growth rates of the plants in relation to time. Compare your results with those of a friend.

Hang sandwich-bag gardens in the room to receive different exposures (north, south, east, and west wall), or on the outside of a building. Compare the growth rates. If there is a difference, how do you account for it?

Add food coloring to the water in your sandwich-bag garden and observe what happens. Can you make a prediction?

Better yet — think of your own ideas and test them!

more...

Cut an inch or two from the top of a carrot or pineapple, set it in a shallow dish of water, and place it in a sunny window. Observe what happens. Try beet and turnip tops too. Try other vegetables.

Seeds from many of the fruits and nuts we buy can be raised into seedlings. Before sprouting, seeds of deciduous fruits and nuts need a period of moist winter chilling. Infer why this is the case. You can supply the chill to break this natural dormancy by storing the seeds in the refrigerator at 40°F. Provide moisture by placing the seeds in plastic bags with wet vermiculite. The length of chilling time needed is:

Almonds	*4 weeks*	*Peaches*	*3 months*
Apples	*2–3 months*	*Pears*	*2–3 months*
Apricots	*3–4 weeks*	*Walnuts*	*3 months*
Grapes	*3 months*	*Grapefruit*	*None*

Plant walnuts about 4–6 inches deep and all the others about 3 inches deep. Watch your forest grow!

Related activities include bis 2, 26, 31, 115; ss 12; sst 10 and 12.

every litter bit helps

Get a big bag and collect some litter in your schoolyard, neighborhood, or shopping center and put it in your bag.

When you return after your litter hunt, empty it from your bag and sort it into several piles; classify it by any method you wish. Have a friend join you to guess the method you used to classify your litter. Was the guess correct?

Count the number of items in each pile of litter and make a graph — any type will do, bar graph, line graph, or histogram. We made our graph by plotting the number of pieces of litter and the kind of litter we collected.

Can you use your graph to answer these questions?

How many kinds of litter did you find?
Which type of litter was most common?
Which type did you find least of? Why?
Which type of litter do you predict a friend would find if you
   sent him or her to the area where you found your litter?
   Try it and see if your prediction is correct.
What other inferences could you make from your graph?

Try a different collection spot. Will you have the same results? Why were your results the same or different?

Obtain a magnet and draw it through your litter while tied to a string. Do you have a new way of classifying your litter?

more...

How would the litter data you collected vary if you lived in a city like New York or Chicago, compared to Olean, New York, or Lafayette, Indiana? How would you compare these areas to a rural area or to your area?

Prepare a list of suggestions for reducing the amount and type of litter you collected. Try your suggestions and then collect litter again and see if your suggestions have worked. Good luck!

Related activities include bis 33, 89; and ss 3.

experimenting by advertising

Each year billions of dollars are spent by companies in extolling the virtues of their products or services and why you should use them or avail yourself of them. Many advertisements emphasize experiments that have been conducted on a product or service and its superiority over a similar product by a competing company.

To get started on your "experimenting by advertising," start collecting advertisements that mention experiments conducted in a scientific manner. They can easily be found in newspapers and magazines.

Some of the experiments can be duplicated in the classroom, but others must be simulated because they would be too expensive. Here's an example of each.

An advertisement from one manufacturer states that a wool carpet cleans better than other types of carpet. Using this advertisement as a beginning, students can identify experimental variables, such as:

> Type of product used to clean carpet
> Types of carpets (100% wool, wool blend, nylon, orlon)
> Thickness of carpet pile
> Color of carpet
> Use of carpet (recreation room, kitchen, baby's room, living
>   room)
> Definition of *clean*

Your students will be able to obtain free carpet samples from carpet stores and develop their own experiments to test the hypothesis that a wool carpet can be cleaned more readily than carpets made from other fibers. They will be able to think of additional variables they want to consider.

After the data have been collected, students may make interpretations based on these data. Did they agree with the claims expressed in the advertisement? Several groups of students may have collected data suitable for graphing.

One advertisement that can be simulated or conducted outside the classroom is the claim by a manufacturer that their color television set has the "best picture." This challenge could be used as an instrument for evaluating if your students can identify experimental variables and then design their own investigations.

It would be impractical to bring many color sets into the classroom, so that this experiment could be conducted as a simulation

Adapted from Gerald H. Krockover, "Experiment Through Advertising," *Science and Children* (January/February 1973), pp. 28–29. By permission.

or by having children go to different stores or households. Some variables might be:

Size of picture tube in set
Age of set
Antenna, cable, or rabbit ears used for reception
Definition of "best picture"
Color
Brightness
Focus

Students can design an experiment they *would do* if they had any equipment they wished. They can then be evaluated on their ability to meet the criteria of skills involved in experimenting.

Students can also be encouraged to develop their *own* advertisements. The advertisements can be classified and individual students should be allowed to select their own advertisements for experimenting.

more...

Is it important to examine for yourself the claims made in advertisements? Why? Where can you turn for help in investigating whether or not advertising claims are reliable? What consumer groups can you name? Make a rating system that evaluates whether or not a commercial's claims are 100% true.

start cutting out those advertisements!

Related activities include bis 47 and 71.

making motion booklets

Motion booklets are an excellent activity for illustrating the motion of an object when the pages are flipped rapidly. The motion of a flower opening or closing, an egg hatching, or a person running are easy to imitate.

On the following pages are samples that can be copied and stapled together to make motion booklets.

try it!

After the motion booklet has been constructed, consider these questions:

Does it make a difference if you flip the pages from back to front or from front to back? What observations can you make?

What difference does the speed with which you flip the pages make? Compare a slow flip with a fast flip and observe differences.

Try to put several motion booklets together to tell a story. How many can you add to tell a complete story?

Can you write a story to go with your booklet? Maybe you can prepare an audiotape to go with your booklet. What about a poem? Or a song?

Using the key for the motion book provided, see if you can find the frames you'd repeat to have the fly circle the frog twice. How would you make the fly circle the frog in reverse? What frames might you repeat three or four times to increase the suspense?

Can you cut out the frames, mix them up, and then put them in order again — without the key? Try it!

Relate this to other science activities, such as the motion of a pendulum, a sphere rolling down an inclined plane, a runner in a track event. Correlate the rate at which the pages flip with the moving object's apparent speed.

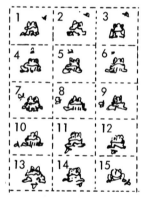

more...

Make a weather motion booklet from the frames provided.

Make a wheel motion machine using the drawing of a tree falling.

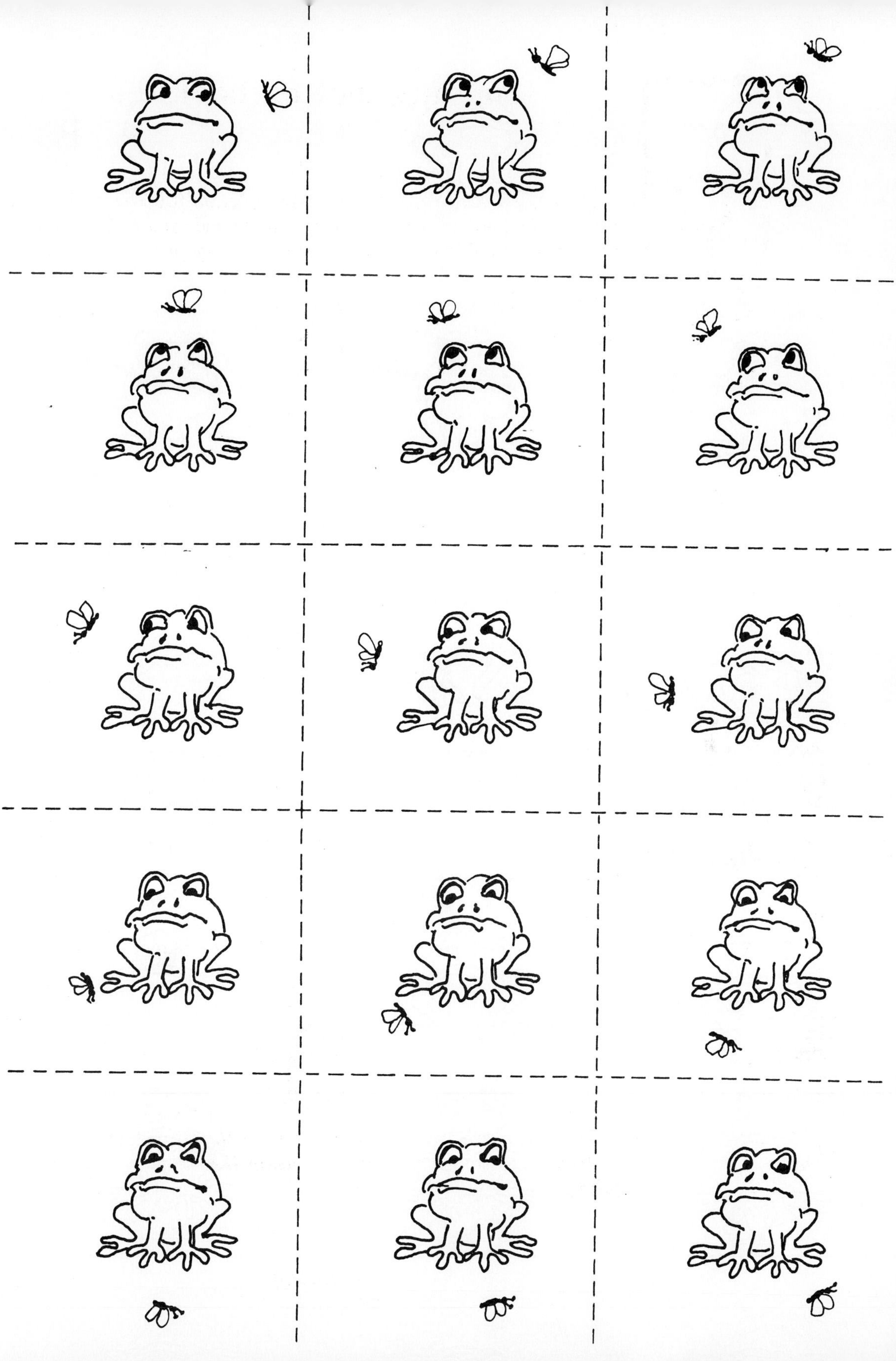

H High **L** Low **—** Cold **=** Warm ▨ Rain

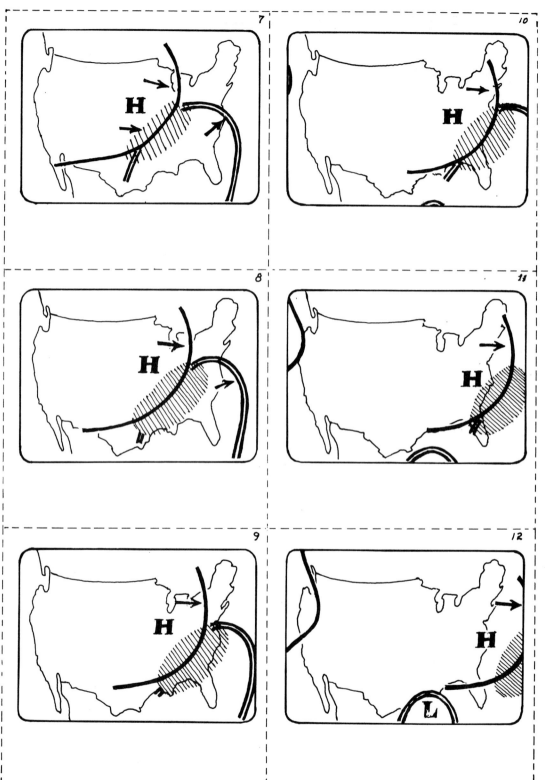

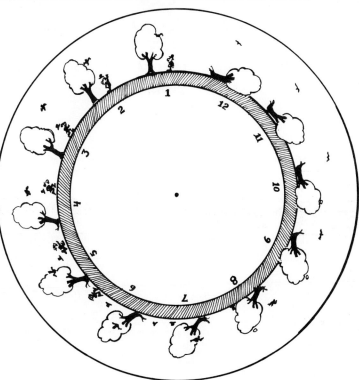

Make moving plant pictures next. You will need 4 white cards the size of a postcard.

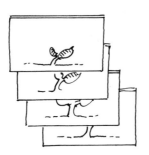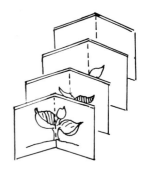

Draw a picture of a young plant on the first card. Draw the sequence of growth on the other cards, keeping to the center.

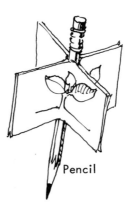

Pencil

Fold the cards back to back. Clip or paste together. Leave a narrow space so a pencil can fit through the center. Twirl your pencil and watch the action. Try motion pictures of someone planting, watering, or cutting a flower. Think of more!

Related activities include bis 46, 80, 116; and ss 21.

water—the miracle liquid

Water is a fascinating liquid. When you introduce activities with water, you are sure to get, at first, remarks like, "Are we going to play with water? Quick, get my water pistol." But anyone looking closely will see that water truly is a fascinating liquid. "Water skin" is one of the natural wonders of the world. A drop of water hanging precariously from a spout clings there until it becomes swollen, too heavy to resist the pull of gravity. Dropping, it quickly forms a sparkling sphere encased in a tough, transparent skin. This same skin forms instantly when water meets other materials. The water molecules squeeze close together when they are in contact with air or other matter, making a dense layer. This squeeze is called *surface tension*. The attractive force of like molecules for each other is known as the *cohesive* force; it makes each drop of water do something to maintain its identity. This cohesiveness keeps it intact until it comes in contact with another material. *Adhesion* makes unlike molecules attract each other more than like molecules. Here are several interesting activities that illustrate adhesion, cohesion, and surface tension:

Sprinkle a few drops of water on wax paper. Does the water spread out or form droplets? With a toothpick, break a drop into smaller and smaller drops. What shape do the smaller drops assume? The attraction (cohesiveness) of the water molecules for each other is greater than their attraction for the wax molecules on the wax paper. How does water on the hood of an unwaxed car compare with that of a waxed car hood?

Why are water droplets round? Geometrically, the most conservative shape in nature is a sphere. It can contain more volume with less corresponding surface area than any other shape. A 5 cm cube has a volume of 125 cm^3 and a total exposed surface area of 150 cm^2. A sphere with the same volume has a total exposed surface area of about 125 cm^2.

Fill a container half full of water. Put several drops of olive oil or salad oil on the surface of the water. With an eyedropper, slowly add rubbing alcohol by carefully letting it run down the sides of the glass. Describe your observations. What questions could you ask yourself to arrive at an explanation of what you observe? Was the oil floating on top of the water? Do rubbing alcohol and water mix? Does the manner in which you added the rubbing alcohol affect the results you observed? Would it make

*any difference if you inserted the eyedropper near the bottom
of the water and then released the rubbing alcohol? How can you
explain your observations?*

Some substances, like soap or detergent, reduce the surface tension of water:

*Float an insect pin or straight pin in a glass with water. A
needle is more difficult, and a paper clip challenges the true
performer. If you have difficulty, place the object on a piece of
wax paper already atop the water, then gently push the paper
away. Drop a small chip of soap or detergent (powder or liquid)
near the needle. Can you explain what you observe next?*

*Sprinkle some talcum powder on the surface of water in a glass.
Dip the soaped tip of a toothpick in its center. What made the
talcum powder rupture?*

Another good extension of this activity is to place two toothpicks in water, and touch a soaped tip of a toothpick between them. With clean water and container, have the children repeat this activity, but now putting a few drops of alcohol between the toothpicks. In all these instances the surface tension has been changed by some added material. The corresponding motion is an adjustment of the floating materials to a new environment.

These same activities could be used to provide practice in quantifying skills:

*Float a piece of wire screen. Gently place some small washers
on it. How many washers do you predict it will take before the
weight exceeds the surface tension of the water? Double the
area of the wire screen. Triple it. What does this do to the number
of washers required to sink the screen? Double it? Triple it? Did
you confirm your predictions?*

Surface tension and adhesion together produce another characteristic property of liquids called *capillarity*. Capillarity lifts water up from under the ground, through porous soil to the roots of plants, then up through stems and leaves. Water moves up a narrow glass tube by the combined action of adhesion and surface tension. The water sticks to the sides of the tube and the molecules at the head of the column are moved upward by the attraction of the drier spot just beyond. The opposing force of gravity is negligible against this advancing action. When the weight of the water and the force of capillarity are equal, the water will stop rising. *Hypothesis:* The smaller the diameter of the tube, the higher the liquid rises in the tube. Can you design an activity to test this hypothesis?

Frozen water floats. Most substances contract when they become colder, more dense. Ice does not. Water at its freezing point expands to about 10% more volume than it has as water. It is less dense than the water it displaces, and so it floats. If it did not do so, we would eliminate frozen water pipes bursting, but we would have other major problems. What problems do you predict would be caused by water freezing and becoming more dense?

Related activities include bis 34, 66, 86, 91, 93, and 107.

make your deposit here

bis 60

You will need a gallon jar or jug and soil, clay, sand, gravel, pebbles, and water.

Put equal amounts of the soil, clay, sand, gravel, and pebbles into the gallon jar. Add enough water so that it is almost full. *Carefully* shake or stir the mixture very thoroughly.

Can you predict the order in which the materials will be deposited (settle out) in the jar?

Stop stirring and let the mixture stand. Observe and record the order with which the sediment settles to the bottom of the container.

Which material settles out first? Can you infer why? Which material settles out last? Can you infer why?

How well did your observations compare with your predictions?

Do you predict that this would be an accurate model for the deposition of sediments on the sea floor?

Can you match the sediment to the rock it comes from, such as clay-shale, sand-sandstone?

Can you prepare a list of variables that would control the rate at which sediments settle? Did you mention size of the particle, shape of the sediment, density of the sediment?

Can you design an investigation to show the effects of shape on the formation of sediments?

Can you analyze the sediment and reseparate it? Try using filter paper and screens.

What if you use salt water instead of tap water or hot water instead of cool water? Will you get the same order and rate of deposition for those sediments?

more...

After a 24-hour settling-out period, insert a soda straw into the gallon jug of sorted earth materials to collect samples of sediments still in solution. Get the samples by putting a soda straw down into the water, capping the straw with your thumb to retain the water, removing the straw and water, and filtering the solution through a piece of filter paper. The solid sediments are retained as the water passes through the filter paper. Allow all the water in the filter paper to evaporate. Weigh the filter paper before and after. The difference is the amount of sediment suspended in solution at the time and the level at which the sample was taken. You can take samples at various depths and intervals.

Record your data. Graph the results, plotting depth against time. Can you extrapolate anything from this graph about materials held in solution?

Related activities include bis 19, 22, 90, and 95.

number of turns, number of tacks

For this activity you will need to make an electromagnet.

How many thumbtacks or paper clips can be picked up by your electromagnet? What variables can you identify that will affect the strength of an electromagnet (measured by the number of thumbtacks picked up)?

Variables you might wish to investigate include: number of batteries, strength of the batteries (number of volts), type and diameter of wire used, type and size of nail used, and number of turns of wire on the nail.

be careful, the wires and the nails can get hot!
handle with care!

You may want to investigate the number of turns versus the number of tacks picked up when everything else is kept constant and one battery is used. A data table can be prepared, comparing the number of turns with the number of tacks. Do your results indicate a trend? Did you notice that as the number of turns increases, the number of tacks picked up also increases — up to a limit? The limit is the strength of the battery and the other variables mentioned earlier.

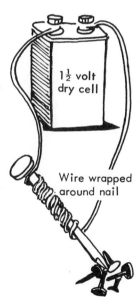

1½ volt dry cell

Wire wrapped around nail

Next you may want to try the same activity, this time using two batteries. Does it make any difference if you connect the batteries in parallel? In series? Batteries connected in parallel have one wire connecting similar terminals of all the batteries involved (for example, the negative or outside terminal), and a separate wire joining all the remaining similar terminals (the positive or center terminals). Batteries connected in series have one wire going from the negative terminal of one battery to the positive terminal of another battery, and so on. You may want to predict the performance of parallel and series arrangements and then test your predictions.

You can graph the data collected for a three-battery system and use your graph to make further predictions:

How many tacks or paper clips do you predict would be picked up by the electromagnet with four turns on the nail?

What is the smallest number of turns that can be used to pick up the greatest number of paper clips?

Does the experimental evidence support your observations in the one- and two-battery systems using the thumbtacks or paper clips?

Do you observe that as the number of turns increases, the

number of paper clips picked up also increases, until a limit is reached?

Predict the limit for a four-battery system, using your results for a one-, two-, and three-battery system.

more...

There is a relationship between magnetism and electricity. Pass a single-wire conductor through a hole in a sheet of cardboard and connect the ends to a dry cell battery. Sprinkle some iron filings on the cardboard around the wire. Tap the cardboard gently with your finger. What do you observe?

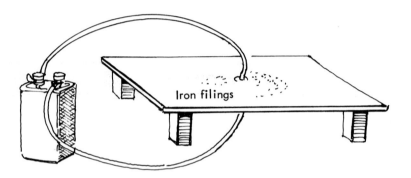

Iron filings

A magnetic field exists around a coil. Thread a length of insulated wire through a sheet of cardboard to form a coil. Sprinkle some iron filings around the coil and connect the ends of the wire to the dry cell battery. Tap the cardboard gently with your finger. What do you observe?

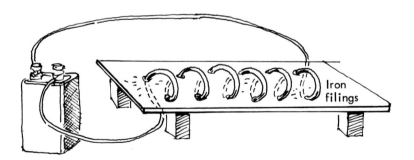

Iron filings

Related activities include bis 68, 75; ss 13; and sst 9.

cemetery etchings

Visit your local cemetery and find a wealth of valuable information.

Record the birth and death dates and sex from about fifty tombstones. Prepare a bar graph of age and sex. Questions that you might consider: Do the data you collected show that males or females live longer? Have males and females lived longer in the last twenty-five years than in the last fifty years? Did fewer children under a year old die in the last twenty-five years than in the last fifty years?

Prepare a line graph of number of years lived and year of birth. What trends do you notice? Do your data support the contention that we're living longer than our grandparents?

What inferences could you make to explain why people died at an earlier age in the past than now?

Using black crayons or charcoal and large sheets of white paper, you can prepare tombstone rubbings, if allowed by local law. If they are not allowed, bring a camera and take pictures.

Related activities include bis 87 and 88.

□

the potato and the spoon, or who forced me?

For this activity you will need a potato, a spoon, a spool, and approximately 120 cm of strong twine.

Tie one end of the twine to a medium-sized potato. Thread the other end through the hole of the spool and tie it securely to the spoon. Have one person hold the spool so that the potato hangs freely beneath it and the thread near the spoon so that it is a short distance from the spool. Next, have the child give the spool a

quick circular motion so that the spoon will spin in a horizontal circle.

Now, can you predict what will happen to the potato? What effect will the motion of the spoon have on the potato? Try it.

Try spinning the spoon at different speeds. Did you observe that if you spin the spoon *rapidly*, the potato will rise all the way up to the bottom of the spool? Did you also observe, however, that if you spin it *slowly*, the potato will move down?

Can you attain a speed for spinning the spoon so that the potato will move neither up nor down?

more...

What objects could you use instead of a potato and a spoon? Try an apple or a ball and a fork.

Can you relate this activity to centrifugal (away from the center) and centripetal (toward the center) forces?

When the potato rises, can you infer which force is greater?

When the potato moves downward, can you infer which force is greater?

When it moves neither up nor down, what can you infer?

For a role-playing activity, let the potato represent the earth and the spoon an orbiting satellite. Can you create these effects: a satellite remains in orbit; then it falls to the earth; and last, it continues to go away from the earth?

Related activities include bis 30, 51, and 112.

pollution poetry

bis 64

Children are often asked to write poems during language arts time. The poems are usually about experiences they've never had, places they've never seen, or people they've never met. It's not easy to write a poem about what a flower thinks of winter.

After children have been involved with pollution activities, they will be motivated to write pollution poetry, plays, or commercials. These were written by children:

Just because coal is cheap
Doesn't mean air is.

      — Dana

Dad: Bobby, go jump in the lake!
Bobby: What lake, what's a lake?
Dad: Oh, I forgot, that was in my day.
      — Wendy

Now's your chance to go to Europe for free.
Take the San Antonio freeway to the coast and drive across
  the ocean.
There's no water in it after the drought.
All you need is a good pair of tires and a lot of determination.
      — Kathy

Dear Polly Polluter:
  We live by a factory and the pollution is horrible. And so is the smoke. I like to hang out my clothes to dry on the line, but they get so dirty. What can I do?
      — Ann

Dear Ann:
  My suggestion is to hang an old sheet over the clothes and they still get dry, but they don't get dirty.
      — Polly

ok, now you try a few!

Related activities include bis 5, 6, 33, and 127.

☐

marshmallow glacier

Steadily accumulating snowfalls eventually compact the lower layers into ice. When conditions are right, these accumulations may form glaciers. A good analogy to show the effect of weight on compaction uses a tall, graduated cylinder or a tall bottle and some marshmallows. The diameter of the cylinder or bottle should be slightly larger than that of a marshmallow. Stack the cylindrical container with marshmallows — one on top of the other. Cut a cardboard disc to fit snugly inside the container atop the marshmallow stack. The cylinder is already marked in units, but if you are using a bottle, attach adhesive tape to its side. Mark the tape in 1 cm or 1 inch units.

Place weights atop the cardboard disc on the marshmallow column.

more...

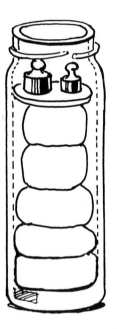

How is compression affected by various weights? Are all the marshmallows equally compressed? Does the number of marshmallows affect the results? What other objects can you use to show compaction? Try packing BB's, popcorn, corn, or peas in uniform containers. How does shape affect compaction? What other factors affect it?

more...

Color the marshmallows with food coloring so that when they are squashed, you can see the layers more distinctly.

Related activities include bis 19, 60, 90, and 95.

chromatography

Chromatography encompasses all the skills of science, from observing through experimenting. It is a winner. It is inexpensive and it is a moving activity; it has action. It is colorful. It can be individual, if you give identical equipment to each child. You need drinking glasses (baby food jars are excellent) and water-color ink markers (primarily with black ink). Selecting one of these markers takes experimenting. Some work better than others, and price does not seem to matter. A black watercolor (water soluble) marker that will separate out into all the component colors seems best. Some manufacturers produce such a marker, which, in separating out, produces only black, which makes the results less spectacular. Water and absorbent paper are necessary. Try filter paper or ordinary paper toweling.

Cut a 10 cm disc out of paper toweling or rectangular laboratory filter paper. With a pair of scissors make two cuts about 1 cm apart from the edge of the disc toward the center. Fold this cut portion back so that it hangs down. With the marker make a heavy dot about 2 cm up from the bottom. Fill your container with enough water so that the hanging part, when resting on the rim of the container, will be suspended in the water, the water making contact below the inked dot on your filter paper or toweling. Because the ink is water soluble, if it is placed below the water level, it will simply dissolve into the water in the container. The action takes approximately 15 to 20 minutes. Water will be observed traveling up the paper. When the water reaches the inked dot, the dot will be dissolved in the rising water, carried up the paper, and spread out as it reaches the flat disc. The heavier components of the ink will be at the bottom of the column, and the lighter ones will be carried farther up the column. Observe and describe the order of color separation.

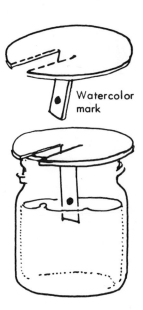

Watercolor mark

If different colored ink markers were used, would one color move more readily up the column than others?

If the temperature of the water were increased, would the diffusion speed up?

If different kinds of paper were used, which one would be preferred?

If the paper were supported vertically instead of resting as a disc on the mouth of the glass, how high would the water rise up the paper? Would it ever stop? Why?

If some liquid other than water were used, would it give better results?

If some soluble material other than ink were used, would that be separated as readily?

If . . .

Related activities include bis 59 and 71.

finding your way

Take the children outside and ask them to face north. If they or you don't know in which direction north is, how could you find out? Compass, stars, sun, policeman, floating magnet? What observations or inferences would you need to make?

Select several major landmarks in your area and ask the children to face in the direction of each. Then, ask them to state which direction each is from north, such as east, southeast, or west.

Many other activities on communication by maps can be utilized:

> Measuring your schoolroom.
>
> Drawing a scale map of your schoolroom.
>
> Locating sites in your town, city, or state with the appropriate map.
>
> Using keys and legends to understand maps.
>
> Using different kinds of maps, including road maps, topographic maps, climate maps, weather maps, and hiking maps.
>
> Have the children prepare a map for their route from home to school, using the shortest, longest, safest, and most dangerous routes.
>
> Prepare a map locating unsafe areas in your school, home, or city, and prepare a letter to go with the map, requesting that the hazard be corrected.

more...

How do road maps differ from weather maps? How are they similar?

How were maps made before there were airplanes? Compare some very old maps with maps made recently. How do they differ?

Can you draw a map to scale? Can you make a map without a compass?

Related activities include bis 19, 74, 125; and ss 27.

☐

just fishin'—with magnets

For this activity, you will need thumbtacks, paper clips, or iron filings; books, magnets, glass, cardboard, wood, cloth, aluminum foil, string, an aluminum pan, a cork stopper, a thin sheet of iron, nails, crayons, buttons, nickels, pennies, erasers, scissors, pins, plastic wrap, and a stick.

Make a fishing pole with the stick, string, and a small magnet. Fasten a paper clip to a candy kiss and put it into a box (representing a pond). Now you're ready to fish. Does the magnet "catch" the candy? Does it attract the chocolate? The paper clip? Or the foil? Test further to find out.

Collect many different items. Infer which objects will be attracted by a magnet and sort them into two piles entitled "will attract" and "will not attract." Test your inferences with a magnet and observe your results. Were your predictions accurate?

Pour some iron filings and thumbtacks onto a pane of glass supported by two piles of books.

cover the edge of the glass with masking tape
for added protection

Move a magnet around on the underside of the glass. What do you observe? Try thin sheets of cardboard, wood, cloth, and aluminum foil between the magnet and the glass plate. Do you still observe an interaction? Try various thicknesses of these objects. Do you observe any differences?

Can you observe magnets attracting through air? Try attaching one end of a string to a paper clip and the other end to a chair. Hold the clip and string up and support a magnet so that it is just above the clip. What do you observe? What will happen if you hold them farther apart? Closer together?

Now, try water. Pour a 1 cm layer of water into an aluminum pan to float a cork stopper freely. Attach a thumbtack to the underside of the cork stopper to stabilize it. Now hold the magnet underneath the pan and observe what happens.

Will a magnet attract through magnetic materials? Try pouring some iron filings or thumbtacks onto a sheet of iron. Move the magnet under the sheet of iron. What do you observe?

more...

Will you get the same results if you use different magnets? Try bar, horseshoe, and U-shaped magnets.

Is the strength of the magnet an important variable? Try arranging magnets from weakest to strongest by the number of identical objects each will pick up.

Try different thicknesses of materials and different media to see if the magnet's force is effective through these materials.

Related activities include bis 61, 75; ss 13; and sst 9.

□

it's official

When is something "official," as opposed to "not official"?

How big is an official softball, baseball, basketball, football, hockey puck, golf ball, soccer ball; swimming pool, football field, baseball field, soccer field, hockey rink, basketball court, golf course?

Compare official high school athletic fields with college and professional athletic fields.

Compare the official national sports facilities, such as Canadian and United States football fields, or Brazilian and United States soccer fields.

What if you compared the weights, colors, and brands of tennis balls? Are orange tennis balls "better" than white or pink ones? Do they bounce higher, last longer? Which is the "best" official golf ball?

How do you calculate official batting averages or free-throw percentages? What is the official ice thickness for a professional hockey match?

How big is a .22 caliber rifle, .38 caliber revolver, 16 mm movie projector?

Or compare 8 mm film with Super-8 mm film — what's the difference?

What is 126-12 film or 135-36 film? Type 108 or 107? Are these official?

Do countries have official flags?

Why are referees called officials?

more...

Why are official standards so useful? What would happen if no official size had been set for a football field? Or no official height for a basketball net? What are unofficial scores for games?

What official things do we use in science?

Related activities include bis 44, 52, and 57.

☐

reducing noise pollution

bis 70

Using shoe boxes or similar containers with sound-absorbing materials such as paper, cardboard, wood, or plastic, find out which material reduces noise best.

Your sound source can be an alarm clock, timer, or other noisemaker.

Fill the box with the material you intend to test (such as shredded paper) and place your sound source (such as an alarm clock) in the material at a known depth. Mark off on the floor a 5 meter distance from the sound source. How far away will you be before you cannot hear the sound (alarm)? How does this distance compare to the distance at which you can hear the alarm when it is unprotected by insulation?

Arrange the materials you select from most effective sound absorber to least effective sound absorber.

If you can obtain a decibel meter (from speech and hearing teachers), graph the decibel level indicated for each material. Many building supply centers will furnish free samples of ceiling tiles of different thicknesses and materials.

more...

Why do some materials reduce noise levels more than others? What contribution does distance from the sound source make?

What if you put a sound source in a thermos? Could you hear it? Why or why not?

Related activities include bis 33, 56, and 89.

☐

soakers

Using different brands of paper towels, different types of cloth, napkins, facial tissues, disposable diapers, cloth diapers, sponges, and cotton, find out how well they work.

Which one wipes up spilled water quickest? What variables need to be considered (type of material, size of material, liquid to be absorbed, surface on which liquid is spilled)?

Would you arrange (rank) the soakers for water in the same order if you used cooking oil or syrup? Predict which soaker would be best; then try it. Try to explain any differences you discover.

more...

Investigate how water moves through soil of different compositions. Use large plastic tubes filled with soil and pour water through them. Compare soils with sand and gravel. Try different liquids.

Related activities include bis 47 and 57.

☐

how does your
light dimmer work?

You will need a bulb, a battery, three wires with alligator clips attached, a piece of diffraction grating (obtained from commercial science suppliers), and a spring. The spring should be made from narrow gauge, good conducting wire, tightly coiled and 20 to 30 cm long.

This activity should be performed in a darkened room. If you cannot get total darkness, darken the room and then do the activity inside a large cardboard carton lying on its side with the top cut out. Construct a closed circuit as shown in the diagram. Attach one alligator-clipped wire permanently to one end of the wire spring. Keep the other alligator-clipped wire in your hand. If you touch the coiled spring near the permanently fixed clip, the bulb will light brightly. With the bulb lit, slide the mobile wire down the length of the spring.

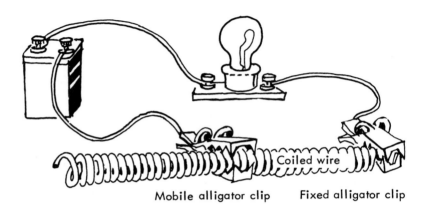

Mobile alligator clip   Fixed alligator clip

What happens to the intensity of the burning bulb? What accounts for this? As you traveled down the coiled wire spring, were you increasing or decreasing the amount of resistance to the electricity provided by the battery?

The movement of the mobile wire up and down the coiled spring is reflected in the burning intensity of the bulb. Can you draw an analogy, explaining how a light dimmer works?

While the bulb is burning its brightest, observe this light through the diffraction grating. Continue observing the burning bulb while sliding the mobile wire down the spring, lowering the intensity of the burning bulb. Observe the spectrum. How does the spectrum change as you look at the bulb burning in these two instances? Repeat this part. What changes do you observe in the spectrum? Is the intensity of the component colors of the spectrum the same throughout? Relate the changes in temperature (burning intensity) of the bulb to the color shift in the spectrum as viewed through the diffraction grating.

more...

In the constellation Orion, three stars are distinctly visible: Betelgeuse (red), Sirius (white), and Rigel (blue). Which do you think is a hot star? A cold star? What evidence can you cite to support your answer?

Related activities include ss 13 and sst 9.

picture it

With an "instant" camera you can express activities and ideas in pictures.

Take pictures of a series of events:

1. A policeman on a motorcycle pulls up to a car in a parking-metered zone.
2. He checks the car and records the registration number.
3. He leaves a ticket on the windshield.
4. The owner of the car notices the ticket and is not happy.

These four pictures can be used for several activities:

(a) Shuffle the pictures and arrange them in order by just observing them.
(b) Write or tape a story to go along with the pictures.
(c) Leave out one of the pictures and have the children make a drawing that they think would be suitable in its place.
(d) Have the children draw a picture that would go before picture 1 or after picture 4.

picture it, short and sweet

Take pictures of theme words: power, pollution, noise, garbage, old, young, happy, sad, creative, new.

Make three pictures out of one (a triple exposure).

Take pictures upside down.

Take pictures in a mirror.

Take pictures of animals, plants, and people — then classify them.

more...

Obtain old scrapbook pictures and concoct a story about them.

Obtain adult and baby pictures of famous people and try to match them.

Cut out newspaper pictures of heroes, statesmen, criminals, and teachers, and, using only the pictures with no names, have children classify the pictures into categories such as teachers, businessmen, doctors, criminals. Can you really tell criminals by the "way they look"? Doctors? Lawyers?

Related activities include bis 23, 32, and 58.

mapping elevations on models

To help understand contour maps and contour lines on a map, students can prepare a model hill or mountain or a valley from wood, plaster of paris (hydrated calcium sulfate), or clay.

Place the model in a container such as a clear plastic shoe box or breadbox with a lid. Mark the side of the container vertically into equal intervals, such as 1.5 cm. Pour water into the container until it reaches the first mark. Put the lid on the container. With a grease pencil, trace on the lid the outline formed by the water where it meets the model. Continue this procedure at successively higher water levels until you have reached the peak of your hill or mountain.

Your end product will be a contour map on the plastic box lid.

An alternative method is to trace the varied water levels on the object directly with a sharp stylus. This will give you contour elevation lines directly on the model.

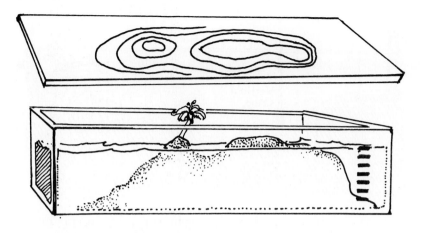

Some questions to consider:

How can you tell if you are going down into a valley or up the mountain by observing the contour lines?

If 1.5 cm = 100 m, what is the height of your mountain?

What other objects would give an interesting contour map? Try an old shoe. A smashed tin can.

more...

How would a weather forecaster use a contour map? Does it measure the same things as your map of the mountain?

Draw a contour map of yourself while sitting in a bathtub. Let the water rise at regular intervals. Can you do it?

more...

For this activity you will need two pieces of string (one long, one short), two sticks about a meter long, a homemade carpenter's level made from a test tube, tape, a Magic Marker, colored water, and a weight of some sort (for instance, a fishing sinker).

Tie the long piece of string to the two sticks and make it taut. Mark off equal intervals along the string with the Magic Marker. Using the colored water, devise a means by which you could make the test tube serve as a carpenter's level. Tape your homemade level to the taut string to be sure that the string is and remains horizontal. Take the remaining piece of string and tie the weight

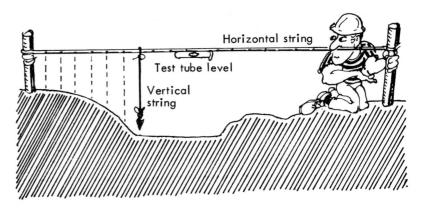

to it. Mark your units of measurement (probably in cm) on the weighted string. Now you have a plumb line that you can use in conjunction with the long piece of string to make a profile of anything that passes underneath the string. By hanging the plumb line adjacent to the marked intervals along the taut horizontal string, you can take vertical measurements that will allow you to make a profile of whatever is being mapped. Go outside and, using your plumb line, fill in the following table. Then you can use the table to make a profile or cross-sectional view of a small hill, gully, and so on.

Horizontal Distance (cm)	Vertical Distance (cm)

more...

Select a 3 x 4 inch section from a topographic map with at least 12 levels of elevation. Cut out 12 pieces of cardboard, each measuring 3 x 4 inches. Following the major contour intervals (such as every 50 or 100 feet), cut out the map section representing the lowest elevation and glue it to a piece of cardboard. Cut the area representing the next highest elevation from the map, glue this piece on the second piece of cardboard, and trim the excess cardboard. Position and glue the second piece of cardboard on top of the first.

Continue cutting off sections of the map, in order of increasing elevation and along contours, until you have completed all sections.

You should end up with a three-dimensional model of the area shown on the map section.

What geologic feature was represented by the topographic map you constructed? Could you identify the structure before the model was made?

What geologic processes could have resulted in the formation of this feature?

Related activities include bis 67, 75; ss 31 and 33.

□

picture it — magnetically

Make a magnetic field picture with paraffin or candle wax, an aluminum pan (large enough for the size of paper you decide to use), sheets of paper (we used 8 x 10 inch), a hot plate, and a piece of cardboard that is the same size as the paper you select.

To make a permanent picture of a magnet's field, melt the candle wax or paraffin in an aluminum pan; use a hot plate, and heat the material slowly.

the heating should only be done under supervision!

While the wax or paraffin is liquid, *carefully* dip sheets of paper into it. Then take the sheets out and allow them to cool until the wax hardens. Place the coated paper on a piece of cardboard.

Pour iron filings onto the coated paper and tap the cardboard gently. Using a magnet and iron filings, the children can design the magnetic field picture that they want.

Carry the cardboard and coated paper (carefully) to a hot plate that is turned on as *low as possible*. Place the cardboard and the waxed paper on the hot plate. As the coated paper warms, the wax will soften, letting the iron filings sink into it. Remove it and allow the coated paper to cool.

You now have a permanent picture imbedded in wax of the magnetic field that was produced by your magnet.

page 129

An alternative method for obtaining a permanent picture of the magnetic field is to pour iron filings onto the shiny side of a piece of heavy waxed paper. Make the field picture with a magnet. Put waxed paper on a cardboard box. Cover the waxed paper and iron filings with a second piece of waxed paper (shiny side down onto the iron filings). Using an iron set on low, "iron" the two pieces of waxed paper together with the filings between them.

be careful when you use the hot iron on the waxed paper!

Can you make different colored pictures in this way? What could you use instead of iron filings? Paper clips? Coins? Tinfoil? Pins?

Can you make pictures that resemble people, places, plants, animals?

Related activities include bis 61 and 68.

□

the jiffy water treatment plant

For this activity you will need straws, a tin can, small rocks, sand, two single-loaf baking pans, lime, alum, and mud.

You can build a rather elaborate model of a water treatment plant quite easily with shallow pans (single-loaf bread pans) as water basins. One such pan might be a settling basin, into which you can introduce water containing lime, alum, and mud. From this basin, lead relatively pure water with a straw or rubber tubing to a homemade sand filter.

Make the sand filter with a can, small rocks, and clean sand. Put two or three little holes in the bottom of the can near one side. Pour the clean sand into the can until it is about half full. Now drop small rocks into the can until it is ¾ full. Hold the filter over a clean pan and siphon the water from the shallow pan through the filter. Water that is relatively clear looking will drop out.

Siphon

Settling basin

Filter

***don't drink this water! it hasn't been treated chemically
and could contain harmful organisms***

*Can you make several observations before and after the water
is treated? Will hot water work better than cold water? Will
this system purify salt water as well as fresh water?*

*What kind of impurities does this type of filter remove? Will
this system purify water mixed with vinegar? Test it with litmus
paper. Can you devise other types of filters to remove impurities
smaller than pieces of dirt? Will some chemicals remove impurities that are dissolved in water?*

more...

Is there such a thing as pure water? Why or why not?

Related activities include bis 8, 33; and ss 17.

how high is pi?

This activity will help the children understand what *pi*, 3.14 . . . , is, and why it is so useful.

Obtain ten or fifteen containers of all sizes, number them, and have the children prepare a data table including the jar number, its circumference, and its diameter.

Have them plot the circumference (measured with a string and then translated with a ruler) on the *y*-axis and the diameter on the *x*-axis for each jar.

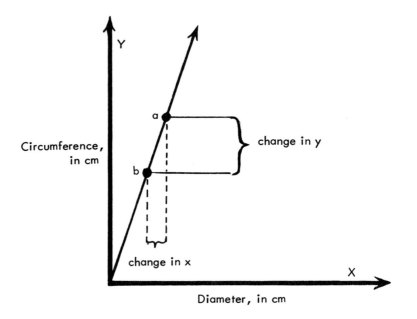

Then have them find the slope of the best line drawn. You find the slope by measuring the change in *y* and dividing it by the corresponding change in *x*, as illustrated in the figure. The units will cancel and your results should be approximately 3.1 to 3.2 (no units), which is called pi (π).

Even though the size of the containers changes, the ratio of the circumference to the diameter is always 3.14, or π.

Now, introduce several unknown jars labeled X, Y, and Z. Give children the diameter of X and Z and the circumference of Y. Have them use their graph to find the corresponding circumference of X and Z and the diameter of Y, which will show how useful pi is: when you know either the circumference or diameter of an object, you know the other measurement too.

If some children do not get 3.14 ± 0.1 for the slope of their graph, they should try to locate their source or sources of error and try again.

A more precise value for pi is: 3.1415926536.

Related activities include bis 29, 121; and sst 11.

□

fire-formed

*this activity must be done in a well-ventilated room
and only under supervision;
you must exercise caution at all times!*

You will need a container of flowers of sulfur, obtainable from a drugstore, paper towels, a propane burner, tablespoon, Pyrex container, and a hammer.

1. With a Bunsen burner or propane tank *slowly* heat one tablespoon of powdered sulfur until it melts. (Don't breathe in the vapor.) Record your observations. Pour the liquid into a paper cone that is in a Pyrex container. Record your observations.
2. Next, slowly melt another tablespoon of powdered sulfur. Pour it into a Pyrex container ¾ filled with cold water. Record your observations.
3. Remove the sulfur samples from the containers when cooled. Keep track of which sample was in which container.
4. After both samples of sulfur have hardened, break them open with a hammer. (Remember to wear safety glasses to protect your eyes.) Examine the fragments with a magnifying glass or microscope.

Can you observe and identify which of the samples cooled faster? What do you observe that supports your answer? Did you notice that one sample has smaller crystals?

You might want to prepare an observational chart, headed *Air cooled* and *Water cooled*, to record your observations. Can you hypothesize on the relationship between the cooling rate of a rock and the size of its crystals?

more...

Using rocks from a commercial rock collection (diorite, gabbro, granite, felsite, basalt, obsidian), plus any other igneous rocks you wish, arrange them from "cooled fastest" to "cooled slowest," by crystal size. Could you also use the depth at which the rocks were formed (near the surface or deep within the earth's surface) to determine their rate of cooling?

Thought for today: Which do you predict would have larger crystals, an igneous rock that was formed from lava in a hot desert or one that was formed from lava that fell into an ocean? Lawrence of Arabia would be proud of you.

Related activities include bis 4, 90; and ss 30.

how many what?

Collect ten or twelve small plastic containers with tops. Rummage through the basement or attic and come up with an assortment of ten to twenty different items, such as poker chips, buttons, pins, stamps, washers, sugar cubes, paper clips, small wooden pencils, thumbtacks, marbles. You will need one of each item for each container. When the containers are prepared with one of each item, place the covers on them. Distribute the containers to the children. When you say, "Ready, get set, go," the children can uncover the container and observe the contents. When you say "stop," they must replace the cover. Then they write down the number and name of the item they saw in the container.

The restriction on the activity may be that the container cannot be spilled out; you may shake the container only to move items about. Excitement is increased by having three to five children observe the contents at the same time. This excitement is contagious. For younger children, use fewer items and a longer observation time — for example: first-graders, 6 items, 10 seconds; sixth-graders, 20 items, 12 seconds. A little experience with this activity and you will know the appropriate number of items and the time necessary. The excitement always grows when you dramatically add items and reduce the time for observation.

This activity stimulates observation. Repeat it, but remember to change the items periodically.

more...

What percentage of the items in the container did everyone name correctly?

Were some items easier to remember than others?

What was the class average?

What was the range?

What could you do to increase the class average?

What could you do to decrease the average?

Which items were most often remembered by most of the class? Why do you suppose that item was remembered most often?

Related activities include bis 1, 40, 53, 101, 106, and 123.

☐

"500" contests

Observations of moving objects and the quantification of these observations are vital in developing perception of the space/time relationship so necessary to describing motion. Experiences developing this skill can be provided in a variety of ways.

Several toy manufacturers market miniature cars with powered racetracks included or notched T-bars for winding up an oversized wheel in the middle of a car. These cars can be used for activities on speed, distance, and time.

By varying the design, children can determine the factors that will make the "fastest" (most efficient) car in "500" contests. They can compete against each other for distance traveled, time traveled, and distance per unit of time or speed. Many variables can be examined, such as type of surface, slope of surface, type of car, and mass of car.

Children can also build their own cars to test in "500" contests.

Paper airplanes, too, provide excellent competitions among students to promote many scientific skills, particularly quantification. Distance traveled, type of paper used, design, and external additions (such as tape and paper clips for ballast), can all be investigated.

Students can observe the characteristics of winning designs and try to improve their old designs.

more...

Kites are also excellent for "500" contests. Homemade kites of twigs and plastic bags are a good start and students can be encouraged to "take off" from these.

Kite height can be measured and related to design, strength and durability, and flying characteristics.

Which material is best for building a kite? Why?
What effect does the tail have? How long should it be?
How should the surface area of the kite relate to its mass?
What additional "500" contests can you think of?

Related activities include bis 30, 45, 61, 114, 117, 118; and ss 19.

☐

perceptual training activities
for developing the senses

FOR VISUAL DISCRIMINATION

1. Match pieces of colored paper with paper cups of corresponding colors. Include colors that can't be matched and will need a new category (a new paper cup).

2. Cover several shoe boxes (four to eight will do nicely) with contact paper of different colors. Have the children bring in objects (pencils, buttons, combs, ribbons, toys) of various colors. Have them classify these objects by color and put them in the appropriate boxes. Later one object can be selected from any of the boxes by a child and identified by its verbal description only.

3. Make color collages from scraps of paper and similar materials. One collage may be shades of red, another shades of blue. Classify the collage according to the number of shades of red or blue observed.

FOR AUDITORY DISCRIMINATION

1. How many ways can you find to make sounds with a piece of paper? One third-grade child found ten, including rubbing it across the desk with his fingertips, letting it flutter to the floor like a leaf, shaking it between thumb and forefinger, snapping by pulling the paper taut between thumb and forefinger, tearing it, crumpling it into a ball and letting it expand, dropping the crumpled paper on the floor, smoothing out the crumpled paper, and blowing on the paper while holding it taut.

Would you get the same results with a different type of paper (we used a piece of ditto paper)?

2. Obtain six pop bottles and fill them with different quantities of water. Arrange the bottles by the sound they make when struck with a pencil, from highest to lowest.

Does the highest-sounding bottle contain the most water?

Would your order remain the same if you changed to another liquid, such as vinegar or cooking oil?

Does the size of the pop bottle make any difference? What if a different type of bottle were used?

Do you get the same order if you fill the bottles with a solid material instead of a liquid? Try crushed Styrofoam, paper strips, animal bedding, sand, gravel, clay.

Does the type of striker make a difference? Try a piece of silverware, plastic, or a rubber mallet.

Play a song!

FOR TACTILE DISCRIMINATION

1. Bring in as many objects as you can and classify them into two piles, smooth and rough.

2. Make a "feel box" by cutting an opening in a cardboard box and glue objects throughout the inside of the box. Have the children draw a picture and list several words to describe how the object feels and possibly draw a map of the objects' positions in the box. Variation: have the objects loose in a bag. Ask the students to describe what they felt in the bag. How many different objects were in it? Were any alike?

3. Make textured pictures with varied materials and objects such as: cloth scraps, yarn, buttons, sewing trims, dry noodles, seeds, straws, and several kinds of paper. Use glue and paste the textured picture to the cardboard to make the picture permanent.

4. Make tactile cards, two of each, with a number of rough and smooth textures. Have the children match them.

FOR OLFACTORY DISCRIMINATION

1. Can you think of two substances that look the same but smell different? Try white vinegar and water or rubbing alcohol and water.

2. Can you think of two substances that look different but smell the same? Try white vinegar and cider vinegar.

3. Fill four jars with substances such as vinegar, water, vanilla extract, and alcohol. Prepare three more jars with the same substances, but add red food coloring to the water, blue to the alcohol, and green to the vanilla extract. Have the children match the substances by smell. Water, vanilla extract, and alcohol will match, but the vinegar will not.

FOR GUSTATORY DISCRIMINATION

1. Have the children plan a breakfast for the class and classify the foods served as sweet, sour, or salty. A good breakfast would be fruit juice, cereal, scrambled eggs, toast and jelly, milk and, of course, coffee for the teacher.

2. Collect pictures of some of your favorite foods from old magazines and prepare a book entitled *Foods I Like*.

Related activities include bis 1, 13–17, and 28.

□

typewriter probability

A typewriter can be used to illustrate how probability and sampling are used for interpretation. A standard portable typewriter has forty-four keys. What is the probability that any one key will be struck?

Have fifteen or twenty children type anything they wish for one minute. Prepare a graph with the frequency of letters typed and the letters. Which letter was typed most? Which letter least?

You could try the same activity using words typed. Which word is typed most frequently?

Do you predict that another sample of ten people would yield the same results? Try ten secretaries, ten fifth-graders, ten teachers. Did you collect evidence to support your predictions?

Are your results the same if you record your data using all males or all females? If you found differences, how can you account for them?

Try an electric typewriter instead of a manual one. Do you still get the same results?

Related activities include bis 40, 43, 78, 87, and 121.

□

extending creature cards

Creature cards, developed as part of the Elementary Science Study Unit, "Attribute Games and Problems," are very popular with teachers and children. They can prepare their *own* creature cards, though, and share them with each other.

We provide you with a sample creature card on the next page; it's an example you can duplicate and use with your children. Once they've got the idea, let them try to make some of their own!

Related activities include bis 1, 13, 23, 32, 109, and 110.

□

All of these are Crockovers.

None of these are Crockovers.

Which of these are Crockovers?

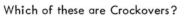

rubber band-ology

A box of assorted rubber bands can kick off a creative sciencing activity. Dump the assorted box of rubber bands onto an overhead projector. The shadows cast on the screen let the children discern some of the properties, such as size and shape. Have them observe as many of the properties as they can. Could you extract a classification lesson from this box of assorted rubber bands? What would some of the similarities and differences be? Remember, don't let your students separate these rubber bands into groups described by vague words like *fat* or *long*.

Have them express themselves quantitatively:
How fat is fat? How long is long?
What other properties can be measured?
How many rubber bands are in the set? How many are in each subset?

Rubber bands have the unique property *elasticity*, which provides many new avenues for investigation. What inferences can you make about these rubber bands? When different ones are suspended from a cup hook and a constant weight is applied to the opposite end, elongating the rubber band, which elongates least? Most?

be careful!

Any objects placed under tension must be carefully handled; accidental quick releases can happen.

Place a known weight on the end of one rubber band. Pull the weight down through a prescribed distance. Don't pull it so far that releasing it could be dangerous. Release the weight. The rubber band should move up and then down until the weight comes to rest. Record the distance of the initial pull. Record the number of times the weight went up and down before coming to rest. Change rubber bands. How does this change the number of times the weight goes up and down? Keep the rubber band constant and vary the weight. Record your data and plot them on a graph. What predictions can you make from your graph?

Can you turn a rubber band into a spring scale?

Students make slingshots out of rubber bands. Does this provide you with an idea for testing different rubber bands and projectiles to determine which shape, size, or other characteristic makes the best slingshot?

take precautions in selecting projectiles —
use soft foam rubber balls or table tennis balls

A variation of this activity is to drive two nails about 5 to 10 cm apart. Hook a rubber band over each nail. Mark off measures in the direction of pull, letting one quantify the distance the rubber band was pulled out. Set an object in the path of the released rubber band. Measure the distance the object is moved by the force of the released rubber band. Graph your results.

more...

Make two marks 3 cm apart on a rubber band. Place the band on a ruler and stretch it to twice its length. How far apart will your marks be? What if you stretched the band to three times its length?

Which is stronger, a rubber band or a piece of string? Make a prediction; then test it!

more...

Let one end of a ruler hang over the edge of a table or desk. Let most of the ruler stick out. Press against the end on the table or desk, and snap up on the other end. What do you observe? Change the length of the ruler overhang. Repeat the snapping of the overhanging portion. What happens to the sound when the overhang decreases?

Related activities include bis 51, 96, 99, and 105.

through the glass rod

All the material you need initially for this activity is a solid glass rod. Almost any rod will do, but one 4 or 5 mm thick by 10 cm long is recommended. Also needed is a strip of paper with four words typed on it. The words are PUN, ECHO, ART, and BOX, and they should all be typed as upper-case letters. Type the words in two colors, preferably black and red. Type the words PUN and ART in black ink and ECHO and BOX in red ink.

Your introduction to this activity can be like this:

Here are two items. Manipulate them and see if you can observe something unusual. Place the glass rod over the words and then lift the rod slowly off the paper. What do you observe?

Looking through the glass rod, you see that the black typed words are inverted and the red typed words appear not to be inverted. In reality, all the words are inverted. Because the selected letters in these words are shaped alike, inversion makes them appear exactly as they were originally. That is why many observers are confused by this discrepancy, leading them to search for an explanation for what they observe.

Students offer explanations like these for their observation: "It is magic paper." "It is a magic glass rod." "It has something to do with the words." Anticipating such reactions, you can ask some directed questions:

Does the paper make a difference? Try several varieties of paper. Type the words in the same way. Use the same rod.

Does the rod make a difference? Try plastic rods, hollow glass rods, or glass stirring rods.

Does the color type make a difference? Retype the same words either all black or all red. Does this change anything?

What do you observe about the words? Are they all upper case? Does this offer an explanation? Try it! Reproduce the words in lower case. Voilà!

Related activities include bis 27, 32, 36, 39, 42, and 126.

□

aluminum boats

Obtain a piece of aluminum foil and make a shape that will float. Float it.

What are the dimensions of your aluminum boat? How much does it weigh? If your boat does not float, redesign it so that it will. What did you have to consider when you made the boat?

Using washers or weights of any type, find out how many weights your boat will support before it sinks. Weigh your aluminum boat with the weights required to sink it. Whose boat held the most weight? Did everyone begin with the same size boat? Find how many weights equal the weight of your boat. Use paper clips, brads, or tacks as weights or "sinkers."

Conduct an aluminum boat contest in your class. Who can make the biggest boat? The smallest? Which supports the most sinkers? Who can construct the longest boat that will float?

Can you keep your boat afloat with a hole in it? Try one above the waterline and one below the waterline.)

more...

Make boats out of other substances, such as: Styrofoam, sheet plastic, wax paper, glass, or clay.

Using different materials, make boats of the same size. Which material will support the most weights?

Does the temperature of the water make a difference?

Does the liquid make a difference? How does your aluminum boat float in soda pop, cooking oil, vinegar, or syrup?

Examine pictures of various types of boats — steamboats, rafts, canoes, sailboats, and rowboats. Why are they shaped as they are?

Related activities include bis 20, 30, 45, 114, 117, 118; and ss 19.

interpreting data

The graph on the next page is taken from a test grass plot that has dandelions growing on it. The data were collected over two years and are based on the number of dandelions counted in the test plot each month for 25 months.

What trend or trends do you notice in this graph?

What is the average number of months between the maximum numbers of dandelions counted? Which months are these?

How many dandelions do you expect in June, 1981? December, 1981? June, 1982? In August, 1983?

In what month do you expect the next maximum number of dandelions to be counted?

Can you identify at least four variables that might have affected the data presented in this dandelion graph?

Where in the continental United States is this grass plot? North or South, East or West?

more...

What other cycles could you use with the children? Animal cycles? Earth cycles?

Have any of the students lost teeth during the year? Ask these children to relate how it happened and whether it hurt. Then take a tooth count. How many children have lost one tooth? How many have lost two? Three? Make a simple, personalized bar graph recording this information and update it during the year.

Set up a classroom display of old and modern almanacs, including the famous Poor Richard's Almanack. *Encourage the children to scrounge in attics and basements for old specimens. Many learning activities can be developed using almanac material, such as comparisons of price, fashion, and weather, and the reading of proverbs.*

Related activities include bis 11, 19, 40, 43, 47, 82, 101; and ss 29.

□

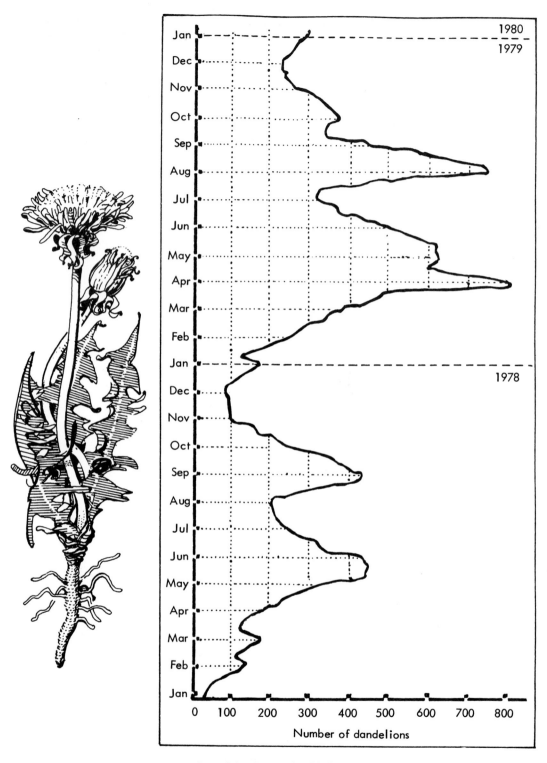

checking changes

Collect objects, such as an apple, egg, cookie, tomato, rock, and dog biscuit, to investigate changes.

What can you do to each object to get it to change? How do you know it has changed? What is your evidence? (An apple can be cut into two pieces.) Can you change the object into another form so that you cannot put it back together to get the same object? (Apples in an apple pie.)

Can you devise a procedure to protect an object from changing, such as an apple from spoiling, an egg breaking when dropped from a height, a piece of bread from becoming moldy? Why should things be protected?

What can you do to a dog biscuit to get it to change? Can it be changed into another form, so that it is not recognizable? (Try soaking it in water for several days.)

Can changes be measured? (The growth of mold on a piece of bread in area per day; the movement of a rock down a hilly slope, in distance per day or week.)

Can changes be classified into: (1) physical, (2) chemical, (3) changes in ideas? Are there other types of changes?

Do living things change? Try comparing baby pictures with school and adult pictures. What did you observe changed most and what changed least? Did the eyes change more than the nose, the mouth area, the ears?

How do dogs change from pups to adults? What about mealworms or butterflies? Can you observe these changes?

more...

Do people change? Is your best friend of a year ago your best friend today? Has your principal changed since the school year began? Have your parents or relatives changed? Describe some of the ways.

Do buildings change? Cities? States? Countries? Laws? Has your street changed? Your home? Your bedroom? What observations can you make about these changes? Are all changes for the best?

Have products changed? Consider cars, trucks, cleaning products, magazines, toys, medicines, deodorants, mouthwashes, toothpastes. Write to some companies and ask them to state how their products have changed and their evidence for saying that these changes are better.

Related activities include bis 2, 4, 10, 23, 31, 36, 43, 55, 103; and ss 29.

☐

pollution task cards

Pollution Task Cards (PTC's) present the child with a problem to solve — they are concise, usually placed on 3 x 5 inch index cards and laminated with a clear plastic material that holds on contact. After you read these examples, copy them and try them with your children. Or make your own.

PTC 1 Investigate your surroundings

Select a specific location in your environment. Describe the general area and the specific site in as much detail as possible. List the desirable and undesirable conditions and propose some improvements for the area. Outline a plan of action.

PTC 2 Solid waste

How much solid waste do you throw away? You will not understand how big a problem it is to dispose of solid waste until you have some idea of how much solid waste has to be gotten rid of each day.

Make a chart on which to record what is thrown away in your home in one day. Ask each member of your family to record on the chart everything that they throw into the waste container.

PTC 3 Sounds in your environment

Using a tape recorder, go outside and find and bring back sounds that make you feel:

1. angry
2. sad
3. beautiful

4. afraid
5. happy
6. tough

PTC 4   Noise in your neighborhood

On your way home from school today, try to describe at least eight noises you hear. Bring your list to school with you tomorrow. Now try to describe the loudness of these noises with a scale of one to ten. Let one be the softest sound and ten the loudest.

Locate and record the sources of at least five of these noises.

Construct a map of the area that will direct your fellow students to the approximate location of each of the five noises.

Distinguish between noises which people can control and those which cannot be controlled.

Design a plan for decreasing noise pollution in the area you mapped.

PTC 5   Return to returnables

Survey your friends, relatives, and neighbors to find out what they do with used bottles. Record your results and report back to the class.

PTC 6   Trash census

Find out the number of people living on your block. Keep a record of how many bags of garbage they put out each week for five weeks. How does the amount of garbage compare to the number of people?

Think of some constructive ways of using trash.

Related activities include bis 33, 56, 70; and ss 2.

☐

bis 90

toothpaste magma
(fight rock cavities)

Using unrolled, half-empty toothpaste tubes, let's pretend that the toothpaste is magma, molten rock.

Squeeze all the toothpaste into one part of the tube. Can you predict what will happen if you press down on the part where all the toothpaste is? Press on that part. What do you observe? Did your observation confirm or refute your prediction?

What do you predict will happen if the toothpaste (magma) comes to a weak spot in the tube (a space between two layers of rocks)? Make a hole in the tube with a pin and observe if your predictions are correct. Try to make the paste come out at different rates — slowly, moderately, rapidly.

Can you design a way of measuring how much toothpaste (magma) erupts in a specific period?

Could you weigh the amount of toothpaste magma collected at selected time intervals under constant pressure?

Additional variables that could be compared: the size of the opening and the amount collected, the time and the amount collected, the amount of pressure exerted and the amount collected. Try graphing the data you have collected.

What could you use for this activity instead of toothpaste? Make sure that it's safe!

Related activities include bis 19, 22, 60, and 95.

☐

observing changes
with rubbing alcohol

***don't do this activity near sources of fire or flame,
and don't breathe the vapors!***

Rubbing alcohol can be used to test many changes:

*How long does it take six drops of rubbing alcohol to disappear
when placed in the palm of your hand? Can you predict how
long it would take three drops to disappear? What about nine
drops? Do twice as many drops (twelve) take twice as much
time; or do half as many drops (three) take half as long?*

*Can you plot the number of drops of the y axis against time
on the x axis? Can you use this graph to make additional predictions?*

*Does the rubbing alcohol really disappear? Can you cite
observable evidence that the rubbing alcohol evaporated? Or
was it absorbed into the skin?*

One child "proved" that the rubbing alcohol was absorbed into
the skin by adding several drops of blue food coloring to the
rubbing alcohol and dropping the "blue alcohol" on his hand.
After the alcohol disappeared a blue stain remained. Suggest an
explanation.

*Can you test the observation that the rubbing alcohol feels
cool on your skin? Can you explain it?*

How much of an area does the rubbing alcohol cover?

Do different brands of rubbing alcohol give different results?

Related activities include bis 1, 13, 14, 15, 21, 28, 81, and 120.

☐

communication with toy constructs

Bees do it, birds do it, even scientists do it — communicate, that is. Commercially available toys that fit together into variations limited only by the amount of equipment and the assembler's creativity (like Tinker Toys) foster skilled communication.

Select and assemble any number and variety of pieces you desire. Select items that have varied shapes, colors, sizes, and materials. This activity is more successful with large groups. You may want to package ten to fifteen or twenty to thirty similar groups of items. To make passing around and collecting this material easy, try packaging it in small, tied, plastic bags.

Have someone step outside and assemble the packaged pieces into any construction of his or her desire and come back in without disclosing the construction. With back to the audience, he or she must communicate, by oral description, pieces and steps for the audience to follow in assembling (with their matching pieces) a like object. At the conclusion, the child holds the construction up for comparison. Usually a lively discussion follows as he or she tries to explain where the description went wrong or what could have been described better.

This game can be repeated and made progressively more difficult by limiting the verbal description: color may not be mentioned but measures may be given (or vice versa), the geometric shape may not be provided, or the type of material may not be included. Each limitation makes the activity just a bit more difficult.

more...

Describe the objects. How are they alike? Unlike? Can you classify their pieces? How?

Describe the properties of the packaged pieces. Do they have mass, length, color? In how many ways can you rank these pieces?

Have two children sit back to back. One selects a piece out of his package and describes it to the other, who must match the description with one piece in his package that fits the description. Set any limitations you wish.

Related activities include bis 24, 44, 58, and 83.

cubes, drops, and wafers

Sugar cubes, lemon drops, and sugar wafers dissolve in water. If you give it time enough, almost everything does.

Start with a sugar cube. Take a glass of tap water. Examine and describe the sugar cube. Drop it in the glass of water. Describe what you observe. How long did it take? Did it raise the water level? How many sugar cubes would it take to raise the water level? How many cubes will dissolve in your glass of water? Does changing the temperature of the water affect any of these results? In what way? How does stirring the solution change the results? Can you accumulate data to support your statement? Does a lemon drop react differently under the same conditions? How about a sugar wafer?

Make some sugar cube constructions with a commercial glue (try Elmer's). Glue eight small sugar cubes together. Make sure you spread the glue evenly across the joining faces of the cubes. Let it dry thoroughly. When dry, place this large cube in a glass of water. If the glue is soluble in water, be careful not to let it dissolve. When the sugar has dissolved, leaving the glue ridges intact, remove this skeleton from the water and let it dry. You will see interesting crystal-like structures. How many geometric shapes can you make? What different effects would other glues provide? Can you make a honeycomb design?

Related activities include bis 8, 42, 47, and 71.

☐

sands of time

Time is an important idea for children to master, and constructing and using a sand timer is an absorbing activity. Children can use it to make timing predictions.

Find out how long it takes for one cup of fine, white sand to run through a cone-shaped funnel made from a paper towel or a pierced, conical paper drinking cup. Experiment with diameters for the opening the sand goes through. Which size of opening will provide the best sand flow? Use this size for these activities.

How long do you predict it will take for 2 cups? Try it! What about 4 cups, ½ cup? Try the same activity with a cup of coarse brown sand. Do you get the same results (time)? If not, is there a relationship between the two activities? Did you obtain proportionally similar results?

Vary the distance between the pouring cup and the cone. Will it take longer if you are closer to the cone? Try it.

Do you observe that the same amount of sand always takes the same time to empty?

Make a one-minute timer. Now find a way to decrease the rate at which the sand flows through. Next, try a way of increasing it. Remember: keep the amount of sand or type of sand the same.

Is a three-minute egg timer really three minutes' worth of sand? Does it really take three minutes for the sand to run through an egg timer? Check one with your timer.

more...

Use your sand timer to make interesting sand pictures. Suspend the timer from a support such as a table, doorway, or chair. Put a sheet of construction paper under the timer. Fill the timer with sand (or try colored sand or cookie-topping sparkles). Keeping your hand over the hole, start the timer swinging. Remove your hand. You will observe that it makes an interesting sand picture. Pour glue over the sand picture and make it permanent, or pour the sand back and make a new one.

Related activities include bis 51, 88, 95; and ss 20.

let's erode

Obtain two pieces of thick cardboard (two or three layers) about 30 x 30 cm, some soil, two basinlike containers, enough leaves to cover one piece of the cardboard, paper towels, and a quart jar. Now you're ready for several erosion activities.

Spread a layer of soil about 3 cm thick on each piece of cardboard. Place a layer of leaves on top of the soil on one of the pieces of cardboard. Slant both boards by leaning them on scrap blocks of wood and have each cardboard empty into a basin.

Sprinkle water from about 60 cm above each piece of cardboard and observe the water flowing down from the soil into the basin.

Using paper towels, compare the amount of soil that has been eroded by filtering out the water. Fold a paper towel into a cone shape, then place it over a quart jar and pour the muddy water from one basin into it. Repeat the filtering with the muddy water collected from the other piece of cardboard.

Compare your observations and then try covering the soil with small twigs. Do you predict that you will get the same results as with the cardboard covered with leaves? Next try rocks or pebbles.

What if you made ridges in the soil at right angles to the slope? What if you planted grass?

and then —

Obtain two wooden, tin, aluminum, or cardboard troughs; a large pan, wooden blocks for slanting the troughs, two containers of the same size, and soil.

Place the same amount of soil in each of two troughs. Then set up the troughs on several wooden blocks so that one slants at about a 45° angle and the other at about a 65° angle.

Fill two jars of the same size with water and predict which trough will have the greatest soil erosion. Pour each jar into one of the troughs and observe which trough lost more soil.

Next place both troughs at a 45° slant and put the same amount of soil into the troughs. Fill one jar with half as much water as the other. Predict which jar of water will move more soil. Check your prediction by trying it.

You may want to measure the amount of soil (by mass) that is placed in the troughs and then the amount that is transported down them. From this measurement you can calculate the percentage of soil transported for each manipulated variable, such as amount of water used, or the slope of the trough (you can use the distance of the trough from the table top rather than angle in degrees).

Other variables you may want to investigate: rate at which the water is poured, temperature of the water, type of soil used, including sandy, clay, and organic; and type of trough used.

Related activities include bis 19, 22, 45, 60, and 90.

□

the obedient can, or
the elastic motor

For this activity, you will need these materials: a coffee can, the plastic cover that usually accompanies the coffee can, a rubber band, weights (lead sinkers or washers), two wooden kitchen matches, a nail, and a hammer.

Using the nail and hammer, punch a hole in the bottom of the coffee can and another in its plastic cover. Both holes must be centered. Smooth the holes with a file. Thread a rubber band through the hole in the bottom of the can. Retain this portion of the rubber band with a matchstick inserted through it. Attach weights securely to the rubber band about midway between the

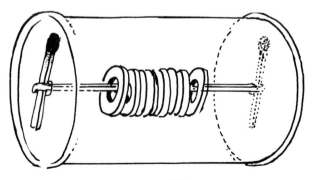

cover and the bottom of the can. Pull the remaining end of the rubber band through the opening in the cover, retaining the end of it with a matchstick. Close the can. Roll it on the floor. Just before it stops, talk to it. Tell it to return to you. It will. It wouldn't dare not to.

The weights secured to the midportion of the rubber band are the force that caused the rubber band to twist. The harder the initial push, the more the rubber band will wind. When the energy given the can by the initial push is used up, the can will stop. The accumulated energy in the twisted rubber band makes it unwind, causing the can to roll back to the sender. The can will return whether or not you speak to it, for it is "obeying" the laws of physics.

Does it make a difference if you use a different size or shape of rubber band?

What difference would it make, if any, if you relocated the weights?

What difference does increasing or decreasing the weights make?

Does the surface the can is rolled on make any difference?

Does the size of the can make any difference?

more...

Punch two holes in the bottom of the coffee can and two holes in its plastic cover. Thread your rubber band through all four holes in a figure eight. Tie the rubber band ends together. Fasten a small weight to the center of the rubber band, where it crosses inside the can. Roll the can away from you. How does this action compare with the original design of "The Obedient Can"?

Related activities include bis 42, 46, 51, 61, 73, 84, and 117.

☐

bis 67

soda-straw investigations

You will need a soda straw (any will do) and a pop bottle of any size. With a ruler and a waterproof marker, divide the soda straw into equal intervals. We used a soda straw 25.8 cm in length and 0.6 cm in diameter, marked off in 2 cm intervals with a 16 oz (0.473 liter) pop bottle filled with 16 oz of water.

Collect evidence to answer this question:

Is there a relationship between the depth to which the soda straw is inserted into a liquid (such as water) and the quantity of liquid in the straw?

Would you get the same data if you used a longer straw with the same liquid and a bottle of the same size? A shorter straw? Does the type of straw make a difference (paper, plastic, bendable, glass)? Do the data change if you use straws with a diameter smaller than that of your original one?

If you substituted syrup for the liquid, would you get the same relationship, keeping all other variables constant? Try vinegar, molasses, motor oil, tomato juice.

Keep the same straw and liquid and use a bottle of a different size. Try a smaller one than you began with and then a larger one. Try jars of different sizes, or a large container like an aquarium.

Have you discovered that as the depth of the straw in the liquid increases, the quantity of the liquid in the straw will also increase? (Did you measure in drops?) Is there a limit to this relationship? Tape several straws together to make one giant straw about 100 cm long to test this relationship.

Related activities include bis 8, 41, 71, and 87.

☐

Adapted from Gerald H. Krockover, "Soda-Straw Investigations," *Science Activities*, vol. 5, no. 5 (June 1971), pp. 24–25. By permission.

who stole our peanut brittle?
an investigation in fingerprinting

An inked stamp pad is needed for this activity. After inking your thumb, press and roll it on paper. Repeat for the other fingers on your right hand. (If the fingerprint smudges or is blurry, repeat until you get clear prints.)

Write down four observations about your fingerprints. Do yours look like arches or loops or whorls? Make several measurements on your fingerprints. Identify which print came from your thumb. Your middle finger. Take your prints to a friend; have the friend identify which of the prints is your thumb. Which print is your middle finger?

Two pieces of peanut brittle have been stolen from our box. Two right-hand thumbprints are found on the box and are shown on the next page.

Write down at least ten observations you can make about the fingerprints of the possible culprits. Does it help to measure any of them? Can you find three ways of classifying the prints? Which print does your thumbprint resemble most?
Can you identify the one who stole our peanut brittle?

more...

Have you ever observed raindrop prints? Try this! Obtain a used nylon stocking, an embroidery hoop, and a box of white powdered sugar. Tightly stretch one layer of nylon across the embroidery hoop. Dust it with a thin layer of powdered sugar, and collect some raindrops. As the raindrops strike the surface, they will pass right through the nylon, dissolving the powdered sugar. This will leave dark spots — the raindrop prints. Measure them.
Snowflake prints can be collected and permanently preserved. Spray a microscope slide with clear lacquer. While the slide is

The three forms of fingerprints:

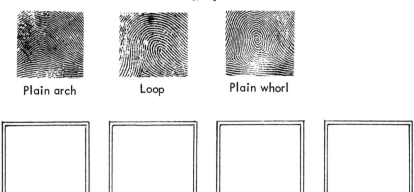

Plain arch   Loop   Plain whorl

Try making your fingerprints here!

Who stole our peanut brittle?

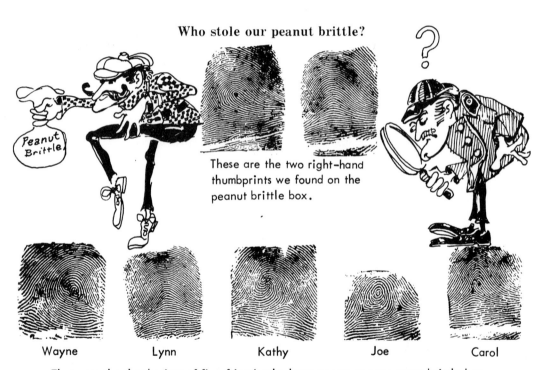

These are the two right-hand thumbprints we found on the peanut brittle box.

Wayne   Lynn   Kathy   Joe   Carol

These are the thumbprints of five friends who have access to our peanut brittle box.

still moist, collect flakes and allow the lacquer to dry. Examine the snowflakes under a microscope.

Related activities include bis 1, 10, 23, 54, 83; and ss 18.

☐

the sound of music

Among our five senses, hearing is the most important after sight. All sound is caused by waves. Audible sounds carry messages to our ears by wave motion. The crash of a bowling ball, the ringing of a bell, the vibrant sound of music, the angry snort of a bull, each tells its story with waves.

Sounds are made by vibrating objects. Strike a tuning fork. Touch it to the surface of a pan of water. What do you observe?

Sounds are generally varied in two ways, amplitude and pitch. The amplitude of a sound wave is an indication of how much energy was used in producing it. The greater the amplitude, the greater the volume. Frequency is the number of vibrations or waves in a specified time. The faster the object vibrates, the higher the pitch.

Materials needed for making sound waves visible are: a small fruit can with both ends removed, a sheet of rubber membrane from a balloon, a broken fragment from a pocket mirror, glue, a rubber band, and a flashlight (see the next page).

Over one end of the small fruit can tightly stretch the balloon membrane. Glue the fragment of mirror to the stretched balloon. Position the mirror fragment slightly off-center. Darkening the classroom, move the can near the blackboard. Hold it away from and at an angle to the blackboard. Shine the beam of a flashlight so that it strikes the mirror and rebounds onto the blackboard, as shown in the figure. Have someone speak, sing, shout, or (softly) blow a whistle into the can. Observe the reflection cast onto the blackboard. Describe your observation.

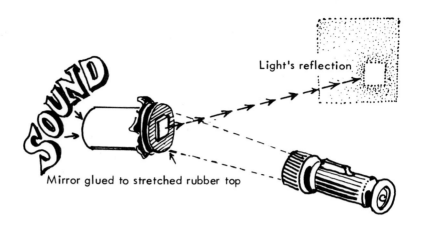

Light's reflection

SOUND

Mirror glued to stretched rubber top

How can the reflection be changed?

Does singing vowels loudly in succession change the reflection? Contrast this with consonants.

How does the reflection vary in relation to the strength of sound used?

more...

How does the vibration of a string, gut, or a rubber band vary as its length does?

How will the pitch change as length does?

Does the vibration of a string depend on its diameter?

How does the vibration rate of a string depend on its tension?

Related activities include bis 17, 84, 113, 122; and ss 26.

rising raisins

You will need a glass tumbler, a commercial carbonated drink, and some raisins.

Fill the glass with the carbonated drink. Place six to ten raisins in the tumbler. They should sink to the bottom, rest a while, and then float to the surface. They will linger a while here, gyrate slowly, and then slowly settle to the bottom. This rising and falling should repeat itself over and over.

What caused the raisins to rise and sink? Will the raisins respond in the same way in tap water? What might be responsible for this action? Try several carbonated drinks. Which gives you the best results?

Observe each raisin at the bottom. Observe it floating at the top. How do they differ? Something had to buoy it up off the bottom and something had to be gained or lost for it to settle to the bottom. What do you think?

How frequently does one raisin rise and sink? How long does it take to make the round trip?

Weigh the raisins before putting them into the liquid. Notice the lightest and the heaviest. Does the mass affect the frequency of the rising and falling raisin cycle?

more...

What other solutions can replicate this procedure? Try vinegar and baking soda. Place some baking soda in the bottom of a glass. Add water till ¾ full. Slowly add vinegar. Add raisins. Does this change the cycle?

Related activities include bis 34, 41, and 48.

bullish or bearish?

Everyone likes to gamble a little. And everyone likes to make money. Give all members of your class an imaginary $1000 bill. Provide a stock report sheet from a newspaper, and have the students decipher the stock market sheet. They should make some observations on the past performances of various stocks. You may want to present or have on hand stock market reports from the last several weeks so that students can backtrack to past selling prices of specific stocks. Have them classify the stocks (transportation, utilities, petroleum, food industry). Using inferences (or predictions), have them invest their $1000 in one or more varieties of stock. Each week have them observe, record, and plot on a graph the changes in value of their stock. From this have them predict when they should sell (or buy). You, or one of the students, can act as the stockbroker to handle the buying and selling of stock. Have the students keep a record of their transactions. Within a prescribed length of time have them report how they did. Who is the best investor?

more...

Some people claim that they see a correlation between the rise and fall of the stock market and the rise and decline of such things as the sale of liquor, aspirin, hemlines. Can you substantiate this connection? How?

Related activities include bis 43 and 87.

air and there

Activities in science involving air are plentiful, usually simple to perform, and often mind boggling. The mind boggling or amazement arises when a discrepancy occurs. You observe something you did not expect and you are not always ready to believe it. Here are some classic air activities. Try them!

FUNNEL BALL

Place a Ping-Pong ball inside a funnel. For better audience viewing, a glass funnel is preferred. Before performing, record how many in your audience think you can blow the Ping-Pong ball out of the funnel. Record how many think you can blow the Ping-Pong ball up in the air one foot. Two feet. Up to the ceiling.

Your attempt to blow the Ping-Pong ball out of the funnel will fail. You can be even more dramatic, repeating the same line of questioning, but inverting the funnel, holding the Ping-Pong ball up and inside the funnel and blowing extremely hard through the funnel stem. The ball will remain tightly nested in the funnel.

OTHER CLASSICS

The same basic scientific principles that are responsible for the Ping-Pong ball staying in the funnel are applicable in several other air activities.

Cut out a 1½ inch square from a 3 x 5 inch index card. Stick a straight pin through the center of the card. Place the pointed end of the pin down into the hole on one end of an empty spool of thread. Hold the spool over your head, place your mouth on the spool, and blow.

do not inhale!

The card will remain in position.

Place an empty pop bottle on a flat surface. Roll up a small paper pith ball. Position the pith ball inside the mouth of the bottle. Try to blow the pith ball into the bottom of the pop bottle. It defies you.

To perform another interesting air activity that captivates everyone's attention, fold a 3 x 5 inch index card so that it forms a bridge. Place the bridge flat on a table cleared of all other objects. The task is to flip the card over by blowing your breath on it, under it, over it, or any way you please. This defies you.

Now it is not the nature of air to be a part of a conspiracy to defy us; it really cooperates and often reveals to us what is happening. However, we don't always observe well. Air usually attempts to establish a balance or equilibrium. Thus, air of high pressure tends to equalize with areas of low pressure and vice versa. When a disequilibrium is set up and an equilibrium cannot be achieved, we appear to be defied.

Did you observe that when you blew on the index-card bridge, the top of the card depressed? Something had to push it down. Would you conclude that the air pressure pressing down was greater than, less than, or equal to the air pressure you were exerting when you blew on the card? The harder you blew the more the card was pressed down.

In the pop bottle activity, the air pressure inside the bottle is equal to the air pressure outside the bottle. You could not blow more air into the bottle because the pith ball deflected the air, causing a lower area of pressure to exist in front of the pith ball than behind it. It is a self-defeating air pressure activity, but it does challenge us to think.

The funnel activity is again a battle of which areas of greater or lesser air pressure are located where. When you blow through the funnel, the air is diverted and reduced around the Ping-Pong ball. The air converges on the reverse side where the air pressure is increased and is greater than that directly opposite; thus, the ball remains in place. A similar activity can be done with a stream of air expelled from a vacuum cleaner and directed at a lightweight beach ball positioned in midair. Try it!

THE DANCING PENNY

Chill an empty pop bottle in a refrigerator. Place it on a flat table. Wet the mouth of the bottle with water. Place a penny over the moistened mouth of the bottle. Now place both hands around the bottle and hold it firmly for about 15–20 seconds. What do you observe happening? Remove your hands. Explain, by reflecting on your observation, what is happening.

CRAZY LIQUID STRING

Locate an empty plastic container which has a squeeze top like many detergent bottles do. Unscrew the top. Clean container and top thoroughly. Thread a twelve-inch piece of cotton string through the hole in the top. It should slip back and forth freely. Knot each end so that the string cannot slip through. Drop the string into the bottle leaving only one knot visible above the top. Replace the cap. When you squeeze the bottle, the string shoots out like a liquid. Air pressure at work!

HOT AIR CONTEST, OR EXHALATION MEASUREMENTS

Who has the most hot air? Following the directions for inverting a container filled with water as outlined in bis 47, invert a half-gallon container of water. Place a strip of masking tape on the side of the container marked to denote pints and quarts. Place a rubber hose into the inverted container. Connect a straw to the hose and seal the connection with clay. Let each child see how much water he or she can displace by exhaling into the container through the straw and hose. It would not be unusual for most children to blow out a quart of air, displacing a quart of water. How do you score in the hot air department? Compare exhalation measurements to the winner's weight or chest measurements. Is there any correlation?

THE TESTY TEST TUBE

For this activity you will need a Pyrex test tube fitted with a one-hole rubber stopper through which a piece of glass tubing has been inserted.

this should be done only by the teacher

The glass tubing should extend 2 inches beyond the stopper in both directions. You will also need a test tube holder, a beaker with colored water at room temperature, and a heat source.

Remove the stopper and place 2 to 3 ml of clear water in the bottom of the test tube. Firmly replace the stopper and place the test tube in the flame. Carefully heat the water to boiling by passing the test tube back and forth through the flame. The glass tubing should be clear and open to allow the expanding gas to escape. Invert the test tube quickly and immerse the open glass tubing below the level of the colored water in the beaker. Wait two seconds. Suddenly, the colored liquid will rush into the test tube and fill it. Retrace your steps and reconstruct what you did to create an imbalance of air pressure. What was the reaction of air to regain a balance?

HAVE A DRINK???

Hold two soda straws in your mouth. Then place only one soda straw into a tumbler of water and let the other straw hang in midair. Drink up?

Make a pinhole at the midpoint of a soda straw. Drink up?
Fill a pop bottle with water and insert a soda straw. Seal the straw to the bottle with clay and pour yourself a drink.

Explain, in each of these situations, why it is so difficult to get a drink.

Related activities include bis 27, 41, 42, and 108.

☐

starchy science

Starch is manufactured by plants and animals as a means of storing sugar. A starch molecule is composed of a long chain of sugar molecules. Many different foods contain starch. A relatively simple test for starch can be made by placing a few drops of household iodine on food. If starch is present, the iodine changes from a reddish-brown to a blue-black color. Remember, read the label on the iodine bottle carefully.

iodine is a poison; do not eat
any food on which you have placed iodine!

You will need:

iodine solution	starch powder
medicine dropper	potato slice
containers for mixing ingredients	bread
glass jar	cooked rice
spoon or stirrer	some butter, sugar, and cornflakes

Stir a bit of starch powder into a small amount of water. Add a few drops of iodine solution. What change do you observe? Record your observations. What inferences can you make? Next, predict what you think will be the results if you try the same procedure with a potato slice, a piece of bread, a slice of apple, a spoonful of cooked rice, some butter, some sugar, or some cornflakes. Record your predictions. What basis do you have for your predictions?

more...

Does the percentage of starch in a food make a difference in testing for starch? Make a 2%, 1%, and ½% starch solution and test various foods. Is there a point at which the starch suspension is too weak? If so, at what percentage?

All green plants require sunlight in order to live. The sun furnishes the energy with which plants manufacture their own food or starch from the carbon dioxide in air and water. This process is called photosynthesis. To verify that plants require sunlight to manufacture starch, try this.

You will need a green plant (almost any plant will do; however, a broad leaf plant such as a geranium works well). You will also need aluminum foil, a saucer, ethyl alcohol, paper clips, and diluted iodine.

Cut a strip of aluminum foil to fit across one of the plant's leaves which will have full access to sunlight. The strip needs to be only ½ to ¾ inch wide. It should stretch across the leaf and be clipped at both ends.

Keep the foil strip on the leaf for several days while the plant soaks up sunshine. After this time, remove the leaf from the plant. Take off the foil and soak the leaf in ethyl alcohol for a few hours to remove some of the chlorophyll (green coloring). Place a few drops of iodine on the area previously covered by the strip and on those areas not covered by the strip. Which area lacks starch? Summarize this activity relating plants and sunlight to starch.

Related activities include bis 88 and ss 29.

bis 104

mass, volume, and displacement

Different amounts of the same substance can be compared by contrasting their volume — that is, the amount of space they occupy. This procedure is especially convenient when we deal with liquids because liquids take the shape of their containers. This is not as easily done with solids.

THE GRUESOME THREESOME GAME

Assemble three sets of three covered jars. One baby food jar, one peanut butter jar, and one large mayonnaise jar constitutes a set. Using a graduated cylinder or some other technique, determine the volume of each jar. Fill all three jars of the first set with unpopped corn. Fill the three jars of the second set with marbles. Fill only the baby food jar of the third set with BB's. Count the pieces of corn, the marbles, and the BB shot in each container. This task need only be done once, and it is time well spent since the materials can be used over and over. Having counted the total number of pieces in each container, permanently record this number (plus the volume) out of sight on the inside of the cap for future use.

Young children in particular have a great deal of trouble when asked how many somethings are in something. Responses range from twenty to ten million. Children need experiences in coming up with "roundhouse" or "ballpark" figures. This activity is a beginning; however, additional experiences to develop the skill further need to be introduced again and again.

Place the jars of set 1 so that they can be seen by all viewers. Ask how many pieces of unpopped corn are in the first container of set 1. Record several or all responses on the blackboard. Depending on grade level, find the median, the mode, and the range of contributions from your students. Tell them the exact number of kernels of unpopped popcorn. Tell them the volume. Now, ask them how many pieces of corn are in the second jar. Record the responses. Give them the exact number. Can they now estimate the volume? For example, three times as much corn should require three times as much volume as the original container. Or you can reverse the process; given the volume (and referring back to the data from the first jar), can they estimate the number? The students should be led from the known to the unknown. Repeat this procedure for sets 2 and 3. Do not rush. Extract the science inherent in this activity.

more...

To extend the Gruesome Threesome Game, pop some corn. Fill a container of known volume with the popped corn. Count the pieces of popped corn, and record this number inside the container cap. Ask the students who have had an opportunity to observe the container of popped corn how much unpopped corn it would require to make this much popped corn. What is the ratio of the unpopped corn volume to the popped corn volume?

Have the students observe the nesting or fit of the components in the smaller jars of all three sets. For example, the corn is triangular and the pieces seem to fit alongside of and between one another. The marbles, by contrast, do not fit as well. The BB's, being smaller spheres, appear to fit better. The volumes of all three jars are the same, and we could say we have equal volumes of corn, marbles, and BB's. But the marbles have the greatest interstices (spaces that intervene between things). Children are prone to think that if you have two equal volumes of two things and you combine them, you double the volume. This is true for similar things, but it is not necessarily true for dissimilar things. Remove half the marbles from the first jar of set 2. Remove half the BB's from the first jar of set 3. Combine the contents of both containers. Do they fill one jar to the top? The BB's filled the interstices or pore spaces and the total volume is reduced.

Try this: Fill a glass to the very top with water — almost to the point of the water crowning over. However, be careful not to let the water spill. If the upper outside wall of the glass gets wet, the desired results are affected. Challenge the students to decide whether you can get anything else into the glass without spilling the water over the sides. Then, slowly add cotton puffs. Keep adding them. You will amaze the students with the number of cotton puffs you can get into the glass. After the water eventually spills over, drain off the water and squeeze the cotton to remove the excess water. Ask the students if they originally thought you could insert such a large bulk of material into a filled glass without spilling the water. Where do the cotton fibers fit? Relate this question to the marble-BB mixture and the availability of pore spaces. Do water molecules have pore spaces between them?

more, more...

MEASURING THE VOLUME OF AIR SPACE
IN SAND

Pour some sand into a graduated cylinder until it is approximately two-thirds full. Record the volume. Using a graduate of similar size, pour water into it until it is about one-third full. Record the volume of water. Slowly pour the water into the graduate containing the sand. What is the volume of sand plus water? What is the volume of the air spaces in the sand? For this activity, commercial sandbox sand is preferable because it is washed and free of dust and debris.

Extend this activity to other materials such as clay, silt, and loam. How do they compare with sand relative to pore spaces?

THE MASS OF A DISSOLVED MATERIAL

Half fill the cap of a small plastic bottle with table salt. Put the cap aside. Pour water into the plastic bottle until it is about half-full. Before combining, use an equal-arm balance to determine the total mass of the bottle, water, cap, and salt.

Pour the salt into the bottle. You may need to shake the bottle to speed up the dissolving of the salt. Find out if the mass changed as the salt dissolved.

When ice melts, it contracts and its volume decreases. Find out if its mass also changes.

Related activities include bis 29, 41, 42; and sst 11.

☐

balloon-ology

Balloons could and should be an integral part of your science program. Their versatility makes them extremely useful in many areas of science investigation.

THE INSIDE-OUT BALLOON MANEUVER

this activity should only be done
under the direct supervision of the teacher

For this activity you will need two 125 ml Pyrex Erlenmeyer flasks, two balloons of equal size and shape (that will fit snugly over the mouths of the flasks), a heat source, a test tube clamp or asbestos gloves, a ring stand, and water.

Place about 10 ml of water in each flask. Stretch the mouth of one balloon over the mouth of one of the flasks. You should observe that the balloon inflates. Place this flask over a heat source. Bring the water to a boil. The balloon inflates. Allow the flask to cool. Placing the flask under cold running tap water will hasten the process. When it cools, observe how the balloon returns to its original shape and position.

With the second flask, bring the water to a boil. Let it boil for several minutes; however, do not boil all the water away. Leave at least 1 to 2 ml in the flask. Quickly cap the flask with a balloon; but

be careful, since much heat
will be retained by the flask

This operation may require more than two hands, so commandeer some help. Having capped the second flask with the balloon, place this flask back on the heat source. Bring the remaining water to a boil. You should observe that the balloon inflates. Remove the flask. Turn off the heat source and allow the flask to cool. A rapid cooling by placing the flask under or in cool tap water makes the demonstration more dramatic. When it cools, you will observe that the balloon deflates and slowly slips into the flask (some kindly guidance by you will insure that the balloon does not get caught and rupture) and readily inflates itself inside the flask.

The question is, Why does one balloon deflate to its original position while the other does not?

Hopefully, the students observed that you did not treat each situation equally. Air expands when heated; therefore, when you capped the first unheated flask, you restricted the future expansion of the heated air to a closed system. The expanded air was trapped within the expanding balloon. When the system cooled, the air contracted and the balloon deflated, everything returning to its original balance. In the alternate situation, you boiled the water first, then quickly capped the flask. Much heated, expanded air escaped. Your quick capping of the flask trapped a reduced amount of air. Thus, when the system cooled, the air pressure outside the balloon was greater than that inside the flask. This disequilibrium resulted in the balloon being forced into the flask and inflating in an inside-out manner.

more...

Can you inflate a balloon inside a bottle?

Place a two-hole rubber stopper into a bottle. Carefully insert two stiff plastic soda straws through the stopper. (You may need to lubricate them.) Make sure the straws are sealed well against the stopper. Attach a balloon to one of the straws and secure it tightly. Now suck in on the straw which does not have the balloon attached. What do you observe? How can you explain your observations? Can you inflate one balloon inside another balloon?

Print your name on a deflated balloon. Inflate it, noting the number of breaths it takes. What happens to the size of the printing as you inflate the balloon?

Inflate a balloon and record its dimensions (volume and mass). Place it in a refrigerator. What happens to its volume and its mass?

Fasten an elongated balloon to the ring on a ring stand. At the other end, attach a paper clip to serve as a hook. Attaching various weights, you can (with caution) stretch the balloon through a fixed distance. Record the vertical oscillations as affected by various weights stretched through various distances.

**anything weighted and placed under tension
by the stretching of an elastic material
needs to be used with careful guidance**

This apparatus can serve as a Wilberforce pendulum. Record the data as you vary weights through a fixed distance and, as you vary distance with a fixed weight, construct appropriate graphs.

Balloons emit sounds. How does the volume of contained air affect the sound emitted when the mouth of a balloon is stretched and air is released?

Is a balloon like a permeable membrane? Using three balloons of equal size, shape, and construction, place equal amounts (three drops) of three different odiferous materials, one in each balloon; for example, perfume, after shave lotion, vanilla extract, and so on. Quickly seal each balloon and wash off any exterior spillage. How many students can identify the contents now? Twenty-four hours later? What can you conclude about the permeability of balloon walls?

How can you determine the volume of air contained within an inflated balloon?

How is bounce affected by the volume of air contained within a balloon? Inflate a balloon and drop it from various recorded heights. Record the rebound of the bounce. Increase the balloon's volume. Repeat the steps, recording the measures. Do they change?

THE AIRBORNE GONDOLA CONTEST

A balloon makes an excellent guided missile. Select three cylindrical shaped balloons and inflate all three so that the volumes are equal. A balance scale will help with this task.

Stretch three thin strings (fishing line works well), on each of which you have threaded a plastic straw, from one length of the room to the other. The straw should be able to slide up and down the string. Keep the string taut. This string will serve as the missile's track. Using tape, attach the inflated balloon to the movable straw and move the balloon to one end. The idea is to release the air by the best means you know in order to propel the balloon as far down the string as possible. Having mastered the

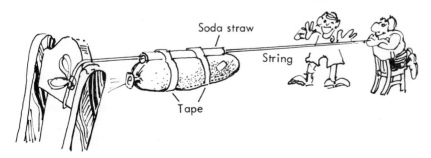

Soda straw

String

Tape

mechanics, you are now ready to find out which balloon will travel the farthest. Also, you could vary the contest by asking:

Will changing the string make a difference?
Will altering the string (rubbing with beeswax or paste wax) make a difference?
Will a different balloon shape make a difference?
Will altering the balloon by the addition of fins or wings make a difference?
Will inclining or declining the string make a difference?

more, more...

NOW YOU SEE IT, NOW YOU DON'T

Attach three 1-foot lengths of flexible tubing to each end of a glass T (or Y). Using thin wire or string, secure the connections tightly. To any two ends of the flexible tubing, attach balloons of similar size and shape. Blow through the remaining flexible tubing. Blow one balloon twice the size of the other. This will necessitate your pinching off by crimping (or by the use of hose clamps) the appropriate tubes so that no air escapes from the input tubing and no air can escape from one balloon to another through the flexible tubing.

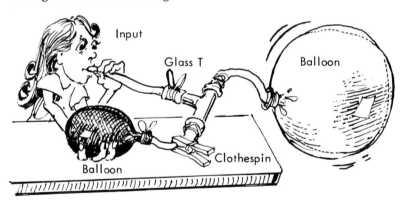

Prompt your students with these questions: What do you think will happen when I open the passageway allowing the free flow of air from one balloon to the other (the input tubing must still remain pinched off)?

Will the larger balloon get larger and the smaller balloon become smaller?
Will the smaller balloon get larger and the larger balloon become smaller?

Will the air distribute itself equally? Thus, will the two balloons end up the same size?

Most students anticipate that the balloons will indeed become equal in size. They are surprised and a bit bewildered. For an explanation, consider the property of elasticity. Is it easier to blow up a new balloon or an old balloon? How does the answer to this question help you find the explanation?

more, more, more...

Using a heavy felt pen, draw various geometric shapes, such as circles, triangles, and squares, on an uninflated balloon. Infer what the shapes will look like when the balloon is inflated. Will the geometric shapes look the same? Larger? Distorted?

AIR-POWERED BOATS

An empty milk carton, a balloon, water, and a competitive atmosphere can make for interesting science.

Lay an empty milk carton on its side, staple the spout end closed, and cut out the top portion. You now have a boat. Blow up your balloon and pinch the end closed. Place the milk-carton boat with the balloon stuffed inside in the water. Release your fingers from the pinched end of the balloon and let the boat go. How far did it travel? What variables affect its motion? Who can make it go the greatest distance? Measure, record, and graph the results.

Most individuals experience trouble finding an accessible waterway that is clean, safe, free of water currents, and yet large enough to permit movements that are measurable. A length of house roof drain, capped and sealed at both ends, makes an excellent water trough for use in this activity. This trough, wet or dry, can be used for many other purposes — for example, an inclined plane.

AN AIR-POWERED CAR

Attach an inflated balloon to a small, four-wheeled toy car or cart. Define a starting point as a frame of reference to determine how far the car will have traveled. Release the air from the balloon and watch the car go!

Related activities include bis 51, 84, 96, and 99.

sugar-coated classification

Have you ever asked yourself, How many watermelon seeds are there in a watermelon? Do all watermelons have the same number of seeds? Or, how many peanuts are in a one-pound jar? These are good, provocative questions that beg investigation.

Popular sugar-coated chocolate candies come in packages of equal weight. The candies inside are multicolored. Does each package have the same number of candies? Does every package have the same number of candies of each color? A brief investigation reveals some interesting things.

Give each student a small package of sugar-coated chocolate candies, and have each respond to these questions: Will each package have the same number of candies? Will each package have the same colors represented? Will every package have the same number of each color? Have the students observe and describe the candies. How are they alike? How are they different? Have the students count the total number of candies. Have the students count the total number of each color. Have them make individual graphs recording the numbers of each color in their packages. Make a composite class graph recording the data. What appears to be the most popular color? What is the average number of candies in a package?

more...

*Try the same thing, using other candies with similar features.
How many potato chips (of the stacked variety) are in one cylinder? Do all the cylinders contain the same number of potato chips?*

Related activities include bis 10, 21, 79; and ss 15.

surface tension of liquids

Water is an amazing liquid. One falling drop of water quickly encases itself in a tough, transparent skin. This same skin forms instantly when water comes in contact with other materials. Water molecules, when in contact with air or other matter, squeeze together forming a dense layer called "surface tension." Surface tension can be measured using a simple device called a tensiometer. This device can be built from scrap lumber, as shown in the illustration.

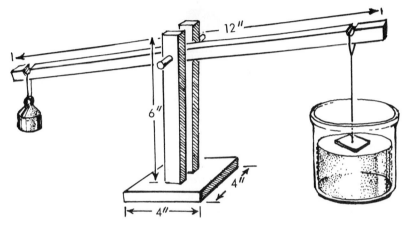

The primary purpose of a tensiometer is to measure surface tension. This is accomplished by cutting a one-inch square of plastic or Plexiglas. This material should be thick enough so that it will lie flat (a thickness of 1/32 to 1/16 inch should work fine). Attach and suspend the one-inch square from the long arm of the tensiometer. The one-inch square should be positioned so that it floats on the water in a beaker. Tap the short arm of the tensiometer to feel the surface tension. Now place weights in a small paper cup. (Commercially available weights are fine; however, small washers work just as well.) Determine the mass (see bis 29) of one washer and you are ready to measure surface tension. Just keep adding washers, one at a time, until the surface tension is broken. Record the mass necessary to break the surface tension.

Does the shape of the geometric figure affect the surface tension? Using plastic or Plexiglas, cut out additional shapes such as rectangles, triangles, and circles. However, make sure the surface area of each shape remains one square inch. This can be accomplished by using the following formulas and dimensions.

rectangle Area = Length × Width **or** ½″ × 2″ = 1 square inch

triangle Area = $\dfrac{\text{Base} \times \text{Height}}{2}$ **or** $\dfrac{1'' \times 2''}{2}$ = 1 square inch

circle   Area = πr^2 **or** $3.14 \times .57^2$ = 1 square inch

Measure the surface tension using these shapes. With the surface being held constant in all cases what happens to the recorded surface tension? Does it increase, decrease, or remain the same?

How is the recorded tension affected by increasing the surface area? Cut out a two-inch square (4 square inches) and measure the surface tension. Is it four times as much as the original one-inch square?

more...

Does temperature make a difference? Use three containers with three different temperatures (hot, lukewarm, and cold) of water. For each recorded temperature of water in each container, determine the surface tension. How do they compare?

Does the liquid make a difference? Measure surface tension using rain water, vinegar, apple juice, cooking oil, and so on. How do they compare to one another?

How does a detergent added to water affect surface tension? Which detergent reduces surface tension the most?

Related activities include bis 9, 27, and 59.

boiling water by cooling

this activity is to be done only
under the direct supervision of the teacher

This activity can serve as an invitation to investigate the concept of air pressure. You will need a 250 or 500 ml Pyrex boiling flask, a tight fitting stopper for the flask, a ring stand, a burette clamp, heatproof gloves, a heat source, and a catch basin.

Half fill the 250 or 500 ml Pyrex boiling flask with water. Using the ring stand and a heat source, carefully bring the water to a boil for a period of several minutes. Shut off the heat and, a minute later, press the previously prepared greased stopper into the mouth of the flask. Using the ring stand, the burette clamp, and heatproof gloves, invert the flask, place it upside down through the ring, and lock it into position.

remember: the water contained within the flask is extremely hot, and a poorly fitted stopper could cause leakage or burns

A catch basin for any leakage from the flask is recommended.

Because of the very low air pressure above the water surface, the water contained in the inverted flask should continue to boil for several minutes. When the boiling action slows down, place a piece of wet cloth over the top of the flask. Evaporation from the cloth cools the top portion of the flask, causing the water vapor to condense quickly. The boiling action continues as long as there is a difference in the temperature of the water that remains in the flask and the air temperature. The cloth positioned on the top of the flask needs to be kept moist.

Related activities include bis 27, 41, 42, and 102.

☐

action metrics

109 bis

Metric education should be an integral part of the science and mathematics programs in the classroom. Rather than using classroom time with repetitive conversion tasks, such as changing miles to kilometers, metrics should be taught as a separate entity and the Imperial (English) system as a separate entity. Children need to be taught to "think metric." Suggested metric activities include:

1. Who's Who in Metrics? How many countries of the world are not on the metric system? Why aren't they? What are the advantages and disadvantages of going metric? Cite examples of products and materials going metric such as cars, tires, soda pop bottles, sewing patterns, and so on.

2. Make your own metric rulers using string, yarn, cardboard, or wood. Mark the appropriate divisions on your metric ruler such as centimeters or decimeters.

3. Find out about your "metric self" by filling in the chart:

My height is	_____ centimeters or
	_____ meters.
The length of my foot is	_____ centimeters.
The length of my arm is	_____ centimeters.
My waist size is	_____ centimeters.
My wrist size is	_____ centimeters.
I can jump	_____ centimeters high.
My friend is	_____ meters tall.
My desk is	_____ centimeters wide.
The shortest distance from my school room to the lunchroom is	_____ meters.

4. Take me to your liter. Using a metric container (one liter or some known quantity), measure the volume of each item in liters. Try a soda pop bottle (_____ liters), a soup can (_____ liters), and a baby food jar (_____ liters). Find three items that hold less than 1 liter of water; three items that hold more than 1 liter, but less than 2 liters of water; and one item that holds more than 2 liters, but less than 6 liters of water. (Estimate the volume of your school milk carton in liters. Check your estimate by measuring its volume.)

5. I'm Amassed! Mass is measured in grams. A mass of one gram is approximately equal to the mass of one (size number 1) paper clip. Using a balance, weigh the following items using paper clips as a unit of measure. Later convert these measures to grams:

Your pencil or crayon	_____ grams
Your empty milk carton	_____ grams
Your shoe	_____ grams

Check the food item containers at home in your kitchen for metric weights in grams. Select five food containers and record the name of each food and its mass.

6. Boy! It's 35° outside. Let's turn on the air conditioner! To help your students relate Celsius temperature to their surroundings, have them prepare a chart that gives the estimated Celsius temperature for:

Your school room	_____ °C
A winter day	_____ °C
A summer day	_____ °C
Ice skating	_____ °C
Swimming	_____ °C
Baseball	_____ °C
Basketball	_____ °C
Your normal body temperature	_____ °C

Remember, your goal is to help children to "think metric," not to use conversion formulas. If there is a need to relate the two systems of measurement, use a chart.

more...

Have the children estimate metric measurements, then actually measure them and calculate the difference.

Develop your own unique standard unit of measure, such as the DeKro, and use it for measurements.

Find out the origin of measurement of units.

Have a metric scavenger hunt.

Draw a metric floor plan of your home or school on centimeter graph paper.

Build scale model metric furniture.

Make your own metric containers.

Make a metric meal for your class — try punch, cookies, and cake.

remember: measure everything metrically

Related activities include bis 83 and 110.

bis110

energy fun activity cards

These Energy Fun Activity Cards (EFAC) are intended to help you introduce energy education activities into your classroom as an interdisciplinary subject. After trying these with your students, add more ideas and extend your cards.

EFAC 1   Cartoons

Draw your own cartoon or cartoon strip about energy wastefulness. Next, make one about energy conservation or try energy alternatives.

Select a cartoon or cartoon strip from the newspaper. Blot out all the original words and turn the cartoon into an energy message.

EFAC 2   Brainstorming

List five ways people waste energy. List five ways people save energy. Design a plan to turn energy wasters into energy savers and now try it. Did it work? Why or why not?

EFAC 3   Reporter

Interview five people and find out how they save energy. Find out if age, occupation, or sex makes a difference in your results. Ask these same five people to suggest ways that their government, business, or home can save energy. Find out which type of energy source people prefer and why.

EFAC 4   Your school

Conduct an energy survey of your school. In what way is your school saving energy? Wasting energy?

Design a plan to help your school save energy and try it.

Does your school use any alternative forms of energy, such as solar or wind? Find out the advantages and disadvantages for your school switching to an alternative source of energy.

EFAC 5   Energy in the news

Using magazines and newspapers, start an energy scrapbook that classifies energy topics by source, conservation, alternatives, advertisements, and wasting energy.

Present your scrapbook to the school library.

EFAC 6   Energy mobiles

Make an energy mobile that illustrates one of these themes: energy alternatives, sources of energy, energy wasters, and so on. Better yet, think of your own theme.

EFAC 7 Energy costs

Find out how many gallons of gas it takes one of your parents to get to work and back home for five days. Find the cost of gasoline per gallon. How much does it cost each five days for gas? Each year?

Next, find out how much gas or electricity costs per unit, such as a kilowatt hour. How much does it cost your parents each month to heat or cool their home? How much does it cost your school?

Develop a plan to reduce this cost and try it.

EFAC 8 Energy city

Draw your own energy-saving city. Include streets, stores, homes, industry, schools, and a park. Label the energy-saving and alternative energy sources you would include in Energy City.

EFAC 9 Don't be an energy egghead!

Make a bumper sticker advertising one aspect of energy, such as conservation.

Make a poster on energy education for your school hallway.

Make an alternative-energy-source bulletin board.

EFAC 10 What a day!

You wake up one morning and find all your sources of energy are gone. No TV, sour milk in the refrigerator, no lights. What will you do? Devise a survival plan for you and your family.

EFAC 11 That's home life

How can you save energy in your home? Prepare a list of things that you can do. Discuss these with your family. Put your plan into action and report your results to the class.

EFAC 12 Make a game

Make an energy game (game board, playing pieces, cards, and rules) illustrating one aspect of energy. Try it with someone.

EFAC 13 Energy museum

Prepare an energy mural entitled, "Ways We Can Save Energy."

Make an energy picture collage.

Paint a mural that presents the history of energy use in the United States.

EFAC 14 Coal

Find out why we don't use more coal as an energy source. Prepare a case for using more coal. Next, try natural gas, oil, geothermal, solar, wind, or nuclear energy.

EFAC 15 Fission or fusion

Find out the differences between nuclear reactors and classify them by type or function. Cite the hazards of nuclear power and how we can overcome them.

Related activities include bis 83 and 109.

soil testing

To test the soil, you will need:

paper cups
litmus paper (red and blue)
vinegar
baking soda
teaspoon
lemon or lime juice
lime (garden variety)
soil samples (coarse sand, clay, and so on)
measuring cup
thermometer

filter paper, paper towel or cloth
oven
coffee cans with both ends removed (all the same size)
rubber bands
screen
large mouth jar
tuna fish cans
knife
beaker or heat resistant jar

Soil temperature varies with depth, season, soil type, time of day, light intensity, and moisture content. Select a site where the depth of the various soil layers is known. Record the air temperature. Read and record the soil temperature at the soil surface and at depths of 5, 10, 15, and 20 cm. Repeat this procedure, comparing shady versus open areas; north- and south-facing hill slopes; wet, dry, or damp soil areas; different soil types. In doing this activity, you will need to make sure that all variables except the one being considered are kept constant. How do the temperatures of the soil and air compare? What is the relationship between soil temperature and soil depth? Which type(s) of soil(s) show the greatest temperature variations? Which type(s) had the least temperature variation? What is the relationship between the moisture content and the soil temperature?

The temperature range in soil affects the distribution of organisms within it. As a result, temperature readings can assist you in analyzing why a population of organisms is found in a particular soil.

Moisture found in soil varies greatly with the type of soil, the climate, and the amount of humus in that soil. The types of organisms which can survive in an area are largely determined by the amount of water available to them. The following method allows students to measure the moisture content of soil before and after it has been dried in an oven. From this information, the percentage of moisture can be calculated.

Weigh an empty beaker and record its mass. Add the soil sample to the beaker and reweigh it. Record the mass. Heat the beaker and soil in an oven set at 100°C (212°F) for approximately 24 hours or until the weight is relatively constant. Reweigh the beaker and the dried soil. Record the mass. Subtract the mass of the empty beaker from the masses of the beaker plus the (1) wet and (2) dry soil to obtain the actual masses of the soil in its wet and dry states. Subtract the mass of the dry soil from the mass of the wet soil. This gives you the mass of the water in the soil. Take this number, divide it by the dry mass of the soil, and multiply by 100%. This gives you the percentage of moisture in the soil sample.

Alternatives to expressing the water-holding capacity of soil as a percentage of the dry weight are available. One such method is to compare the water-holding capacity of two or more soils which differ in humus content and particle size.

Collect two or more soil samples in cans such as coffee cans. Using a rubber band, secure a piece of filter paper or cloth to the base of each can. Oven-dry each sample of soil. (Try to get samples from places where grasses have been grown, such as playgrounds, gardens, and so on.) Fill each can approximately two-thirds full of the soil sample and label it. Place each can on a screen above a beaker or jar. Pour equal amounts of water into each can. Measure the time that elapses before water begins dripping into each jar, how long the water continues to drip into each jar, and how much water eventually passes through each soil type.

Infer why some soil samples are able to absorb large amounts of water while others cannot. Prepare a graph of your data. Which soil sample absorbed the most water?

The *percolation rate* or speed of moisture infiltration into the soil can be measured using a can with both ends removed. Work the can about 4 cm into the ground. Pour a measured amount of water into the can. Measure the time required for all the water to enter the soil. Repeat this procedure in two or three other locations with the same soil to obtain an average. Try different soil types. Which soil type(s) absorbed the water most rapidly? Cite advantages and disadvantages of fast infiltration of water into the soil.

page 187

What about slow infiltration? Repeat this same activity using muddy water and observe. What differences are perceived? Relate these findings to percolation rates and erosion. Try a measurement over the mouth of a worm burrow. Infer how the activity of worms helps to prevent flooding.

In every sample of oven-dried soil, a certain percentage of its volume is occupied by air. This is called the *pore space* and it is found between the solid soil particles. In moist soil, some space is filled with water and some with air. The amount of pore space varies from one type of soil to another. Let's measure the pore space in two soil samples and compare them.

Oven-dry two soil samples for 24 hours at 100°C. Measure the internal diameter and height of a tuna can. Attach filter paper to one end of the can using a rubber band. Place a second rubber band at the base of the can. Weigh the can and dry filter paper. Record the mass. Wet the filter paper and reweigh the apparatus. Record the mass. Add 8 to 10 g of soil at a time to the can. To settle the soil, tap the top of the can after each addition. When the can is full, level off the top and then tap the can. Continue to add soil to the top and level it off until only very slight settling occurs. Level the top of the can. Place the can in 1–2 cm of water and leave it overnight. By morning, a portion of the soil will have expanded above the top of the can. Remove this with a knife blade drawn across the top of the can at an angle. Weigh the apparatus containing the remaining wet soil. Record the mass. Dry the soil in the can for 24 hours in an oven set at 100°C. Cool the can and its contents. Weigh the apparatus and record the mass. Repeat the procedure with the second soil type.

Using the following formula, calculate the percentage of pore space in the soil sample:

Percentage of pore space =
$$\frac{\text{Mass of wet soil} - \text{mass of dry soil}}{\text{Internal volume of can}} \times 100\%$$

Here are some formulas that will help:

Mass of wet soil = (Mass of can + wet paper + wet soil) −
(mass of can + wet paper)

Mass of dry soil = (Mass of can + dry paper + dry soil) −
(mass of can + dry paper)

Internal volume of can =
$$\pi \left(\frac{\text{Internal diameter of can}}{2}\right)^2 \times \text{height of can}$$

Which soil type has the largest percentage of pore space? Infer why air is necessary in soil. How might water be drawn from pore spaces under normal conditions? How might rain storms or changes in the atmospheric pressure bring "fresh" air into the soil?

more...

Try chemical soil tests to find out if your soil samples are acidic or alkaline (basic).

Dissolve a teaspoonful of each of two alkalines (baking soda, lime) in separate half-cups of water. Put a teaspoon of each of two acids (vinegar, lemon juice) in two other cups of water. Dip blue litmus paper in each cup, using a separate strip for each. What color change do you observe take place when blue litmus paper is moistened with an acid? With an alkaline? Now do the same with strips of red litmus paper. Next, put a teaspoonful of each soil sample into separate cups. Add half a cup of water to each and stir. After the soil has settled, test it with blue and red litmus paper. Which soils are alkaline? Which are acidic? Which are neutral? (Neutral soils cause no color change in the litmus paper.) Take the soil that tested acidic. (If you have none, add a teaspoonful of vinegar to a neutral or alkaline soil.) Add a pinch of lime, and stir. Test it with litmus paper. Have you changed the soil to alkaline? If not, add another pinch of lime and try again.

Cite reasons why a farmer adds lime to his soil.

Investigate why fertilizers are added to the soil. Why are different fertilizers used for different purposes? Prepare a chart showing the uses of fertilizers and the compositions of the various fertilizers.

Find out what kinds of plants and animals live in the soil. Prepare a classification scheme for these plants and animals.

Related activities include bis 2, 31, 115; ss 12; and sst 10.

☐

you turned the tables on me

To do this activity, you will need a record player and a cardboard circle cut to fit the turntable.

Have you ever tried to walk in a straight line across a merry-go-round while it was in operation? It was difficult to do, wasn't it? To observe what happens on a spinning turntable, try this activity.

Cut a cardboard circle to fit the turntable of a record player. If the cardboard doesn't spin with the table, fasten it down with tape that sticks on both sides. With the turntable spinning, use a pencil, pen or crayon and try to draw a straight line on the cardboard. What do you observe happens? Explain why it happens.

Next, try drawing a circle on the spinning cardboard without moving the tip of your pencil. Then try using two pencils at once to draw a small circle and a large circle at the same time without moving either pencil. Compare the circumferences of the two circles. Compare the length of time it took to draw the two circles. Under which pencil was the turntable moving faster? This activity should help explain why you didn't make a straight line when you moved the pencil across the spinning cardboard.

Pretend that you are a ladybug walking across the turntable in a straight line. Suddenly someone turns on the record player. Describe your path. Make a drawing of what this path might look like.

Try changing the speed of the pencil as you move it across the cardboard. What patterns do you observe as the movement of the pencil changes?

What will your line look like if you draw your pencil from the outer edge of the spinning cardboard to the center? Test your prediction.

If your record player has different speed settings, investigate their effects on the pattern drawn by the pencil. What could you substitute for a pencil? Try a steel ball rubbed on a black inked stamp pad.

more...

Until about five hundred years ago, most people, including scientists called astronomers, believed that the stars were revolving, or moving in a circle, around the earth once each 24 hours. The people thought that the earth was motionless and at the center of the universe! We now know that the earth is spinning around like the cardboard on the turntable. Using a globe that turns, a partner, and some chalk, you can observe the effect of motion as a result of our earth's rotation. Have your partner rotate the globe in a counterclockwise direction. Place your chalk on the equator and attempt to draw a straight line toward the North Pole. Record your observations and relate this to our turntable activity. Try it again, only move toward the South Pole. What do you observe? Relate your chalk lines to an air mass moving northward from the equator or a rocket ship launched northward.

Related activities include bis 30, 51, and 63.

□

let's make waves

OCEANOGRAPHY ACTIVITY CARDS (OAC)

OAC 1
You are planning a deep sea dive in the ocean. Prepare a list of the materials and equipment you will need and how you will use them.

OAC 2
Make the Cartesian diver in bis 41, and observe the air space in the eyedropper. Try varying the amount of water in the eye-dropper before placing it into the container. How does this affect the performance of your Cartesian diver? Pretend your eyedropper is a submarine. State the ways that the submarine will use air and water combinations to go up and down.

OAC 3
Using a Slinky, try making waves. What do you have to do to make large waves? Do all the waves you make travel at the same rate? Does it take more energy to make a series of large waves or a series of small waves? Can you arrange the Slinky so that the wave is reflected back to you from the other end? By stretching the spring and suddenly pushing it in at one end, you can make a compressional wave. Does the compressional wave have the same characteristics as the wave you made in the first experiment? Tie

one end of a rope with a knot in the middle to a doorknob. Extend the rope to its fullest length and jiggle it from the free end. Waves pass along the rope toward the doorknob. How does the rope itself move? Describe the motion of the knot. Relate this model to the motion of water particles in a wave. Think of other models that would represent the same thing and try them.

OAC 4

Dissolve two tablespoons of salt in a glass of water. Place one hardboiled egg, still in the shell, in the salt water and one in a glass of plain water. What do you observe? How can you explain these observations? Now try this. Insert single thumbtacks in the erasers of two pencils. Place one pencil in a glass of plain water and one pencil in a glass of salt water (tack ends down). The pencil should float in an upright position. Record your observations. Infer which water (plain or salt) is denser. Try testing other objects in plain and salt water to observe flotation levels.

OAC 5

Using the wave tank described in ss 26, initiate some waves in the contained water and see if you can measure either the wavelength or the speed at which the waves travel. Make a circular wave pattern with your finger. Now make a wave of different lengths. Next, change the speed at which the waves move across the water. Float a toothpick in one corner of the tank. Make waves with your finger in the corner diagonally across from the toothpick. Describe the motion of the toothpick. Put a drop of food coloring on top of the water near the toothpick. Again make waves in the corner diagonally across from the toothpick. Describe the way the food coloring mixes with the water. A wave carries energy as it moves. Observe how the toothpick moves when the waves hit it. Describe other ways to move energy from one place to another; for example, when a baseball hits the catcher's mitt. List other examples. Make some straight waves with a short ruler at one end of the wave tank. What happens to the waves if the tank is tilted so that the water edge does not quite touch the opposite end of the tank? Find a way to change a straight wave into a curved wave.

OAC 6

Pretend you are an ocean diver. Write a story about an exciting dive that you have made. Why did you make the dive? Where did the dive take place? At what depth were you? What observations did you make? How did you feel? Provide some illustrations for your story.

OAC 7

Select a sea plant or animal that you would like to learn more about. Find out what it looks like, its size, what it eats, some of its ordinary and peculiar habits. Draw a lifelike picture of this animal. Find some stories in the library about this plant or animal to read. Create your own ocean plant or animal and tell others about it.

Related activities include bis 17, 84, 99, 122; and ss 26.

□

test your chark here

To build a Chark, you will need:

1 soda straw	1 metric ruler
glue	1 meter stick
1 sheet of notebook paper, any size	1 balance
	1 pair of scissors

Prepare a data table, and record the following information as you obtain it: length of the short strip (mm), length of the long strip (mm), mass of the small loop (g), mass of the large loop (g), distance to the center of gravity (mm), length of the straw (mm), diameter of the small loop (mm), diameter of the large loop (mm), total mass of the Chark (g), and glide distance (m).

To construct a Chark, cut two 25-mm-wide strips from notebook paper. One strip should be cut from the full length of the paper and the other strip from the width. Glue the ends of the strips so that each forms a loop. Place a dot of glue on the inner surface of each loop, in the area of the previously glued joint, and press the soda straw down into the glue.

Test glide your completed Chark. Record the distance of your test glide in the data table.

Approximate the center of gravity on the straw and measure its distance to the nose. Also weigh your Chark.

Your challenge is to modify the design of the Chark so that it will glide a distance of 10 meters. What changes will you make? You might want to try loops of different shapes, weighting the nose with paper clips, larger or smaller loops, wider or narrower strips, longer or shorter straws, and so on.

Draw a picture of your new Chark. Record the new dimensions in a data table, and test glide the Chark. Did it travel 10 meters? If yes, congratulations! If not, try another modification on your Chark.

more...

Compare the performance of your Chark with a standard paper airplane. In what ways are they alike? In what ways are they different? Design a conventional paper airplane that will outperform a Chark.

Pretend your Chark is similar to a real jet airplane. Which Chark parts correspond to the parts of the airplane?

Related activities include bis 20, 30, 45, 80, 86, 117, 118; and ss 19.

initial growing

The materials you will need to make initials grow are:

    floral foam or Styrofoam
    seeds
    plate

Outline your name or initial on a square of the floral foam. Press seeds (such as beans) approximately 1.5 cm into the foam, following your outline. Space the seeds about 1 cm apart. After planting, place the foam on a plate and keep the foam moist. Observe what happens each day until your seeds sprout your name or initial.

more...

Using the foam and seeds, try making a collage, your family crest, or your school emblem.

Make seed pictures by drawing a design on cardboard. Then brush a coat of slow-drying glue over the entire design. Select seeds of different colors, sizes, shapes, and so on. Place them on the cardboard to complete the picture. Prepare a classification scheme of your finished product using color, type of seed, or any other property you choose.

Wet a large sponge and squeeze out most of the moisture. Sprinkle it with grass seed. Tie a string to the sponge and hang it in a sunny window. How many days does it take for the seeds to sprout and cover the sponge with green grass?

Related activities include bis 2, 26, 31, 55, 111; ss 12; and sst 70.

get the drift?

One of the great scientific debates now taking place argues whether the continents have been fixed in position throughout their history or whether they have drifted to their present locations. To illustrate the drifting of the continents, duplicate the next pages for each student in your class. Have your students prepare a motion booklet (see bis 58), by cutting out each drawing and stacking them up in numerical order with number 1 on the top and number 12 on the bottom. Making sure that the twelve pages line up, staple them on the left-hand side. Quickly flip through the pages and observe the movement of the continents. Trace the movement of specific continents. What would have happened if the continents had remained as shown on frame 4? Speculate upon the implications of this to our climate, culture, and problems associated with traveling from one country to another.

CONVECTION CURRENTS AND CONTINENTAL DRIFT

To illustrate the relationship between convection currents within the earth's surface and continental drift, try this activity (under the direct supervision of the teacher).

You will need:

> 1 Pyrex glass container (approximately 9 x 13 inch)
> water
> tongs
> decorative wood bark (lawn chips)
> food coloring
> stand for the container
> heat source (burner, candle, or lamp)
> eyedropper

Place the container on the stand, and fill it approximately one-third full of water. Put the bark chips in water, and clump them close together. Heat the container with the heat source.

Observe what happens as the water begins to heat up. Place 4–6 drops of food coloring to help you observe the path of the convection current.

Record your observations as the water is being heated. Trace the path of the convection current. Infer the cause of the convection current. The uneven heating of the water causes the convection current to be set up. Relate the convection current to the theory of continental drift. Classify each piece of equipment

200 million years ago

190 million years ago

180 million years ago

150 million years ago

135 million years ago

100 million years ago

65 million years ago

30 million years ago

10 million years ago

World at present

25 million years in the future

50 million years in the future

in this activity with its real counterpart on earth. For example, the heat source would represent the _____ of the earth. (Did you say "core" or "center"?)

PLATE TECTONICS GAME

Construct a Plate Tectonics Game for your class. The object of the game is to determine the original arrangement of the continental plates by collecting data from the six continental stations (Utopia, Oz, Mordor, Gondwana, Laurasia, and Etrusca), and a team should aim to visit every station. Dice can be rolled by each of the six teams to decide the order of movement. To begin, a team must roll a 7 or below. A roll of 2 through 7 sends the teams to the number of the station thrown; that is, a 2 sends the team to Utopia, a 3 to Oz, and so on through 7. At the station the team will find the Continental Station Data Cards; this information should be recorded on a data sheet.

In the next round, a roll of 2 through 7 sends the team to the number of the station thrown; an 8 causes loss of a turn and a review of the glossary; a 9 allows the team to go to the station of their choice and draw two cards from the data box; a 10 requires the team to give up one piece of data on their data sheet; an 11 allows the team to go to the data box and draw a card; and a 12 allows the team to go to the station of their choice and draw one card. The data box is a shoe box with a hole in the lid and four copies of each station card in it. The glossary should include definitions of the following terms: *subduction zone, trench, ridge, island arc, seismic activity, index fossil, coral reef, salt dome, unconformity, plate, diapir, magma,* and *trilobite.* In addition, a geologic time scale should be provided for each team.

Continental station data cards

2. Utopia

Utopia has diapirs that cooled from high acidic magma.	There are proliferous brachiopods found in the fossil record of Utopia.	There is deep-seated seismic activity with andesitic volcanic rocks. (Volcanic activity is of explosive nature producing vesicles.)
While standing on the shore of Utopia, you will look out to the sea and see many island arcs rimmed with coral reefs.	While observing fossil data, you will find trilobites from the Upper Cambrian period.	There are numerous unconformities between the Upper Cambrian and Permian periods in Utopia.
While walking around Utopia, you will find granite of high quartz content with a very coarse grain.	Utopia contains areas of high heat flow.	One can find many rugose corals while in Utopia.

3. Oz

While scuba diving, you will see that the sea floor rocks get younger to the west.	You will find many fern fossils of the Pennsylvanian in Oz.	Beware of the seismic activity 1000 km offshore; it's shallow though.
The black shale of Oz contains ammonite.	One may observe red sandstone abundantly.	One can find many echinoids on Oz which display characteristics of both primitive and advanced forms.
Oz contains only a few brachiopods in its fossil record.		

4. Mordor

There are echinoids of primitive form located on Mordor.	Have your Oz tank ready to explore the ocean — the sea floor rocks get younger as you go to the east.	Take notice of the fossilized Volkswagen.
Don't trip over the many mastodon bones.	Watch out for the salt domes of Mordor.	The black shale of Mordor contains abundant ammonite fossils.
Mordor contains proliferous brachiopods in its fossil record.	Mordor has many unconformities between the Upper Permian and Lower Cretaceous.	

5. Gondwana

While hiking on Gondwana, notice the granite of high quartz content with the very coarse grain.	The white sandstone of Gondwana is very beautiful.	Beware of the mold of a 1962 Volkswagen in a river bed.
Add this to your fossil information — many trilobites from the Upper Cambrian period.	Magnetic data indicates the continent has drifted southeast of its original location (approximately 4000 km).	There are many unconformities formed between the Cambrian and Permian periods.
The diapirs of Gondwana cooled from highly acidic magma.	The coal beds contain excellent energy for the industries of the area.	

6. Laurasia

Within the black shale, one may find only a few ammonite fossils.	You may observe fossils of the Mississippian period on Laurasia.	One may find evidence of blocking limestone of the Permian era in Laurasia.
The echinoids of Laurasia display characteristics of both primitive and advanced forms.	The granite of the mountains in Laurasia is very fine grained.	Laurasia was once heavily glaciated because of the thick soil and mature sediments.
There is shallow seismic activity 1500 km offshore.	Magnetic data indicates that Laurasia has drifted 2500 km southwest of its original location.	

7. Etrusca

Etrusca contains blocking limestone of the Pennsylvanian period.	Notice the proliferous brachiopods in Etrusca.	While scuba diving, you may notice the sea floor gets younger as you move to the west.
The echinoids of Etrusca display the characteristics of both primitive and advanced forms.	Etrusca is an area of deep-seated earthquake activity.	Volcanic activity of the explosive nature created andesitic volcanic rocks (area of high heat flow).
Etrusca was once heavily glaciated — evidence of thick soil and mature sediments.	Etruscan black shale contains abundant ammonite fossils.	

Data box cards

(Make 4 of each.)

Station 1	Station 2	Station 3
One can find many rugose corals while in Utopia.	There are large deposits of red sandstone in this area.	Don't trip over the mastodon bones.
Station 4	**Station 5**	**Station 6**
The magnetic data indicates this continent has drifted southeast of its original location (approximately 4000 km).	The echinoids of Laurasia display characteristics of both primitive and advanced forms.	Etrusca is an area of deep-seated earthquake activity.

By participating in this game, your students have collected data, analyzed it, and attempted to solve a problem just as scientists do. Did they find out that the following continental stations go together?

2 and 6
5 and 7
3 and 4

more...

Construct continental drift jigsaw puzzles for your class. Select six frames from the "Get the Drift" activity and trace each one on a heavy piece of paper. Cut out the continents and glue the remaining ocean area to a piece of heavy cardboard. Your puzzle is now complete. Have your students put the six puzzles together, paying close attention to the placement of the continents and which ones are moving. Place the finished puzzles in the sequence in which continental drift occurred.

Related activities include bis 46, 58, 80; and ss 21.

□

spooling along

It is a basic tenet of survival that anything that moves merits attention. This tenet is also basic to student interest. Things that move usually are more captivating than inanimate objects. If something moves, one can concern oneself with how far, how fast, and under what conditions it moves. Perhaps this is a partial explanation for the continued interest in and success of the rubber-band mobile.

Rubber bands do not create energy; rather, they possess energy. If you stretch or twist a rubber band, you are putting additional energy into the system. As a result, its potential to do work is increased. Rubber-band mobiles are easy to make and prime material for much sciencing.

MAKING A RUBBER-BAND MOBILE

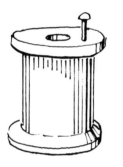

You will need rubber bands; one empty, wooden, thread spool; two wooden kitchen matches that have had their heads removed; a piece of hard soap (or a candle) from which a ¼-inch-thick wax (or soap) washer can be fashioned; and a small nail.

Drive in the nail close enough to the spool hole so that the nail, when driven in, goes into the main body of the spool. If only plastic spools are available, predrill a small hole and glue in a small nail. A sheet metal screw works equally well.

Notch one side of the ¼-inch-thick wax (or soap) washer to accommodate the long match.

Washer

Cutting a wax (or soap) washer is not difficult. Carving the hole through the center of the washer requires a little more patience. Working carefully with a pocket knife, you can do it. However, a cork borer works better and more efficiently.

As an alternative to carving out wax or soap washers, plastic beads of ⅜ inch diameter may be used. The sphericity of the beads greatly reduces the friction where the bead comes in contact with the spool. The broad surface of the carved wax or soap washer, while being lubricated by the composition of the wax or soap itself, causes much surface drag. The beads must be larger than the diameter of the spool hole. You should make enough bead washers for the entire class. The students usually can furnish spools, and beads or inexpensive necklaces can be purchased in craft stores or the five-and-ten. The increased efficiency of the rubber-band mobile is impressive. The beads must be prepared by enlarging the holes in them to accommodate passage of the rubber band. A vise, an electric drill, and a ⅛ inch drill bit will quickly accomplish the task. Don't despair; the students will love you for it.

Assemble the rubber-band mobile by threading the rubber band through the bead washer and the spool hole. Loop one end of the rubber band over the larger match stick and loop the other end over the shorter match stick which is located at the spool end with the nail.

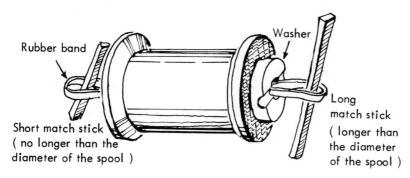

Wind the larger match stick ten to twenty turns, place the spool on a flat surface, and release. The spool should move forward. With a plastic bead washer in place of the wax washer, it will race forward.

Inasmuch as the rubber-band mobile is something that moves, you should be able to collect substantial data relative to the rate of speed, distance traveled, the relationship of turns to distance traveled, and so forth. These involvements afford many opportunities to record data, to plot data on graphs, to infer, to predict, and to experiment.

This activity provides numerous opportunities to be creative. Who can design and construct a rubber-band mobile that will travel the greatest distance? Travel the fastest? Climb the steepest hill? Traverse the roughest terrain? Or, pull the heaviest load? Remember, you are not limited to one spool, or to spools, or to the size of a spool. Try using other wooden wheels. Double or triple the number of rubber bands you use. Alter the surface of the wheels for greater traction. Reduce friction by improving on the wax or plastic bead washer. The variety of directions in which this activity can move is limitless.

more...

This activity can be extended to the design and construction of rubber-band cars. Some criteria for design limitation should

be set by either you or the class; for example, the car must be made of only common household materials, and it must be self-propelled by no more than two number 32 rubber bands (3 x ⅛ inch). A teacher-made car to serve as a pacesetter would serve the class nicely!

Emphasize the science involved in this interesting activity; for example, applications to simple machines, kinetic energy, potential energy, propulsion, ratios of various components (wheel diameter to axle diameter). With everything made ready, with science topics taught and learned, line up your cars and have a real, rubber-band mobile rally.

ladies and gentlemen, start your engines!

Related activities include bis 20, 30, 45, 80, 86, 96, 114, 118; and ss 19.

the great glider contest

Paper objects that students construct and randomly sail through the air (much to the dismay of teachers) are improperly called *paper airplanes.* They should be called *paper darts,* for more often than not, when thrown, these paper constructions fly only in a straight line. By contrast, a paper glider is not thrown; rather it is lofted. You push it slightly and the forward weight carries it through the air majestically.

Gliders may be constructed in a myriad of shapes, varying dimensions, and materials. The designs are endless and creativity can run rampant. Three basic designs are furnished. These serve only to initiate creativity. You and your students will undoubtedly improve on these designs and come up with many new ones.

Which glider design

stays aloft the longest?
travels the greatest distance?
reaches the greatest height?
is most acrobatic?
is most aesthetic?

more...

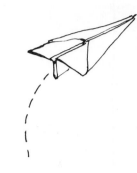

Construct a graph plotting the weight of the glider versus the distance traveled (or weight versus time aloft).
Determine the exposed surface area of the glider.

Related activities include bis 20, 30, 45, 80, 86, 114, 117; and ss 19.

☐

Glider 1 *

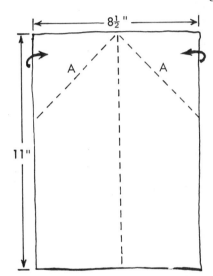

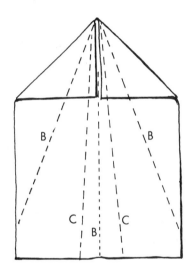

Crease first on dotted line A, then line B, and then line C

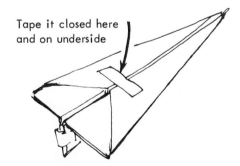

Tape it closed here and on underside

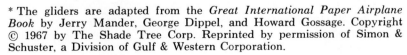

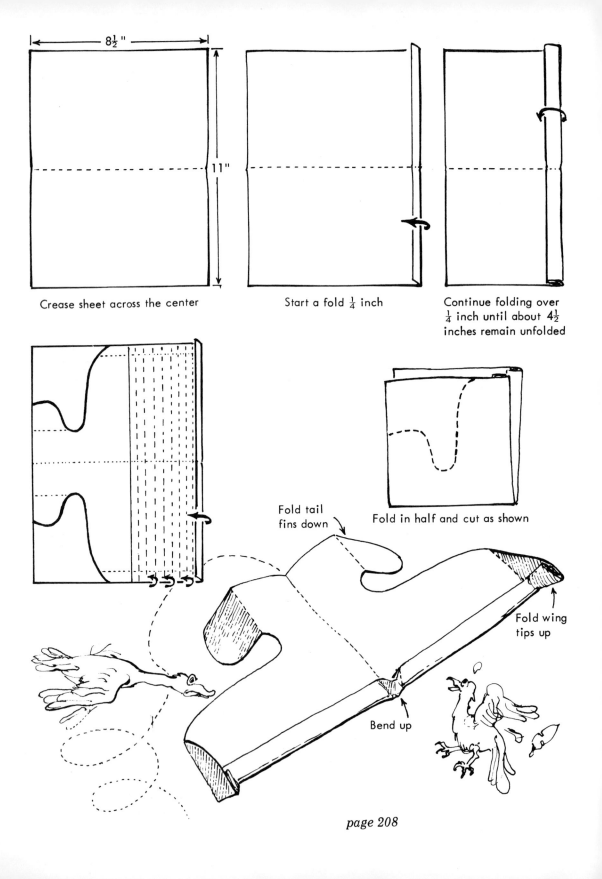

8½"

11"

Crease sheet across the center

Start a fold ¼ inch

Continue folding over ¼ inch until about 4½ inches remain unfolded

Fold in half and cut as shown

Fold tail fins down

Fold wing tips up

Bend up

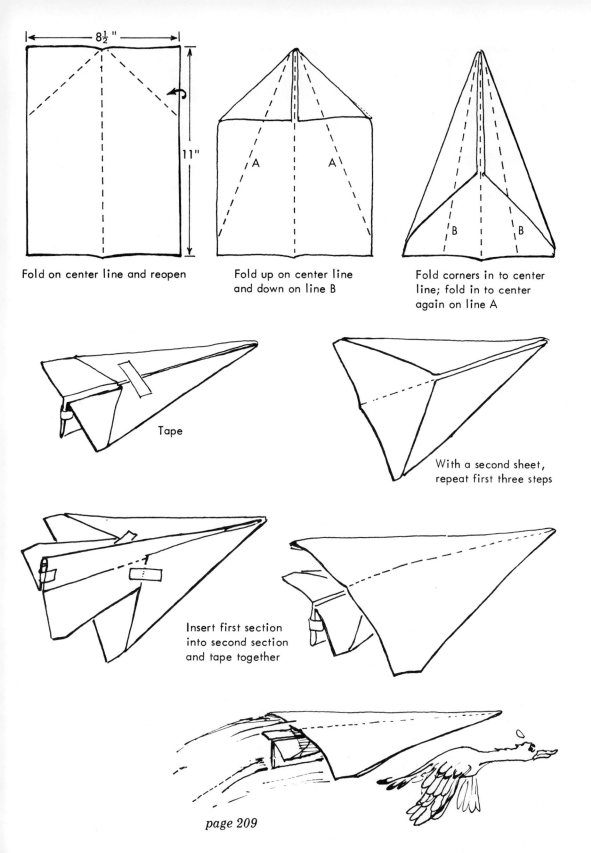

8½"

11"

Fold on center line and reopen

Fold up on center line and down on line B

A   A

Fold corners in to center line; fold in to center again on line A

B   B

Tape

With a second sheet, repeat first three steps

Insert first section into second section and tape together

free as a frier fly

Three diagrams of the frier fly have been furnished for your use. Frier Fly A and Frier Fly B are parent flies. These can be designated by you (or the students) as to gender. Have the students observe and describe one of the frier flies. Now have them observe and compare the two frier flies. How are they alike? How are they different?

Offspring usually come to resemble their parents in certain major respects, but differ from their parents in many minor respects. Offspring do not inherit features such as curly hair or blue eyes, but they do inherit genes which give rise to curly hair or blue eyes. Each parent passes on one set of genes to the offspring. Each feature is influenced by at least one gene from each parent. Genes that control the production of a feature are called *dominant* (denoted by *D*). Those genes whose features can be hidden by another are called *recessive* (denoted by *d*).

Frier Fly Z is a nondescript frier fly. Seven differences can be observed in the seven areas noted.

Reproduce the diagrams of Frier Fly A and Frier Fly B. Give students a copy of each. The students should print a large *D* (dominant) on each of the seven sections of Frier Fly A. Have the students label all seven sections of Frier Fly B's features as recessive (*d*). Now have the students cut up the copies of the two frier fly diagrams. These fourteen pieces should be intermixed, and each student should assemble a new frier fly using any mixture of dominant (*D*) features and recessive (*d*) features. The new frier fly pieces should be pasted on another sheet and labeled Frier Fly O. Have the students pair off, each contributing his or her Frier Fly O as a parent. Assembling the data, they should be able to infer what the frier fly offspring generated from the parent O frier flies will look like. The students should record this information on a chart.

Feature	Contribution from Parent 1		from Parent 2		The Offspring's Features	
1. body	fluted	( )	not fluted	( )	_____	( )
2. wings	striped	( )	not striped	( )	_____	( )
3. tail	sharp	( )	blunted	( )	_____	( )
4. legs	cylindrical	( )	curly	( )	_____	( )
5. neck	threaded	( )	bayonet	( )	_____	( )
6. antenna	split	( )	whole	( )	_____	( )
7. nose	2-pronged	( )	3-pronged	( )	_____	( )

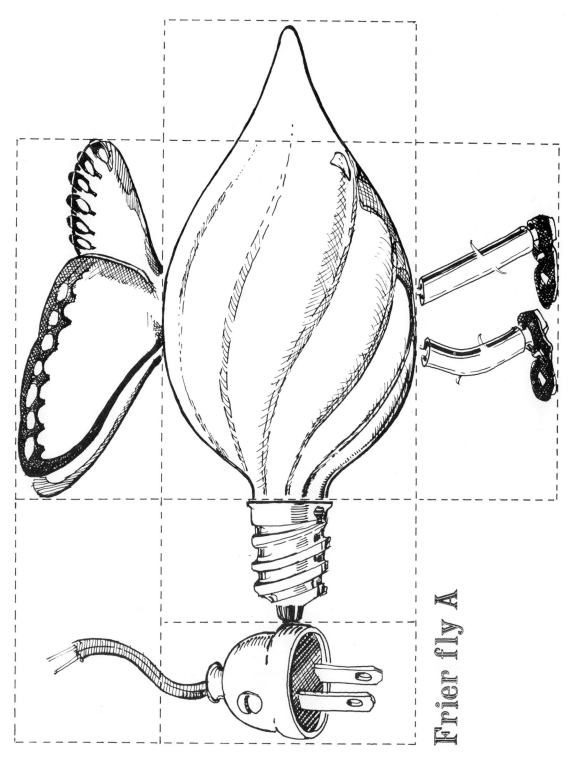

Frier fly A

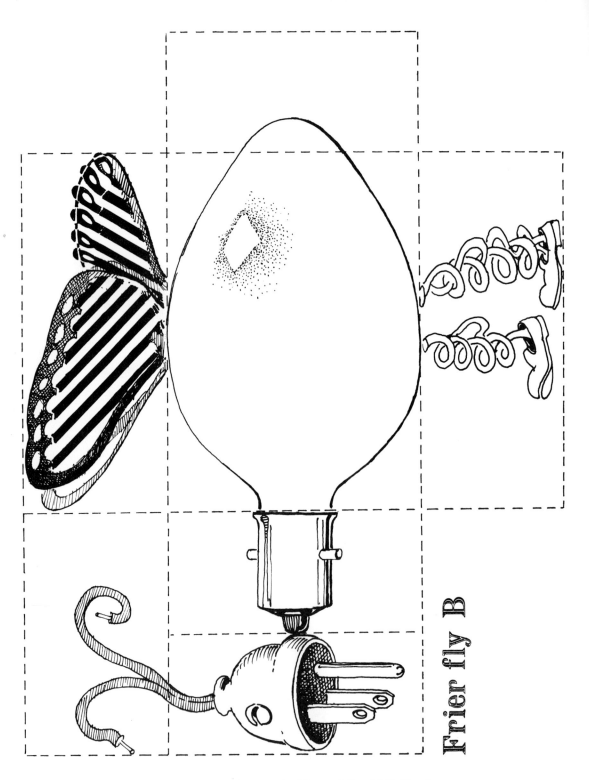

Frier fly B

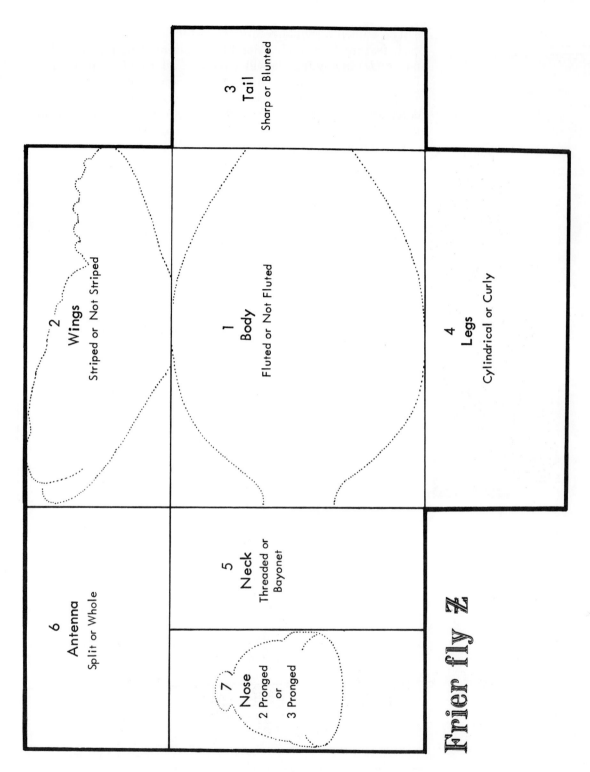

2
Wings
Striped or Not Striped

1
Body
Fluted or Not Fluted

3
Tail
Sharp or Blunted

4
Legs
Cylindrical or Curly

6
Antenna
Split or Whole

5
Neck
Threaded or
Bayonet

7
Nose
2 Pronged
or
3 Pronged

Frier fly Z

The students should record the letter designation (*D* or *d*) for each feature from each Frier Fly O parent. One recorded dominance (*D*) in any feature will make that inferred feature dominant (*D*) for the offspring. Two recorded recessives in any feature (*d*) will make that feature recessive (*d*) for the offspring. Write a description of the offspring, detailing the features. Try to infer the next generation from other frier fly parent matches.

Related activities include bis 1 and 98.

the student indicator

This is a short exercise with high level of interest. The science content has to do with temperature, surface area, and expansion.

Cut a four-inch replica of a child from a piece of celluloid or plastic sheet. Make the feet and head large and generous. Place the piece of plastic flat on the palm of one student's hand. Use the following evaluation scale.

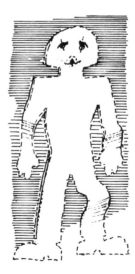

Celluloid cutout

If the plastic child:

moves its head, ...	you are alive.
moves its feet, ...	you are a good dancer.
moves its head and feet, ...	you are the cheerleader type.
curls on its sides, ...	you are wrapped up in yourself.
turns over, ...	you are an A student.
is motionless, ...	you need vitamins.
curls up entirely, ...	you are the teacher's pet.

The explanation for movement is the transfer of heat from the palm of your hand to the plastic. Differences in movement are caused by the uneven heat absorption of the plastic.

Rub your hands together. Now, place the plastic in the palm of your hand. What do you observe?

Related activities include bis 1, 13–17, 32, 91; and ss 12.

□

calculator manipulations

You will need calculators for these activities — just about any kind will do.

Start in the box in the upper left hand corner with the numbers at the bottom of the box, 5×7. Then find the box that has the answer to 5×7 at the top of the box. Continue by doing the operation at the bottom of that box (the answer to 5×7 is 35, and the operation at the bottom of the box with the answer is $8 + 2$). Now find the box that has the answer to $8 + 2$ at the top, and so on, until you arrive back at the box with 56 at the top.

Finish

56 5×7	22 $6 + 17$	39 7×7	2 6×3	76 $96 \div 4$	18 5×3
15 $10 + 12$	35 $8 + 2$	1 $12 - 3$	52 21×5	21 $10 \div 5$	88 $27 \div 9$
117 19×3	12 9×10	55 10×10	10 3×7	43 $29 - 10$	9 $102 \div 2$
100 $5 + 7$	68 8×7	23 13×3	90 17×4	57 11×5	79 $94 - 42$
24 8×11	3 $59 - 16$	19 $47 \div 47$	51 $132 - 53$	105 $129 - 12$	49 19×4

Start is to the left of the first row.

Which of the following operations will result in a larger number than shown in the readout on your calculator? Which one do you predict it will be?

$1 \times 2 =$
$1 \times 2 \times 3 =$
$1 \times 2 \times 3 \times 4 =$
$1 \times 2 \times 3 \times 4 \times 5 =$
$1 \times 2 \times 3 \times 4 \times 5 \times 6 =$
$1 \times 2 \times 3 \times 4 \times 5 \times 6 \times 7 =$
$1 \times 2 \times 3 \times 4 \times 5 \times 6 \times 7 \times 8 =$ (and so on)

The idea of the next activity is to get from *Start* to *Finish* following the instructions in each box and using the numbers beside the boxes to arrive at *Finish* with 0 in your calculator readout. Try the activity. Then make up your own.

Start $0 - 6$ $\boxed{+}$ -18 $\boxed{+}$ 10 $\boxed{\times}$ -48 $\boxed{\times}$ -16 $\boxed{\div}$ 8 $\boxed{+}$ -6 $\boxed{\div}$
-50 $\boxed{\times}$ 9 $\boxed{-}$ 5 $\boxed{\div}$ -2 $\boxed{-}$ -1 $\boxed{+}$ 2 $\boxed{\div}$ 2 $\boxed{+}$ -2 $\boxed{\div}$ 10 $\boxed{\times}$
-13 $\boxed{-}$ 79 $\boxed{\times}$ -1 $\boxed{-}$ $1 = 0$ Finish

To do a fourth activity, you will need two calculators and two players; each player must use either all even or all odd numbers (one person can choose all even, the other all odd). Each player enters one of his or her numbers into his or her calculator. The person who chose odd numbers selects an operation ($+, -, \times, \div$) and both players enter it and then enter another one of their numbers (each person may use his or her numbers only once). Then both players press the equal button. Now the person who chose even numbers selects an operation (multiplication may be used only twice during the five rounds of the game). Both players enter it, then enter another one of their numbers, and press the equal button. "Odd" says another operation, and "even" says another operation and the round is over. The person with the highest or lowest — you set the rules — number wins the round. The person winning five rounds wins the game.

To do a fifth activity, you need a calculator and a tape measure. Measure your classroom (metrically, of course), by measuring from the middle of one wall to the middle of the opposite wall, and then measuring from the middle of the adjacent wall to the middle of the wall opposite.

Measure from A to B and from C to D.

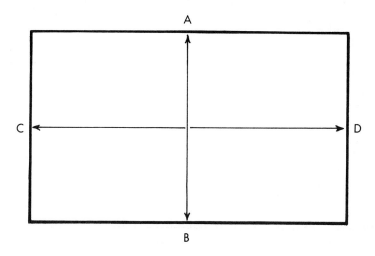

Stand on one side of the room and, using your calculator, divide by 2 the distance between you and the wall opposite you. Now measure off that distance from the wall where you are standing, and move to that point. Subtract the distance you moved from the original measurement and from this new point, measure that distance, divide it in half again (divide by 2), and move to that point. Now subtract that amount from the remaining distance to the opposite wall, divide by 2, and move to that point. Continue the process, until you get across the room, if you can.

You will discover what the philosopher Zeno discovered over 2000 years ago. You cannot get across the room completely because, from whatever point you find yourself, you will always be moving only half the distance to the opposite wall. You will get very close, but not all the way.

more...

Try the last activity, dividing by 3 or 4 each time instead of 2.

Since you measured the room in both directions, move across it in the other direction this time dividing the distance by one-third.

Two much! How many times can 453871 be divided by 2? 10? 20? 30? Try it. Next, try 75684.

Find a way to get to the number 560 in 10 steps. Use at least two numbers at a time and use all the operations at least once. This will get you started:

1. $8 \times 1 = 8$
2. $8 + 2 = 10$
3. $10 \div 10 = 1$
4. $1 \times 40 = 40$
5. $40 - 1 = 39$
6. You continue.
7. You continue.
8. You continue.
9. You continue.
10. You continue.

Next, try 3000 in 12 steps or 142 in 7 steps. Try your own number and steps.

Write an equation and have another person solve it for x using a calculator.

Try: $(20 + x + 5) \times 2 = 100$
$$x = ?$$
Was the calculator readout 25?

Try: $(6 \times x) + (5 + x) - (3 - x) + (20 \div x) = 28$
$$x = ?$$

See, you can get as complicated as you wish with this bis.

Was the calculator readout 2?

Related activities include bis 29, 77, 82; and sst 11.

□

catsup-bottle oceanography

This activity concerns several properties of water, principally density and temperature. Relative to oceanography and these properties, one could ask the following questions: Which is lighter, fresh water or salt water? Which is lighter, warm water or cold water? The answers to both these questions are fundamental to a study of the motion of ocean waters.

To respond to these questions, you will need two catsup bottles, food coloring, salt, hot and cold water, and a piece of cardboard (a 3 x 5 inch card should do nicely).

Fill a catsup bottle with cold water. Fill another bottle with warm, colored water. Cover the top of one bottle (either bottle) with the cardboard square. Invert the bottle, holding the square of cardboard across the mouth of the bottle. Be prepared for spillage by working over a sink or a catch basin. Position the mouths of the bottles so they are matched and balanced one on top of the other. Holding both bottles steady (some help now would not be interpreted as a sign of ineptness), slip out the cardboard square. What do you observe? If little is observed, invert the bottles. Now what do you observe? What can you conclude about warm and cold water and ocean movements? Which is lighter — warm or cold water?

Repeat this same procedure, using one bottle of salt water and one bottle of colored fresh water (temperatures should be relatively the same). If nothing is observed, invert the bottles. What can you conclude about salt and fresh water and ocean movements?

more...

If warm water rises over cold water, and fresh water floats over salt water, how will warm salt water and cold fresh water interact? Try it!

Related activities include bis 17, 84, 99, 113; and ss 26.

☐

bis 123

guesstimations

How many:

raisins are in a box of raisin bran?
chocolate chips are in a bag of chocolate chips?
slices of bread are in a loaf of bread?
segments are in a grapefruit?
blades of grass are in your lawn?
leaves are on one tree in your yard?
cars are in the schoolyard parking lot?
bicycles are in the schoolyard rack?
stars are in the sky?
floor tiles are on the classroom floor?

You can see how this line of questioning could go on and on. And it should. Not enough to wear out your welcome, but enough to keep the skill of estimating "how many" improving.

It is difficult to "guesstimate" with some degree of accuracy until one develops some strategy for estimating. One way is to subdivide whatever is being guesstimated into manageable components; for example, to respond to how many cornflakes are in a cereal box, mentally subdivide the box into quarters, eighths, or any other convenient fraction. Calculate the capacity of the subdivision and multiply this figure by the denominator of the fraction you used. Most strategies bring you closer to the exact number than sheer guessing. Challenge children to develop strategies in responding to your queries necessitating estimations.

more...

How many:

hairs are in a person's head?
scales are on a fish?
feathers are on a duck?

Find a million somethings.
Find a billion somethings.
Find a trillion somethings.

note: they cannot all be stars

Roll a piece of plasticine flat. Sprinkle in numerous colored sparkle flecks. Work the clay until the flecks are distributed throughout. Roll it flat again. Or make any shape you wish. Tear the clay shape in half. How many flecks are visible? Estimate how many are contained within the entire solid.

Related activities include bis 40, 43, 79, 82, and 87.

☐

cutting up

Old magazines have a variety of uses. Here is one use that fits science, health, art, mathematics, social studies, and reading: Provide children with a varied selection of old magazines (of course, those that meet community standards). The greater the mix of magazine topics, the better the results of this activity.

Have students rummage through these old magazines and cut out appropriate pictures that can be reassembled to depict:

    foods for a balanced meal
    a variety of topics, such as a vacation, the possibility of a move
       to another area
    articles for survival (you set the conditions; for example, on the
       moon, in Las Vegas, or up the Amazon River)
    articles revealing a variety of feelings and moods
    articles for a specific hobby (for example, rock collecting)
    articles involving a sport, an art, or mathematics (metric)
    a social event (for example, a mass rally, a rock concert)

A CREATIVE CUT UP

Have the students cut out pictures of any five items they like; for example, an automobile tire, a can of soup, a boy and his dog, a tree, and a guitar. Each student then places the five pictures in a shoe box. All these pictures should be thoroughly shuffled by you. Each student, without being able to see, picks out any five pictures at random. Assign each student five (or ten) minutes to conjure up a creative oral story utilizing all five items in the pictures. Or the student can write a story using the five pictures as a basis.

□

star clock and calendar

Ancient people had the same time allotted to them in a day that we have. Our time, however, is occupied with inventions of modern technology such as cars, television, movies, and so forth. Ancient people, not having these distractions, turned to and observed that ever-present stellar performance occurring nightly in the sky.

Ancient people thought that the earth was the center of all things and that everything revolved about the earth. It has been firmly established that this is not so. The earth instead revolves about the sun. One full revolution takes 365¼ days. Concurrent with this solar revolution, the earth rotates about its axis once every twenty-four hours. The stars appear to rotate one full turn in twenty-four hours and to make one full revolution in one year. Because the earth rotates about its axis in a counterclockwise direction, the stars appear to move in a clockwise direction in the heavens. It is this daily rotation and annual revolution that provides a changing but cyclic stellar performance which is the reason the stars can serve as a clock and a calendar.

Place an umbrella directly over your head. Think of the North Star as being positioned exactly at the top of the umbrella shaft where it exits the umbrella.

Divide the underside of the umbrella into four quadrants, and chalk in the Big Dipper, the Little Dipper, and Cassiopeia.

Place the umbrella over your head. Hold the umbrella motionless and rotate (walk) under the umbrella in a counterclockwise direction, imitating the motion of the earth. In what direction do the stars appear to move?

Standing under your umbrella, rotate it and orient the constellation Cassiopeia in a northerly direction. Cassiopeia is a

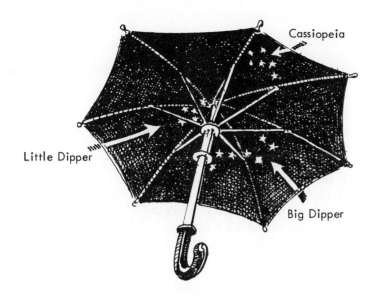

Little Dipper

Cassiopeia

Big Dipper

constellation that is easy to locate. Five bright stars in this constellation appear to form the letter *W*. An imaginary line joins Cassiopeia and the Big Dipper. These two constellations appear to turn in a circle around the northern sky. They make a kind of seesaw with the North Star as the middle support. Simulate the movement of the earth (which takes 24 hours to complete one full rotation) under the umbrella. In 6 hours, you would have moved through an area equal to one-fourth of the umbrella area (or 90° or one quadrant). As you rotate you are seemingly leaving Cassiopeia behind. In one one-quarter rotation, you traverse 90° in azimuth and leave Cassiopeia 90° behind. How many degrees do you traverse in 1 hour?

For each 15° of traverse that you advance, Cassiopeia is left behind that same amount. One full rotation brings you back full circle to the original starting point. If you were to fall asleep under the stars while camping and you noted Cassiopeia's position at 10:00 P.M., and if you woke up in the middle of the night and Cassiopeia appeared to have moved 45° in azimuth, three hours would have passed. It would now be 1:00 A.M. Suppose it had appeared to have moved 90°; what time would it be? The stars do tell time.

The earth makes one yearly revolution about the sun. The earth, moving in its orbit about the sun, causes the various constellations to seem to move across the sky. Note the position of the Big Dipper. Record the time, date, and relative position of this constellation. Repeat this procedure at the same time and day, only one month later, for several months. What do you observe about the position of the constellations? What can you infer about the path of the Big Dipper? Predict the location of this constellation six months from your initial observation. Nine months. One year.

more...

Underexposed and discarded 35 mm slides can be perforated with pinpoints to depict various constellations. These slides can be projected on a screen or used in a viewer to familiarize children with the various constellations.

Using a flashlight, a nail or punch, a tin can, and a hammer, you can construct a very useful device for viewing constellations. Select a constellation. Using a punch, make a replica of one constellation in the lid of the tin can. Be careful to distinguish brightness of stars by enlarging specific holes. Darken the room. Insert the lighted flashlight into the tin can so that the light will shine through the punctured holes. Observe star images produced on the ceiling by the light rays shining through the holes. The stronger the flashlight the better the results.

Earlier, we instructed you to hold the star-chalked umbrella directly over your head. Inclining the umbrella shaft approximately 23° would more accurately portray the sky as viewed from earth. Chalk in some additional stars near the outer edges of the umbrella. Tilting the umbrella to coincide with the inclination of the earth's axis, and keeping your line of sight focused in a level line approximating a horizon line as viewed on earth, rotate the umbrella. If you confine your sight to looking straight ahead parallel to an imaginary horizon and rotate the umbrella, some stars will appear to disappear, or as we say "set" and later "rise." Do all stars rise and set?

more, more...

CATCHING STELLAR DEBRIS

If your house gutters are not directly connected to storm sewers, there is a good chance that water from them spills out onto the lawn or a driveway. A roof makes an excellent catch-surface for the collection of micrometeorites of nickel-iron composition whose origins were most likely in the asteroid belt. These micrometeorites, having landed on the roof's surface, are washed down by rainwater. Sweeping roof gutters or the outpouring areas of various drains with a magnet allows for the collection of these magnetic visitors from outer space. They usually will be spherical and, if fresh when collected, shiny.

page 224

A microscope slide, thinly coated with petroleum jelly and exposed to the sky in a location where it will be undisturbed for a period of twenty-four hours, will also catch micrometeorites. Examine these under a compound microscope. Determine the mass of the collected micrometeorites. Knowing the area of the slide, calculate the mass per square cm. The total surface of the earth is calculated at 5.10×10^{18} cm^2. Estimate the mass of micrometeorites striking the earth in each twenty-four-hour period.

Related activities include bis 19, 67, 74; and ss 27.

hand shadows

Using your hands and a light source to cast shadows, make the hand shadows shown on the next pages.

Have other students observe the hand shadows and try to guess what they are. Invent your own shadow figures.

more...

Have each child trace a silhouette of a plant in the room on a large sheet of paper. Collect the silhouettes and have the children match them to their respective plants.

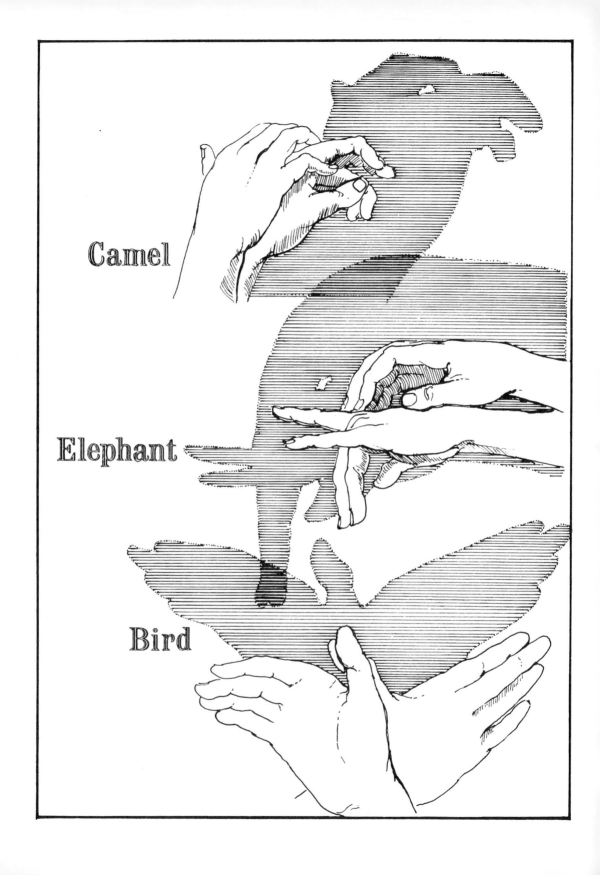

Camel

Elephant

Bird

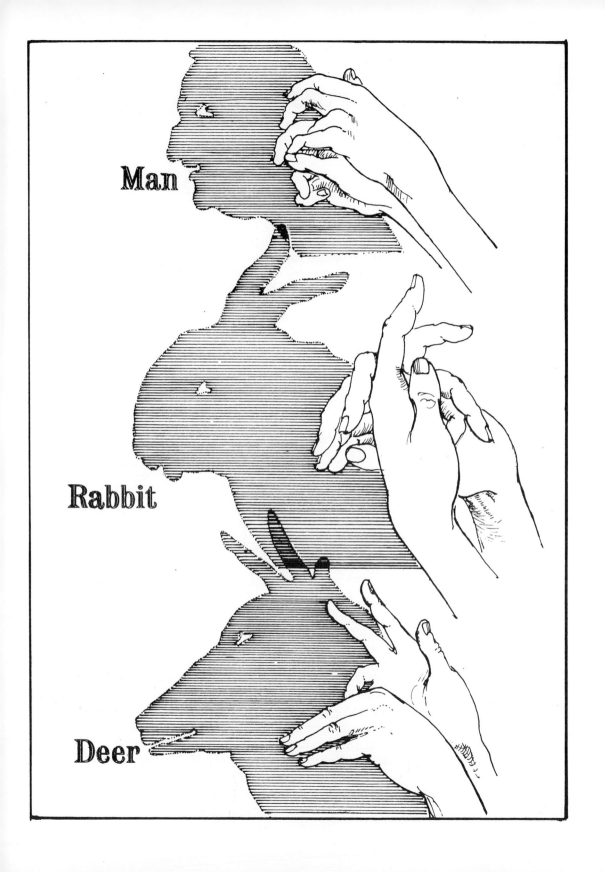

Man

Rabbit

Deer

Try other objects.

1. Make a drawing of your favorite plant or animal on a sheet of lightweight cardboard. Color it in.
2. Turn the drawing over and draw an abstract design (a simple one) on the back side.
3. Cut along the abstract design lines to make a plant or animal jigsaw puzzle. Dot the back side of each piece to distinguish it from the front.

Using different, uncut pieces of geometric solids (a cube, a rectangular solid, a sphere), a screen, and a flashlight, cast shadows onto the screen. From the reverse side, have the students view and infer from the shadows the different geometric shapes that generated the shadow. Combine by stacking one or more geometric shapes. Repeat the inferred observation.

Related activities include bis 23, 27, 36, 39, 42, and 85.

a feeling forecast

Select a weather symbol and write a paragraph expressing how the weather condition the symbol represents might affect you. Draw a picture of yourself as you will look on that day. For example, try:

A rainy day makes me . . .
I wake up and find snow and feel . . .
Sunny days make me feel . . .
A tornado watch makes me feel . . .
When I observe lightning, I . . .
When there are fluffy white clouds in the sky, I . . .
Dark, stormy clouds make me . . .

 High   Low

 Clear   Overcast

more...

Write sentences to tell how you might feel and what you might do in different types of weather. Try:

It is the first snowstorm of the winter.
It is a beautiful April spring day (22°C). There is a pleasant breeze.
It is a hot, humid summer day with no breeze. It seems unusually quiet. The sky has become very dark with an odd, greenish cast.
It is a warm day. It has been dry, dry, dry for so long. Finally, a gentle, steady rain begins to fall.

 Calm   Cloudy

List several times when your plans were changed due to the weather. Write how you felt when your plans had to be altered.
Describe the type of weather you really enjoy. Draw a picture (showing an activity you like to do in this type of weather).

Related activities include bis 5, 6, 28, and 64.

how much dust is in the air?

For this activity, you will need 3 one-gallon, wide-mouth, glass jars; two gallons of distilled water; 3 three-quart pans; and a balance.

Pour a quart of distilled water into each jar and mark the water level. Label the jars and pans 1, 2, and 3. Cover the top of each jar with a piece of wire-mesh window screening folded down over the mouth and fastened with light wire. Set the jars outside, about five feet above the ground, in an area you wish to test. Since you will need to expose the jars for 30 days, make sure they are in a place that will not be disturbed by people or animals.

Check each jar from time to time, record your observations, and add distilled water to keep the water at the level marked.

After 30 days have elapsed, pour the water from jar 1 into pan 1, place the pan on a heat source (such as a hot plate), and carefully evaporate the water. Repeat for jar and pan 2 and 3. Add more water from each jar to its pan until all of the water has been evaporated. You may need to rinse out each jar with additional distilled water until all the material collected in the jar has been transferred to its pan.

Prepare a data table and record the mass of the pan with the water and dust; the mass of the pan and the dust; and the mass of the pan. Subtract to obtain the mass of the dust in milligrams. This is the amount of milligrams collected in 30 days (one month) per the surface area of your jars.

more...

An air pollution commission measures dust fall in tons per square mile per month. To change your results to these units, measure the inside diameter of the mouth of the jar and find the area of the jar mouth in square centimeters.

Area = pi (π) times radius squared (r^2)
(Radius = ½ diameter)

Use the following formula to convert to tons of dust per square mile per month.

Tons of dust/square mile/month =
Mass of dust (mg) ÷ area of jar mouth (cm^2)
$\times$ 28.6 (conversion factor)

Use a vacuum cleaner with a piece of tissue or filter paper over the vacuum hose opening and find out how much dust is in your classroom. Examine the tissue or filter paper through a hand lens or microscope. Try to identify some of the particles. Using your vacuum cleaner, test other locations and compare these areas to your classroom.

Take squares of nylon stocking and mount them on cardboard frames from which the center has been cut out. Hang them up outside the house or school in areas where you want to test for air pollution's effect on clothing, especially the effect of sulfur oxides in combination with water to form sulfuric acid. Damage to the squares of nylon would appear as broken fibers, best visible under a lens of some sort.

Into a small piece of wood, hammer two nails and stretch a rubber band between them. The rubber band will crack and break in the presence of ozone. The time it takes is relative to the concentration of ozone. Place samplers indoors and out. Electric motors generate ozone, so put the rubber band near an operating appliance.

Related activities include bis 89 and ss 21.

□

osmosis: crossing
the impermeable barrier

To observe the effects of osmosis (the passage of a liquid through a membrane), try this activity. Before you begin, collect:

>   4 raw eggs in their shells
>   4 jars with caps that have a
>   7–8 cm opening
>   4 pints white vinegar
>   4 pints white corn syrup

Set up four jars as follows: jar 1, all vinegar; jar 2, 2 parts vinegar and 1 part water; jar 3, 2 parts vinegar and 2 parts water; jar 4, all water. Carefully place one raw egg (still in the shell) in each jar, making sure that each egg is completely covered by the liquid. Cap the jar and observe the egg after 1 hour, 3 hours, 1 day, 2 days. Record your observations.

Did you observe bubbling in the jar with vinegar (jar 1) and that the egg floats in the vinegar solutions (jars 2 and 3)? Did you also observe that in each of the vinegar-water combinations, the hard eggshell dissolved and the egg grew larger? You might infer that the water went through the shell into the egg.

After two days, pour off the vinegar in jar 1, put clear corn syrup in the jar, and observe the egg for a period of one day. Record observations after 1 hour, 3 hours, 1 day. Did you observe that the shell of the egg in the syrup became indented? This was due to the fact that the water left the inside of the egg and went through the shell into the syrup to even the concentration. The syrup went through the shell into the egg, but did not occupy the same amount of volume as the water.

more...

Relate the shell of the egg to a cell wall. The cell wall allows certain materials to pass through the wall to the cell's interior. Other materials are retained and do not pass through.

Compare the effect of the concentration of the water to the all-vinegar and all-syrup container shell. Try using different concentrations. Or try using a salt solution. Why doesn't the syrup go through the shell of the egg? Try making a diagram to explain your answer.

Put salt water in one container and plain water in another. Place dried fruit (apricots, prunes, or apples) in each container. Observe each container after 1 hour, 3 hours, 12 hours, 1 day. Infer why the fruit in the salt water does not change.

Related activities include bis 59 and 107.

shoestring sciencing □ss

sciencing

more for less

How many times have you made a major expenditure for science equipment that annihilated your science allotment? How many times have you received the equipment with wild anticipation, only to find that you could have duplicated the materials or gotten comparable ones for a tenth or a twentieth of the original cost? Convenience costs money. Catalog purchasing is tidy, convenient, and costly. Sometimes it is a disaster. Occasionally, however, it is an absolute necessity. By and large, you can realize tremendous savings by purchasing your own science materials and supplies or by purchasing the components to construct equipment of your own design. This flexibility in purchasing or acquiring materials by any means possible allows you to acquire exactly what you need in the quantities you need for your class. One innovative teacher in a large suburban school saved her district more than $200,000 in one year by making equipment for district-wide use and having children help her assemble the materials.

Catalog shopping can be replaced by repeated tours of supermarkets, lumberyards, junkyards, garage sales, discount stores, drugstores, auctions, stationery stores, cellars, attics, school supply cabinets, and home closets. This takes time and energy, but the results are well worth the effort.

Many school supply closets contain a lot of science equipment that has yet to be discovered by teachers. You may find microscopes, beakers, test tubes, and tuning forks, all yours for the investigating.

Section Two of *Creative Sciencing*, called "Shoestring Sciencing" (ss), is designed to provide you with many ideas for sciencing that involve a minimum of equipment and cost for a maximum of science. Successful shoestring sciencers collect and save almost everything, from string to tinfoil. You never know when you may need sixty baby food jars, ten shoe boxes, or forty-five aluminum pie plates immediately. The key is to anticipate and be ready. To succeed in creative sciencing inexpensively, adopt the substitution habit. Substitute a baby food jar or a peanut butter jar for scientific glassware. And:

WHEN YOU NEED	SUBSTITUTE
Aquaria	Gallon jars
Crayfish homes	Plastic swimming pools
Flashlight casings	Toilet paper rolls
Vials	Used pill bottles

page 234

Eyedroppers	Soda straws
Weights	Fishing sinkers
Spheres	Marbles
Containers	Coffee, film, tobacco, tuna, soup cans
Wheels	Skates, bicycles, toy cars
Mirrors	Aluminum foil on cardboard
Graduated cylinders	Baby bottles or medicine cups
Shelves	Cardboard boxes
Density objects	Clay, copper tubing or pipe, iron or aluminum nails
Mobile supports	Coathangers
Dowels	Broomsticks
Trays	TV dinner trays, pie trays, margarine tubs, school lunch trays
Jars	Pop bottles, wine bottles, mayonnaise jars, pickle jars, catsup bottles
Measuring sticks	Scrap lumber, licorice, string, or straws
Wire or string	Fishing line
Screening	Nylons
Stirring rods	Tongue depressors
Scoops or shovels	Plastic bleach bottles
Culture dishes	Plastic margarine tubs
Timers	Old alarm clocks

are you getting the idea?

Ask the students to bring in needed articles. Advertise in the school newspaper (you may have to start your own). Parents can provide many things you need, from corks to old typewriters. One teacher inherited an old but usable sewing machine. At the end of the year you can have one huge garage sale. Activities in this section will get you started in creative sciencing, on a shoestring if necessary. We hope that you can extend the intent and purpose of shoestring sciencing to shoestring art, mathematics, social studies, and anywhere else it will do some good.

science, 76¢ worth

Hardware stores, grocery stores, department stores, and toy counters should all be considered sources of both the hardware and the software of science. A large bag of wooden odds and ends (cast-offs from commercial woodworking houses) was our first purchase. In the bag were ninety wooden items, ranging from cylinders, spheres, cone frustums, and rectangular solids, to spindles, spools, buttons, discs, chessmen, tool handles, and barrel- or mallet-shaped objects. It cost 76 cents. What can you do with 76 cents' worth of odds and ends?

Six months and a hundred children later, we had uncovered many uses for these seemingly extraneous wooden odds and ends. A few of these uses are presented as they apply to science in its many applications.

Observing (through the senses)

Sight

raw wood	shapes and sizes
colored pieces	curved lines
shellacked pieces	straight lines

Touch

texture	grooved
hardness	waxy
polished	

Hearing

rolling sounds	bouncing sounds
sliding sounds	contact (striking one against
tumbling sounds	another) sounds

Smell

odors of different woods

Classifying (similarities and differences)

sizes
colors
shapes

Adapted from Alfred De Vito, "Science, 76¢ Worth," *Science and Children*, vol. 6, no. 8 (May 1969), p. 16. By permission.

Using numbers and measurements

How many items in the set?
How many items in subsets of the set?
Rank height, length, and width of pieces in some order within the subsets.
How much do the pieces weigh?
Find the surface area and volume of the pieces.
How far down an inclined plane will the pieces roll, slide, or tumble?

Bonus uses

building blocks
various constructions
shadow game (identification by shadows)
pulleys

wheels
pieces for the creativity bin
displacement in water activities

Related activities include ss 2 and sst 1.

□

recycling helps
science education

Examining what we throw out as we clear the household of daily trash can furnish a steady supply of science equipment — all free and expendable.

To help you assemble some of the hardware that teaching science requires, we suggest that you start collecting materials now. Save everything that looks remotely usable, even though its use may not be immediately apparent. As you progress through your science program you will run into times when you need something perfectly ordinary that you can't come up with in a hurry. How would you get hold of thirty catsup bottles, fifteen pie plates, or a dozen egg cartons on demand? The only way to do it is to collect things in advance.

Adapted from Alfred De Vito, "Found Science Equipment," *Science Activities,* vol. 8, no. 5 (January 1973), p. 15. By permission.

Who knows how many materials could be recycled from trash into your science program? This list is a beginning.

Glassware

pop bottles

catsup bottles

wine bottles plus corks

mayonnaise jars

pickle jars

Containers

cups (plastic and paper)

egg cartons

gallon jugs (glass and plastic)

coffee cans

margarine tubs

small plastic (tomato or berry) containers

aluminum TV dinner trays

pie trays

plastic containers

Wooden objects

spools

broomsticks

dowels

curtain rods

clothespins

scraps of wood

Miscellaneous

old golf and tennis balls

marbles

balloons

bottle tops or caps

boxes (plastic, cigar, cardboard)

aluminum foil

cellophane wrap

insulation materials

parts from old toys and kits

linoleum squares

ceramic tiles

copper pipe and tubing

nuts and bolts

screws and nails

washers

leather belts, pocket books, wallets

coat hangers

old 35 mm slides

film cans

tobacco cans

coffee cans

cardboard (shirt inserts)

string

fishing weights

leftover paints

charcoal

milk cartons

paraffin

clay

soda straws

blotters

BB shot

crayons

old pots, pans, trays

flowerpots

sand, dirt, gravel, and sawdust

mirrors

eyeglass lenses

springs

wire (various materials)

glass

eyedroppers

baby bottles

wheels (skate, bicycle)

old manila folders

scissors

old clocks

stirring rods

old silk stockings

pill bottles

straight pins, tacks, thumbtacks	paper tubes (toilet, towel)
old radios and television sets	cheesecloth
	needles
screening	thread
elastic materials	iron filings
pieces of fabric such as corduroy, silk, cotton	flashlights
	batteries

As you go ahead capitalizing on recyclable household items, you will be accused of being cheap, insensitive, uncouth. You may even be labeled "The galloping guru of the garbage set." New interest in recycling trash will make your avocation respectable. It will also help children learn science.

Related activities include bis 56, 64; and ss 1.

☐

a basic rock-forming
mineral calculator

ss

The three major rock groups are igneous, sedimentary, and metamorphic. Rocks are classified primarily by texture (grain size), mineral composition, and structure (arrangement of particles). Each of these properties, adequately observed and described, contributes information that can help identify an unknown rock sample. This presentation is limited to one technique for assisting students in identifying basic rock-forming minerals that determine what rocks are made of.

Minerals are the components of rocks. A formal definition of a mineral calls it a naturally occurring inorganic substance, having a definite chemical composition and usually a distinctive crystal form. More than 2000 minerals are known. At first, the task of identifying minerals for rock classification appears awesome. Fortunately, however, only a few (roughly 1%) of the known minerals

Adapted from Alfred De Vito, "A Basic Rock-forming Mineral Calculator," *Science Activities*, vol. 4, no. 4 (December 1970), pp. 36–40. By permission.

make up most of the rock in the earth's crust and so are called rock-forming minerals. Reasonable mastery of nine basic minerals can provide students with enough working knowledge to identify the mineral constituents of common rocks. These minerals are quartz, orthoclase feldspar, plagioclase feldspar, biotite mica, muscovite mica, pyroxene, amphibole, olivine, and calcite.

To know a mineral variety you need information on distinctive physical and chemical properties such as luster, hardness, streak, color, specific gravity, rupture (cleavage and fracture), transparency, crystal form, and other special items such as magnetism and reaction to dilute hydrochloric acid (HCl). These properties are not all-inclusive; they are only the ones that help us identify the nine basic rock-forming minerals.

You will want to provide materials such as a hand lens, tweezers, a penny, a dull steel knife blade, a piece of window glass, a streak plate, a balance for determining specific gravity, a small hammer, a magnet, and a dilute HCl bottle. Then, let the students establish the properties of a suite of minerals provided by you. For the moment they need not identify any specific minerals. It is important for them first to become familiar with the techniques for establishing and describing specific properties of minerals. You should give applicable information about these properties, describing them generally, as follows.

THE PROPERTIES

Luster

The way the surface of the mineral looks in reflected light is luster. How does it look? Is it glassy, pearly, waxy, dull, or what? Minerals are divided into two great groups by their luster. One group is opaque and has a metallic luster like that of metal. This group is called metallic. The other group may be opaque or transparent but does not have a metallic luster. This group is labeled nonmetallic.

Hardness

The resistance a mineral offers to scratching is hardness. Minerals are scaled in hardness in a range from 1 to 10; 1 is very soft and 10 is extremely hard. To determine the hardness of a sample, pick up a grain of the material with tweezers and try to scratch your fingernail. If it does not scratch your fingernail, the specimen is softer than your fingernail. A fingernail has a hardness of 2.5; therefore, the specimen must have a hardness of less than 2.5. Do the same thing with a penny. A penny has a hardness of 3. If the specimen scratches the penny, it is harder than the coin and has a hardness greater than 3. (How much greater than 3, we don't know.) You must continue until you find a substance the specimen will not scratch. A steel knife blade is about 5.5 in hardness and window glass is 5.5 to 6.0. Diamonds have a hardness of 10.0. Diamond is the hardest mineral. The standard (Mohs') scale of hardness is:

1. talc	6. orthoclase feldspar
2. gypsum	7. quartz
3. calcite	8. topaz
4. fluorite	9. corundum
5. apatite	10. diamond

A Mohs' hardness scale collection of rocks is extremely helpful in establishing more detailed comparative hardnesses.

Streak

Streak is the color of the ground-up or powdered mineral, which can be found by rubbing the mineral on a ceramic streak plate or household ceramic tile. The color of the streak may be similar to the color of the gross mineral, or it may be quite different. The color of the mineral's streak is usually constant even though the color of the mineral may be quite variable.

Color

Color is the most obvious physical property of a mineral. Yet because it is so variable, it is not a reliable property for identification.

Specific gravity (relative density)

Specific gravity is a number expressing the ratio between a mineral's weight and the weight of an equal volume of water at 4° C. If a mineral has a specific gravity of 2, a specimen of that mineral weighs twice as much as the same volume of water.

$$\text{Specific gravity} = \frac{\text{Weight in air}}{\text{Weight in air} - \text{weight in water}}$$

This property can be difficult to use if a balance is not available. Therefore, the work with specific gravity may be crudely relative. Most common minerals have a specific gravity of 2.5 to 3.0. Minerals less than 2.5 feel "light" and those more than 3.0 feel "heavy" for their relative size.

Rupture (cleavage and fracture)

A rupture in which the mineral splits along planes parallel to crystal faces, and with smooth flat surfaces along these places, is called a cleavage. Some minerals have but one cleavage direction, others may have two, three, or more. Any breakage other than cleavage is called a fracture.

Transparency

Transparency is the degree to which minerals will transmit light. Transparent minerals allow full passage of light; they are clear like a windowpane. Translucent minerals allow light to pass, but not images. Opaque minerals show no passage of light.

Magnetism

The reaction of the specimen to a magnet is another property. Is the specimen attracted or not?

Hydrochloric acid test

Does the application of dilute HCl cause any reaction? Does it bubble or effervesce?

dilute HCl *must be handled carefully*

HOW TO MAKE THE CALCULATOR

The mineral calculator is a simple device to help students identify the nine basic rock-forming minerals. In a standard manila folder, make nine parallel 1 inch slits, equally spaced, across the width of the folder at the centerfold. Keep a vertical separation of

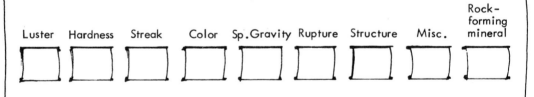

about ¾ inch between these parallel slits. Place labels corresponding to the properties of minerals over each pair of parallel slits. From the wide section of another manila folder cut nine strips, equal in width to the openings you have cut. Divide each strip vertically into ¾ inch spaces. Label the top of each strip to correspond with each label on the first folder. Now write the specific properties pertaining to the strip headings in the individual frames you have marked on each strip. Here is what you should include:

Under *luster:* list metallic, vitreous or glassy, resinous, pearly, greasy, silky, and hard or brilliant.

Under *hardness:* list the numbers 1 through 10, with examples of materials of that hardness. In order of increasing hardness, your examples would be: talc, gypsum, calcite, fluorite, apatite, orthoclase feldspar, quartz, topaz, corundum, and diamond.

Under *streak:* list green, blue, red, brown, white, colorless, yellow, orange, black, and gray.

Under *color:* list brown, dark green, light green, white, gray, black, red, yellow, and blue.

Under *specific gravity:* list the ranges between 1 and 2, 2 and 3, 3 and 4, and so on, up to "greater than 9."

Under *rupture:* list conchoidal and uneven, uneven and splintery, uneven and one direction, uneven and two directions, and fibrous.

Under *structure:* list sugary, glassy, and green; long, narrow crystals and cleavage; flexible, thin, elastic sheets; twinning, striations, and cleavage; and short, stubby crystals and cleavage.

Under *miscellaneous characteristic properties:* list magnetic, nonmagnetic, reacts to HCl acid, doesn't react to HCl, transparent, translucent, and opaque.

And for your last strip, of course, you should list the nine rock-forming minerals.

Thread the strips through the parallel slits from the back so that only one frame of each strip is visible at one time. Then give the student the nine rock-forming minerals and the materials for determining specific properties as described in the individual strip headings. With each mineral, the student determines a specific property and threads the corresponding strip through the calculator so that an applicable frame for that property is shown in the calculator. Continuing this procedure for all the properties for eight frames, the student has a description of a specific rock-forming mineral. He then moves the last strip through, matching one of the named rock-forming minerals with those properties. For help in starting out, the student has the text definitions of the nine rock-forming minerals in Table 1 and the working definitions that follow.

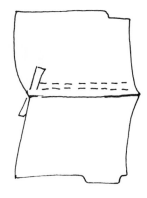

THE MINERALS

Quartz

Quartz is a translucent or transparent mineral with no cleavage. It resembles pieces of glass and may be white, milky, smoky, pink, clear, purple, or (rarely) green or brown. It is transparent to translucent, has a glassy luster, and scratches glass; its broken surfaces can be curved or smooth. It is a glossy mineral with a slightly grayish cast. It is resistant to weathering, has a hardness of about 7, and occurs in light-colored rocks. Because it is resistant to weathering, quartz as a weathered product is one of the main constituents of sandstones and siltstones. It may be distinguished from calcite by its hardness and lack of effervescence with hydrochloric acid.

TABLE 1 □ TEXT DEFINITIONS OF THE NINE BASIC ROCK-FORMING MINERALS

	Luster	Hardness	Streak	Color	Specific gravity	Rupture[1]	Transparency	Remarks
Quartz	glassy, waxy	7.0	white	usually colorless, or any color	2.65	conchoidal[1]	transparent to translucent	no effervescence in HCl
Orthoclase feldspar	glassy to pearly	6.0	white	white, pink, gray, red	2.4–2.7	uneven, two directions	translucent	massive, hard; has cleavage
Plagioclase feldspar	glassy to pearly	6.0	white	white, gray, blue green, pink	2.7	uneven, two directions	translucent to opaque	twinning; striations[2]; has cleavage
Biotite mica	glassy to pearly	2.0–2.5	white, gray	black, brown, green	2.7–3.1	uneven, one direction	transparent or translucent	thin, elastic sheets
Muscovite mica	glassy to pearly	2.0–2.5	white	colorless, gray, white, yellow	2.7–3.0	uneven, one direction	transparent	thin, elastic sheets
Pyroxene	glassy to pearly	6.0	grayish green to white	olive green, brown, white, black, gray	3.1–3.5	uneven, splintery	translucent to opaque	short, stubby crystals; 90° cleavage
Amphibole	glassy	6.0	dark green, brown	dark green, brown, black	2.9–3.5	uneven, splintery	translucent to opaque	long, narrow crystals; 60° and 90° cleavage
Olivine	glassy	7.0	pale green, white	yellow green to green yellow	3.2–3.6	conchoidal[1]	translucent	granular, sugary, glassy grains
Calcite	vitreous[3] to dull	3.0	colorless	usually colorless, tinted by impurities	2.72	rhombohedral[4]	transparent	effervesces in HCl; varieties show strong double refraction

[1] Describes a fracture with smooth, curved surfaces like the interior of a shell.
[2] A series of minute parallel lines.
[3] Glassy.
[4] Cleavage in three directions, but not at right angles.

Copyright © 1976 by Little, Brown and Company (Inc.)

Orthoclase feldspar

The feldspars are pink, white, gray, bluish, and red. When found in rock, feldspar appears dull. But flashes of light will reflect from the tiny cleavage surfaces when light strikes some surfaces just right. These cleavage surfaces clearly separate the feldspars from quartz, which has no cleavage. Orthoclase has cleavage in two directions, approximately at right angles to each other.

Plagioclase feldspar

Most plagioclase is a grayish-white glassy mineral that, like orthoclase feldspar, breaks easily on two sets of flat cleavage surfaces to produce light-reflecting facets. One cleavage surface of plagioclase has striations (minute parallel lines) representing separation planes between tabular or sheetlike crystal twins. Twinning striations are a clear sign of plagioclase.

Biotite and muscovite mica

The micas have close to perfect cleavage parallel to the base. They are elastic and their luster is vitreous to silky or pearly. They are easy to separate by color. Muscovite is clear and colorless; biotite is brown or black. Both have soft, shiny, flat flakes.

Pyroxene and amphibole

Pyroxene and amphibole are both dark in color, usually ranging from dark green to black. They cannot be readily distinguished from one another except by cleavage angles (under a microscope). Hornblende is characterized by long, hard, black grains.

Olivine

Olivine is green to greenish brown and weathers easily so that it leaves the rock brown with iron oxide stain. In pure form, olivine occurs in sugary mineral aggregates. The tiny grains sparkle like quartz; however, quartz and olivine seldom occur naturally together in igneous rock. They can occur together in sedimentary rocks. Olivine is native to the darkest rocks, those which are severely deficient in silicon.

Calcite

Calcite is a carbonate. It effervesces in dilute HCl. It is low on the hardness scale (at 3). It is usually white: in the pure crystalline form calcite may resemble clear glass, but more commonly it is a chalky white in rocks. Several varieties show strong double refraction; that is, one dot seen through these forms of calcite will appear as two.

The mineral calculator can be extended by reducing the windows, changing the strips, strip titles, and associated data, to involve the classification of rock by utilizing mineral composition, structure, and texture.

Related activities include bis 4, 26, 65, 78; ss 6, 14; and sst 13.

playground equipment

Science is more often taught indoors than outdoors for many reasons, yet the inside is not necessarily the best place to practice sciencing. The outdoors can be a cornucopia for making abstract ideas concrete. When you're teaching difficult science concepts, playground equipment can be used to advantage.

The teeter-totter or seesaw

This piece of equipment can be many things for a science teacher. It can be used as a mammoth equal-arm balance, with children of equal (or unequal) weights appropriately positioned to bring the balance into equilibrium. You could position yourself on one end and see if one or more students at the opposite end can balance the teeter-totter. It can be an example of the lever or inclined plane, or it can teach about efficiency of machines.

The swing

The playground swing is no more than a pendulum. Children swinging can be taught about pendulums dramatically. They become part of the pendulum's mass. They can experience motion, rest, vibration, frequency, displacement, and amplitude. They can also experience positions in a complete vibration, reinforcing understanding of potential energy and kinetic energy.

The slide

A slide will help you demonstrate an inclined plane when you roll objects of varying masses down the inclined plane. Everyone can observe the time and distance and calculate the rate of speed.

Roll objects down the slide to determine how mass affects speed. You can change the slide's surface to reduce or increase friction and measure the effect on speed.

Jungle bars

The equally spaced, intersecting bars nicely introduce two-dimensional and three-dimensional space. Establish one horizontal bar as the x axis, one intersecting vertical bar as the y axis. Label each as a number line. Designate another bar perpendicular to the plane containing the x and y axes. Label this the z axis. Number it, too, in a number-line fashion. You now have designated a three-dimensional grid system. Have children provide three plots (x, y, and z) and locate the point in space. Then have them do the reverse. Locate a point in space. Have the children designate the coordinates.

The merry-go-round

This apparatus can help you get across the ideas *rotation* and *revolution*. Not every playground has a merry-go-round, but a bicycle wheel is a suitable substitute. Uniform circular motion, rotary motion, angular velocity, angular acceleration, moment of inertia, angular momentum, Newton's three laws of motion, and other notions can be extracted from the spinning wheel or the merry-go-round. It is all there for the investigating.

In how many ways can you work playground equipment at your local schools into creative sciencing ventures?

Related activities include bis 51, 94; and ss 20.

☐

mobiles

Are you interested in an inexpensive art, mathematics, science, or language arts activity? Then have children make mobiles, interesting art projects that can be take-home presents and can reinforce measuring skills and the technique of balancing objects. Creative writing activities too can be tied to making mobiles. They are also excellent classifying activities.

How many types of materials can you make mobiles from? Try twigs, dowels, straws, tubes, cardboard cylinders, pipe cleaners.

What can you hang from mobiles? Try hollowed eggs, rocks, geometric shapes, pictures, spheres, cloth, flowerpots, fruit.

remember: mobiles can be dangerous!

Be careful where you hang them, and make sure that the support can handle the weight. Also, mobiles with shapes that have sharp points may be hazardous. Make sure to round off all sharp edges.

Try making theme mobiles: pollution, colors, shapes, paper, plastic, liquid, minerals.

Can you invent a mobile that makes sounds?

Related activities include bis 39 and ss 9.

☐

rock or mineral? a puzzle

Students pick up, observe, and collect rocks. Rarely do they pick up minerals, but rocks are made of minerals. This is a brief exercise in distinguishing a rock from a mineral.

The label *rock* is attached rather loosely and often interchangeably to many things that are or are not minerals. A mineral is a naturally occurring substance that has a characteristic internal structure formed by regularly arranged atoms or ions within it; its chemical composition and physical properties either are fixed or vary within a definite range. A rock, by contrast, is an aggregate of minerals. But definitions do not always clear up ambiguities in interpretation.

ROCK OR MINERAL PUZZLE

Have the students make cutouts (oak tag board will do) of the four geometric shapes provided in the illustration, constructing

Adapted from Alfred De Vito, "Rocks and Minerals — A Puzzle," *Science Activities*, vol. 3, no. 3 (April 1970), pp. 35–37. By permission.

sixteen cutouts of each shape. These cutouts should then be colored and labeled. Have them color four cutouts of each shape white and label them as quartz; four more of each shape should be colored pink and labeled as feldspar; another group of four each should be colored black and labeled as mica; and the remaining cutouts should be colored green and labeled as hornblende.

The four minerals are the basic components of granite. The average granite contains 60% feldspar, 30% quartz, and 10% dark minerals (biotite mica or hornblende).

Each cutout represents a mineral. Depending on the grade level, this shape can be more closely related to something specific about a mineral, such as chemical composition. What makes a mineral a mineral?

Take the pattern below as a model, from which you can make a ditto master or an overhead transparency. The teacher, the child, or both can, from the array of individual mineral cutouts, construct a figure representing a rock or a mineral. Students can build it by superimposing the individual cutouts on the ditto; you can put a transparency with colored overlays in an overhead projector.

How does a rock differ from a mineral? Which is which? If the finished puzzle is entirely composed of similarly colored cutouts, the mosaic will represent a cross-section of a mineral. If two or more colored cutouts are inserted into the mosaic, the cross-section will represent a rock.

By varying the amounts of granite's mineral components, deleting some minerals or changing the names of some (identifying feldspar specifically as either orthoclase feldspar or plagioclase feldspar), you can alter the granite construct or puzzle so that it will be identified as syenite, quartz-diorite, diorite, or gabbro.

more...

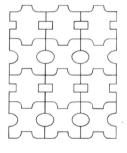

Extend the puzzle activity by having the students estimate the percentages of the mosaic's mineral components. The puzzle can also depict interlocking grains, a characteristic trait of igneous and metamorphic rock.

When we study rocks, composition, structure, and texture are important. The rock puzzle may be expanded to include these, but it is primarily designed to help distinguish a rock from a mineral.

Related activities include bis 4, 26, 66; ss 3, 14; and sst 13.

plaster of paris constructs

Plaster of paris can be bought in hardware stores, hobby shops, art supply houses, or discount stores, and is excellent for preparing casts or molds. It comes as a fine white powder that you add to water (*not the reverse*) until it has a pasty consistency. Because it usually hardens (sets up) in about 10 to 15 minutes, you should have your project well in mind before mixing the plaster of paris with water. It generates heat while it is drying, so that caution is recommended. Also, wash your hands immediately after using plaster of paris and keep it away from all mucous membranes

eyes included!

Any remaining material *should not be washed down a sink drain;* put it in a trash container designed for solid waste.

With plaster of paris you can make many materials for creative sciencing: casts of animal tracks, tire tracks, people tracks, and plant tracks; models of mountains, hills, and valleys; objects for observation of various shapes, sizes, colors, and weights; and people casts, including hands, fingers, elbows, knees, toes, and feet.

Try making casts from plaster of paris to which you've added food coloring, sand, soil, gravel, or rocks.

Try using a straw to blow over, into, and under the plaster of paris while it is still soft. How does the surface texture change?

Try varying the thicknesses of the plaster of paris. Can you make buildings with it? Homes?

Try plaster of paris maps of cities, states, nations. Try maps of highways, rivers, rock formations, and topographic maps.

Try making impressions (to be inferred) in plaster of paris casts before they harden by using chicken wire (press down and remove it), screen wire of different sizes, assorted sizes of wire screening. Make impressions with nuts, bolts, screws, nails, washers.

Related activities include bis 18, 38, 62; ss 11, 18, 33; and sst 13.

□

build a buzz box

The buzz box is a simple battery-operated device that buzzes when a child chooses a correct answer on a teacher-constructed punch card. Make the punch cards from manila cardboard cut to 3 x 5½ inches. Print three choices on most of the cards. The child takes the punch card to the box, puts the card on the box, and picks one of the three. If this selection brings on a buzzing sound, the answer is correct.

A classification card looks like this:

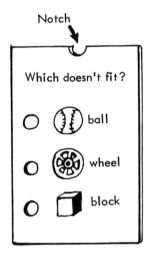

The child should select the square block because it is not round. A buzzing sound informs him that the answer is correct. If he does not hear a buzz, he will know he must try again. The possibilities for classification are endless. Color, shape, toys, pictures of animals, chemical formulas in chemistry class, are easy to adapt to the buzz box. It can also be used for nomenclature, chemical cycles, and classifying plants and animals in biology class, and for symbol recognition and calculations in mathematics and physics classes. Buzz boxes are excellent for rock and mineral identification in earth science class.

If you would like to make one or more buzz boxes for your classroom, just follow the steps listed here. To make more than one, just multiply the parts accordingly.

Adapted from Gerald H. Krockover and Diane Bobb, "Buzz-Boxes — An Aid to Individualizing Instruction," *Science Activities* (April 1972), pp. 26–29. By permission.

Materials needed

1 perfbox with Perfboard top, 3¾ x 6⅛ x 2 inches

1 solid copper-clad plate, 3⅝ x 6⅞ inches

1 DC buzzer, 1½ to 3 volts

1 solderless test probe, 5 inches

1 aluminum battery holder for two AA batteries

2 AA cell batteries

6 round-head machine nuts and screws, 4/40 x ¼

1 18-inch single-stranded, insulated copper bell wire

Equipment needed

1 drill (either hand or electric) with 7/64 inch drill bit

1 sharp knife

1 soldering iron and solder (rosin core)

1 screwdriver

1 pair metal shears

Assembly directions

Remove the four screws from the Perfboard on top of the perfbox.

Mount the battery holder on the inside of side A of the perfbox (see the diagram on page 254). Use two machine screws and nuts.

Mount the buzzer on the bottom of the perfbox on the inside.

Attach the test probe to one end of the single-stranded wire (remove about 1 inch of the insulation from the ends of the wire first) and solder the other end of the wire to the end of the battery holder that faces side B. (Make sure the batteries are removed.)

Solder one of the wires from the buzzer to the end of the battery holder that faces side D.

Drill four holes in the Perfboard top and copper-clad plate that has been cut to fit the Perfboard top. Use four of the machine screws and nuts to hold the plate and Perfboard top together.

Solder the remaining wire from the buzzer to the copper-clad plate at E.

Using pieces of clear plastic tape, block off portions of the "live" areas on the copper-clad plate so that not all areas will buzz.

Attach the copper-clad plate to the Perfboard top with the four machine screws.

Install the batteries in the battery holder and mount the Perfboard back onto the perfbox.

Things to remember

Make sure that all the connections have been soldered.

Install your batteries.

Have several different "live" areas on the copper-clad plate so that correct answers can be arranged differently on the punch cards.

page 253

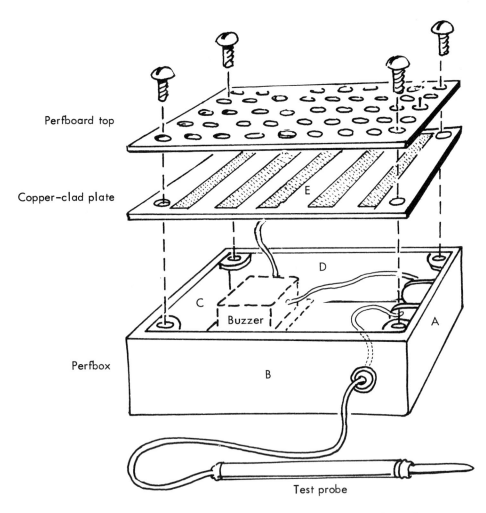

Perfboard top

Copper-clad plate

E

D

C

Buzzer

A

Perfbox

B

Test probe

Check to make sure that your buzzer works. Some buzzers need to be adjusted by a small screw on the back. Make the adjustment before you mount it in the perfbox.

Make a master pattern of the "live" areas (which buzz) and "dead" (taped) areas (which do not buzz) on your copper-clad plate so that you can prepare your cards properly.

Now you are ready to prepare your cards. Remember to vary the locations of the correct answers and to give your children plenty of time to experiment. Maybe they will enjoy making their own punch cards. Many teachers have found it useful to cut a notch or some identifying mark in their cards to distinguish top from bottom, and to match this mark on the buzz box, insuring correct placement of the cards.

The noise is minimal, the cost is nominal, and the educational possibilities are endless. The only limitation is your creativity and imagination. Build a buzz box today!

page 254

more...

Build a butter-tub buzz box from a two-pound plastic butter container (or a similar-sized container) by placing the battery and wires in the butter tub. Attach the buzzer or a light bulb to the lid of the butter tub (see the diagram).

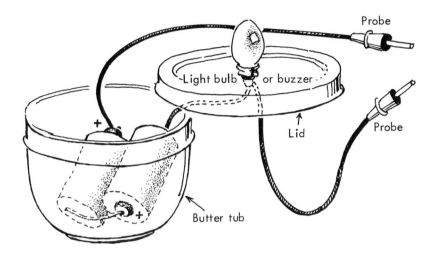

Make question-and-answer cards for your butter-tub buzzer by using aluminum foil and file folders. See the next illustrations. The aluminum foil should be cut in thin strips $\frac{1}{8}$–$\frac{1}{4}$ inch wide. Each strip should be stretched from the question to the correct answer and fastened with tape. Your designation of the location of questions and answers should be plotted in advance, staggering the location of questions and answers to avoid a set pattern of re-

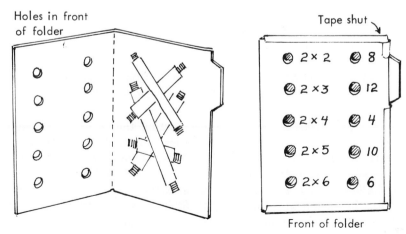

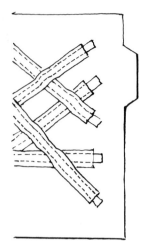

sponses. Crossing aluminum strips one over the other will establish a multiplicity of responses. Unless this is desired, you must insulate any crossovers by placing a strip of masking tape over the bottom aluminum strip. Taping the entire strip provides insurance that holding the card up to the light will not reveal established patterns. Cover each aluminum foil strip with masking tape up to the exposed holes.

Prepare a file cabinet full of butter-tub buzz-box cards. Let the students help themselves to this approach to individualized instruction. Make cards for all areas of the curriculum. Have the students make their own remediation cards.

Build a buzz box with switches instead of a probe.

Use variations for buzz-box cards: computer cards, old greeting cards, index cards, old plastic charge cards.

Related activities include sst 6 and 7.

Masking tape
over aluminum
strips with
ends exposed

catsup-bottle balance

Expensive, delicate balances are excellent pieces of equipment, but each is slightly different and takes some familiarization to master. Simple equipment fabricated by students is often preferable. A homemade balance can provide you with the number and simplicity of balances you need.

You will need a bottle, cork, a dowel, a paper clamp, string or bead wire, two small aluminum potpie pans, and two large safety pins.

The bottle serves as a base, supporting the balance arm and providing the elevation that the weighing pans need to swing freely. Almost any bottle will do. Large catsup bottles, because of their shape, seem to work best. Add sand or water to the bottle for ballast. Fit a cork snugly in the bottle.

The balance arm is cut from 5/16 inch wood dowel about 28 to 30 cm long. Make your measure an even number so that later it will be easy to find the midpoint of your dowel. Three small holes must be drilled in the beam, one of them in the center. Measure this midpoint accurately. Here will be the fulcrum or pivot point, and the more accurate you are initially, the fewer problems you'll experience later. Drill the other two holes, one about 3 cm in from

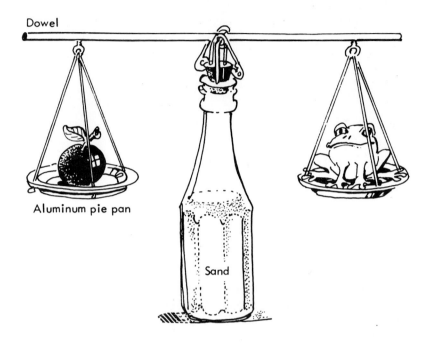

Dowel

Aluminum pie pan

Sand

each end. Make the distance in from the ends equal. You have several options on the drilling. You can prefabricate the dowels for the entire class or turn it into an applied mathematics lesson. The students will make mistakes, but nothing catastrophic. All inconsistencies in the balance can be compensated for with a rider or a bit of clay appropriately placed on the dowel.

The center support system for the balance is two large safety pins opened and stuck into the cork. The loops in the pins make the rest for the axle that is inserted through the hole of one pin, through the dowel, and through the hole of the second pin. This axle can be cut from a large heavy-duty paper clamp. A piece of wire cut from a light coat hanger works well too. Bend the wire into an L shape. Each arm of the L should be about 4 cm long.

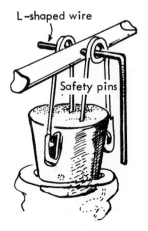

L-shaped wire

Safety pins

The pin should be spread far enough apart so that the balance beam can swing freely. Glue the wire where it enters and leaves the dowel, and let it dry. When dry, the L-shaped wire and dowel swing as a unit. Through the holes on each end thread fine bead wire or string (or use cup hooks). Hang your aluminum balance (potpie) pans from each arm.

page 257

If the balance does not balance, compensate by adding weights to the appropriate arm in the appropriate place. Devise a system of weights. One gram equals how many paper clips, staples, thumbtacks, paper matches?

Related activities include ss 4, 5; and sst 2.

☐

box-board buildings

Single, dual, and Tri-walled cardboard can be used to construct any number of building projects. Cardboard can be glued, nailed, pegged, taped, tied, and slotted together for sturdiness.

Make a simple table or stool by notching two pieces of cardboard into an **X** and then cutting an additional piece for the surface. Sizes and shapes can be adjusted to suit your needs.

You can make three-dimensional rectangular or cubic blocks by gluing, stapling, taping, or nailing six pieces of cardboard together. They can be painted in bright colors, taped with colorful tape, or decorated with decals.

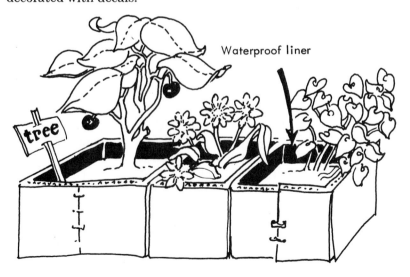

Waterproof liner

tree

A large cardboard garden box can be made by cutting the ends out of several boxes and gluing or taping them together. The box can be lined with large plastic sheets such as heavy duty painter's dropcloth or protective tarpaulins (or use plastic trash bags). Then fill ¾ full with soil and you have a garden in your room.

Many puzzles can be made from several pieces of cardboard glued together or from dual or Tri-wall construction. Shapes, numbers, and letters can be cut out with a jigsaw and decorated by painting or coloring.

Appliance boxes and fiber barrels make excellent study carrels or private areas.

Cardboard boxes can be stacked for good bookshelves.

Cardboard boxes can be cut up to make banjos and kites.

more...

Try building with cardboard tubes — make chairs, tables, shelves, flashlights, telescopes, cameras.

Next try auto, truck, and tractor tires, discarded bulk ice cream containers, scrap bricks, pegboard, and geometrically shaped buildings.

Notice: good sources of Tri-wall cardboard, along with cardboard carpentry ideas, are:

Building with Cardboard   Tri-Wall Containers, Inc.
Education Development Center   100 Crossways Park West
55 Chapel Street   Woodbury, N.Y. 11797
Newton, Mass. 02160

Related activities include ss 2 and sst 8.

☐

animal homes

Children enjoy finding animals and bringing them into the class-room. Homes for them can be quite expensive if you purchase them commercially. You will find here many ideas for animal homes that can be constructed from scrap or materials obtained at a minimal cost. Most important, children can build these homes with very little supervision. Try making some for your classroom.

ANT HOMES

Because ants are easy to find, let's begin with ant homes. You will need these materials: three plastic food jars or sandwich boxes (preferably clear), soil, and glass and plastic tubing. To construct the ant home, drill a hole (of a slightly smaller diameter than that of the tubing) at the ends of each of the three boxes, as shown in the diagram. The holes drilled in the end boxes can be used for ventilation. These two holes can be fitted with a piece of glass tubing drawn out to a narrow tip so that the air gets in *but* the ants don't get out.

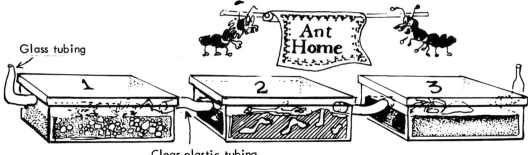

Glass tubing

Clear plastic tubing

The simplest way to move an ant colony in is to take a section directly from an anthill and transfer it to the middle plastic con-tainer. An alternative method is to place the colony in a jar cov-ered by a piece of cloth held tight by a rubber band. Make a hole in the cloth, insert a piece of plastic tubing, and extend the other end of the tubing into the new nest (the middle plastic container). Let the jar stand in water that has been previously heated to 80 or 85° F. The ants will move through the tubing to the nest.

Several interesting activities to try (you will think of many others) are:

Put soil and a damp sponge in the other two containers. Place some food (sugar) in the first container and observe the activity. Do you predict that all the ants will migrate to the first container with the food and then stay there? What really happened?

Next, try to find out what type of food ants like best. Place different foods in containers 1 and 3. Remember to keep the damp sponge in both containers with the food.

Do ants prefer sand or dirt for homes? Try both.

In what temperature do ants live best? Place the food in container 2 for this activity and vary the temperature of containers 1 and 3. Try placing one of the containers on ice cubes or warmed rocks.

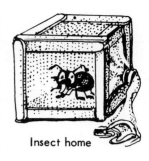

Insect home

Test the ants' reactions to light by placing a cloth over one container. Try different colors of light and record your observations.

For another interesting activity, place the food in container 2; put one species of ant into container 1, and a different species into container 3. This activity can be related to several social studies activities such as urbanization of our environment, crowding, and overpopulation.

These homes are also excellent for studying mealworms, pill bugs, caterpillars, roaches, earthworms, and ladybugs. Remember, with creative sciencing activities the well never runs dry!

INSECT HOMES

Insect homes can also be built from Popsicle sticks or tongue depressors that have been glued together. You can cover the sticks with screening to keep the insects in the home or you can put the Popsicle frame inside an old silk stocking — either way you have a good insect cage.

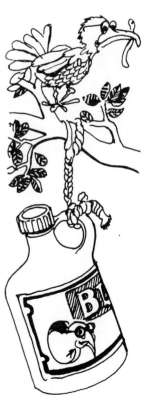

Bird home

BIRD HOMES

Try making bird homes to hang in trees outside the home or school. These can be made from bleach bottles (thoroughly cleaned), gourds, coconut shells, and gallon or half-gallon milk cartons.

SMALL ANIMAL HOMES

Homes for chipmunks, mice, gerbils, and hamsters are extremely valuable and not hard to make at all.

You will need a gallon *glass* jar with a screw-on lid and wide mouth and ¼ inch wire screen. Tools needed include a scratch awl, a pair of tin snips, solder, and a soldering iron.

Punch a hole in the center of the lid large enough to take the tin snips. Start in the center and snip in a spiral direction until you are about 2.5 cm from the edge and have a round opening.

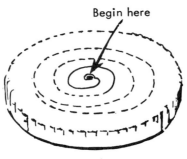

Cutting the top: outside view

Attaching the screen

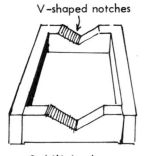

V-shaped notches

Stabilizing base

Cut the wire screen to fit inside the lid and solder at the points indicated in the diagram. If you want to keep your cage from rolling, you will need a stand. To make one, you'll need a one meter length of a 1 x 2 inch or 1 x 4 inch wooden board, nails, a saw, and a hammer.

Cut either the 1 x 2 or 1 x 4 inch wood into two 15 cm pieces and two 12.5 cm pieces. Make a **V** notch with the saw in the 12.5 cm pieces; these are the ends of the base upon which the cage will rest.

Nail the two 15 cm pieces to the two 12.5 cm pieces. Make sure that the ends fit *inside* the sides, as shown in the illustration.

If you need a water bottle for your animals, you can use an empty medicine vial or bottle, a one-hole cork stopper, a piece of 8 mm glass tubing, a triangular file, and a propane burner.

Before working with glass tubing or the propane burner you may want to check the appropriate skills and techniques sections later in the book (sst 3 and 4).

Bend the tubing over the propane burner so that it fits the angle needed to go through the screen and into the cage.

Fire-polish the end of the glass tube so that the animal will not be cut when drinking.

Now *carefully* insert the tubing.

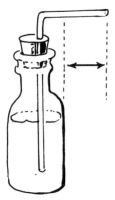

Water bottle

don't force the tubing — it can break and cut your hand!

You must wet it first with water or lubricate it with glycerine.

Use a piece of wire to hold the inverted bottle in place on the lid of the cage.

Small animal home

EGG HOMES

To make an incubator, you will need:

1 Styrofoam cooler
1 lamp cord
1 thermostat (available at farm stores or science supply houses)
1 thermometer
1 sheet of glass, 20 x 25 cm
1 light socket

1 aluminum pan for water
1 sheet of ½ inch wire mesh (small enough so that chicks won't fall through it)
1 light bulb, 40 watt
plastic electrical tape
fertilized eggs from a hatchery

Window taped in place

Preparing the cooler

Prepare the cooler by cutting an opening at the bottom of the end of the cooler (through which you can change or fill the water pan).

Next, cut a hole for the light socket at the top of the end.

Cut a rectangle in the top approximately 3 cm smaller than the sheet of glass. Tape the glass in place.

Split the cord close to the light bulb and wire it to the thermostat. Tape carefully with electrical tape and tape the wires to the side of the cooler. Now connect the lamp cord to the socket.

Place the water pan in the bottom of the cooler and place wire mesh about halfway down in the cooler. Check to be sure that it is secure.

Tape the thermometer to the side of the cooler and adjust the thermostat so that the light bulb turns off at 100°F.

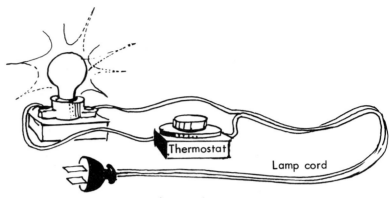

Electrical system

Remember to turn the eggs twice daily (put an **X** on one side of each egg to keep track), and keep the water pan filled.

Your finished incubator should look like this:

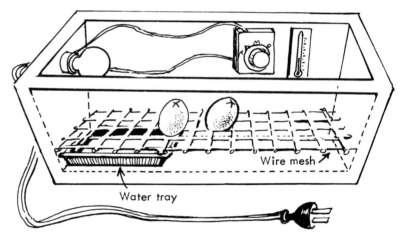

Egg home assembled (without top)

MAKE A HUMMINGBIRD FEEDER

Obtain a 20 dram *untinted* prescription vial from your local drugstore. Heat an ice pick or nail and punch a pair of holes on opposite sides of the plastic vial near its open end. These holes should be extremely small so that insects are kept out and the liquid kept in. Make sure that the holes are very close to, but not covered up by, the bottom of the cap when the cap is in place.

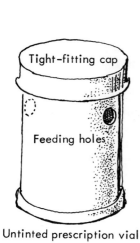

Tight-fitting cap

Feeding holes

Untinted prescription vial

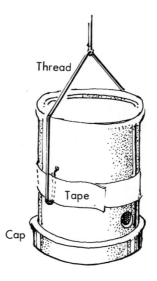

Thread

Tape

Cap

To make a hanger for the feeder, use a couple of feet of thread or fine wire and secure the ends of the thread or wire with tape, as shown in the illustration. For extra holding power, fold the ends of the thread back over the tape and wrap a second piece of tape around the vial.

To fill the finished feeder, take off the cap and hold the vial upright, then "top it off" with nectar, cap the container tightly, and quickly invert the tube (so that the feeding holes are at the bottom). Initially, a small amount of liquid may leak out of the feeding holes, but the leakage will stop as a vacuum is created inside the vial.

The hummingbird food can be a commercial nectar mix of the granular type, or you can make up your own sugar solution. Instant nectar can be purchased at pet supply stores or supermarkets. To make your own syrup, stir four or five heaping teaspoons of *granulated* sugar into a cup of warm water. Add enough vegetable dye red food coloring to give the mixture a scarlet hue. Which colors attract hummingbirds best?

Decide on a good location in the shade, near flowers, for your feeder and observe the results of your efforts.

Related activities include bis 12, 18, 38; and ss 7.

□

root observation chamber

When you are observing how plants grow, it can be interesting to observe, measure, and infer how the roots as well as the stems and leaves show their growth.

A root observation chamber can be built from plate glass with beveled edges (a glass company will bevel the edges for you). You will need 3 sheets of 15 x 60 cm; 2 sheets of 7.5 x 15 cm; and one sheet of 7.5 x 60 cm. You will also need to apply silicone caulking (from the hardware section of a discount store) to hold the glass in position. Plan on a 1.5 cm overlap where the front and back sections join the base.

You may want to make a holder from 1-inch thick wood boards cut to 60 cm lengths and nailed to a base as shown in the sketch.

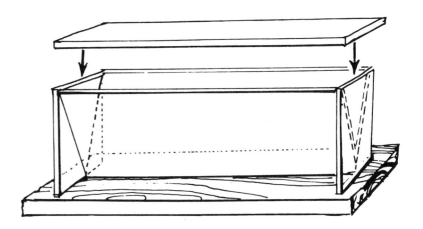

Check for leaks with water and, after the observation chamber has been sealed and allowed to set for 24 hours, fill it half full with soil or other material. Then plant some seeds.

Once the seeds have germinated, you will be able to observe the root growth, its branching, and its rate of growth.

No glass? Try Plexiglas or plastic sheeting. Try a wooden stand using 1 x 2 or 1 x 4 inch boards. Try the ends of two shoe boxes as a stand.

more...

Build a plant maze box out of wood or cardboard, as shown in this illustration:

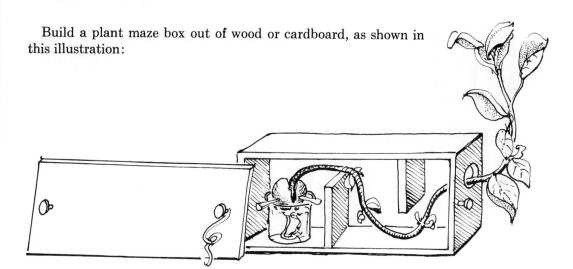

Plant a sprouting potato in a pot of moist soil. Place it in the corner of the maze. Put two obstructing partitions inside, leaving small gaps at the box top and bottom. See the illustration. Close the box and set it near a window or bright light. Explain your observations. Plant onion, carrot, and radish sprouts. Observe their development.

Make individual root observation chambers using milk cartons. Cut off the pyramid top of a half-gallon milk carton. Cut out a window on one side only, leaving about a half-inch border all around that side of the carton. Cut a piece of glass or Plexiglas to fit behind the window, leaving enough surface area for gluing. Waterproof glue, silicone caulking, or pruning paint may be used for a tight seal. Since roots tend to grow straight down, the window must be slanted (the carton tipped) to keep the roots growing against the glass so that all of their action is visible.

Use your root observation chamber to show the movement of water through various kinds of soil.

Show how water moves through soil layers by placing the following layers in your root observation chamber from top to bottom: soil, sand, soil, sand, gravel. Observe how the water builds up before it can move from one layer to another.

Related activities include bis 2, 26, 31, 55; sst 10 and 12.

Plexiglas window

circuit boards

With two 12 x 18 cm pieces of pegboard, brass paper fasteners, solder, a soldering iron, and bell wire, you can make a circuit board by following these steps:

1. First, decide which circuit you want to make. Keep a small sketch as a record to help in assembling it.
2. Put brass paper fasteners into each terminal hole. Turn the board over. Solder one end of a precut wire with the insulation removed from each end to terminal 1 and then to terminal 3, like this:

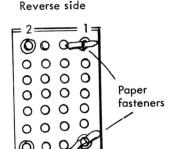

Reverse side

Paper fasteners

Side view

3. Check your soldering job by turning the pegboard panel over and checking to see if a light bulb lights when the wires are touched to terminals 1 and 3.
4. Make any other circuits that you wish, such as a wire from 2 to 4.
5. When your circuit board is wired to your satisfaction, use a matching piece of pegboard as a backing and tape with masking or similar tape.

Circuit boards can be used to infer wiring diagrams by observing when a light bulb lights or a bell rings. For a basic beginning, if you touch terminals 1 and 3, the light bulb is observed to light. You infer from that that a wire connects terminals 1 and 3. You can draw the wiring diagram. To check your diagram, peel back the masking tape and observe the inside of the board. Was your inference correct?

Now let's proceed to a more complicated circuit board!

Suppose our four-terminal board is wired like this:

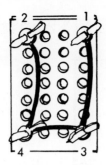

Even though no wire connects terminals 1 and 2, the light bulb tester would still light, because you still have a complete circuit between terminals 3 and 4. You would be unable to infer the "correct" diagram.

To test this inference, create an analogy by making a circuit-board terminal consisting of two brass paper fasteners connected by a paper clip, like this:

As long as you keep the paper clip connected to the two fasteners at the terminal, it will act as one terminal. If you remove the paper clip it will "break" the circuit.

Now let's return to our circuit-board problem, but this time we will use the two-fastener terminal to help explain our original model. The wiring diagram will be:

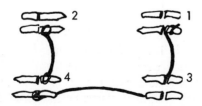

As long as paper clips connect both two-fastener terminals, you can infer that a wire goes from 1 to 2 (the light bulb will light).

Four possible diagrams explain why 1 and 2 light up:

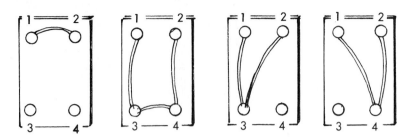

You could make these four boards and all would result in the same observation: 1 and 2 light up. But they all have *different* wiring diagrams!

Which diagram do you have? Using the two-fastener technique, you can figure out the diagram.

You may remove *one* and *only one* paper clip at a time and you may *not* check that terminal, but you can check all others. Record your observations. Replace the paper clip and then remove a different paper clip, following the same rules. Repeat this procedure until you have checked all terminals. You should be able to correctly infer the wiring diagram. Then you can open your circuit board and check your inference.

No pegboard? Use cardboard, shoe boxes, canceled check boxes, Perfboard, manila folders.

You may want to wire your light bulb into the circuit board. Substitute a buzzer for the light as an indicator for a complete or incomplete circuit.

No paper clips? Try pieces of aluminum foil, tin foil, lead foil, gum wrappers.

No wire? Try paper clips (bent into a wire) or thin strips of aluminum foil.

No solder? Try plastic, masking, or adhesive tape.

more...

Next try six- or eight-terminal boards.

Design a burglar alarm system, a window alarm system, and a door alarm system.

Related activities include sst 6 and 9.

a tin-can crystal viewer

To help you view crystals, you may want to make a tin-can crystal viewer.

Use a one-pound coffee can. Remove the lids from both ends. Keep the plastic top to use as a viewing table. Obtain one light socket, a lamp cord, and a 40 or 60 watt light bulb, and arrange as in the diagram.

It is wise to punch many pinholes in the plastic lid for cooling.

You can place crystals or any transparent or translucent object on the plastic lid for viewing. Try looking at alum, salt, sugar, Epsom salts, cream of tartar, and washing soda crystals. Observe their sizes, colors, and shapes.

Related activities include bis 4; ss 34; and sst 13.

☐

edible four-layer earth

You will need a large mixing bowl (the larger the better) for this activity. To end up with a frozen model of half the earth, you will need these materials:

green ice cream	Dragées (little metal-like
graham crackers	edible silver spheres)
chocolate ice cream	vanilla ice cream
with nuts	red food coloring
yellow ice cream	green food coloring

Before constructing the edible earth, you may wish to make a scale model cross-section, or relate the size of the sections to known objects, such as the mantle to the size of a grapefruit and the outer core to the size of an egg.

Make each layer and then freeze in the mixing bowl (one layer at a time).

The four layers to make in order are:

1. Crust: use green ice cream and crushed graham crackers. Freeze this layer.
2. Mantle: chocolate ice cream with nuts (rocks). Freeze this layer on top of crust.
3. Outer core: yellow ice cream with a few Dragées sprinkled throughout. Freeze this layer on top of the mantle.
4. Inner core: gray ice cream (made by adding equal amounts (drop by drop) of red and green food coloring to vanilla ice cream), and a greater concentration of Dragées. Freeze this layer on top of the outer core.

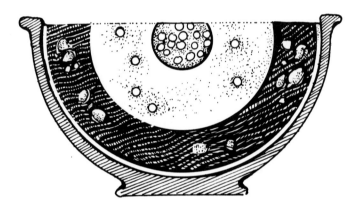

When your model is finished you can observe the layers, compare them, and then best of all,

eat them!

Related activities include bis 10, 21, 54, 60; and ss 18.

the printing kit

Children involved in the act of printing will use many language arts skills and techniques, from spelling to sentence construction to story writing.

An inexpensive printing kit can be made by purchasing about five dozen wooden clothespins, a stamp kit that has a rubber sheet containing the alphabet and numbers, and a stamp pad. These items are sold as a complete kit at discount stores, especially at Christmas time. Individually cut out the letters and numbers. Then, with small brads, nail (or glue, using epoxy) each to one of the clothespin tops. A good holder for arranging alphabetized and numerically labeled clothespins is a cardboard box, used as a stand: The stamp pad or pads can be placed in the middle of the box.

Depending on the ages of the children who will be using the kit, you may want to put a dot on the side of the clothespin to show the direction in which to hold the clothespin, so that the letters will be properly oriented.

Children enjoy printing their names, sentences, spelling words, and starting their own newspaper (jokes and sports columns are most popular).

If you want to get your children involved in duplication, a hectograph kit is excellent. These are available with complete directions from stationery or large department stores.

Now you're ready for a visit to the local newspaper and a return visit from their reporter.

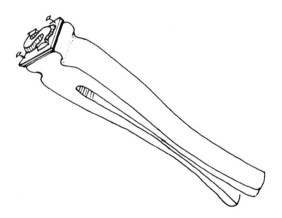

Related activities include bis 25, 44, and 92.

the dekro water treatment plant

Water treatment plants are usually built to remove floating solids (wood, leaves, rubbish) with screening; large nonfloating solids such as silt with a settling basin; suspended solids with filtration; dissolved chemicals and discoloration with alum; bacteria with chlorine; and dissolved gases with carbon. You can illustrate how a water treatment plant operates by building the DeKro Model Water Treatment Plant.

You will need six plastic freezer dishes, four 1½ inch pinch clamps, 60 cm of 7 mm glass tubing, 30 cm of rubber tubing, 1 glass chimney, charcoal bits, 10 g of alum, chlorine bleach, wire mesh window screen, scrap lumber, gravel, coarse sand, fine sand, and two baffle plates (from stores that sell replacement pads for humidifiers).

This is the setup:

1. Use scrap lumber to support the seven levels for a gravity flow.
2. Dirty water goes into the settling tank, where large nonfloating solids settle to the bottom and floating solids are screened out.
3. Alum is added in the mixing tank to neutralize dissolved chemicals — stir to mix thoroughly.
4. Settling tank with screening filters fine solids.
5. Then a charcoal filter removes dissolved gases.
6. Chlorine bleach is added to kill microbes as the water passes through the filtering bed consisting of pebbles, coarse sand, and fine sand, in that order.
7. The "treated" water goes into the catch tank and comes out "clean."

caution: this water is not for drinking!

This model plant *simulates* the procedures and methods used in actual water treatment plants. It is *not intended to be used to produce drinking water.*

Now, you're ready for the local municipality's tour of the water treatment plant.

Related activities include bis 59, 60, and 76.

☐

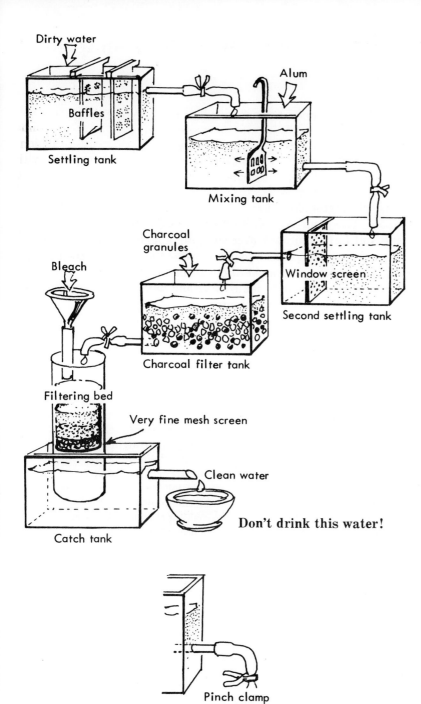

Dirty water

Baffles

Settling tank

Alum

Mixing tank

Charcoal granules

Window screen

Second settling tank

Bleach

Charcoal filter tank

Filtering bed

Very fine mesh screen

Clean water

Don't drink this water!

Catch tank

Pinch clamp

Water transfer system

making hardened-flour shapes

To make hardened-flour shapes, use these ingredients:

> 4 cups *unsifted* flour
> 1 cup salt
> 1½ cups water

Mix all ingredients together thoroughly and knead for five minutes. Use your hands, kitchen utensils, or cookie cutters to shape and form figures. Water will glue dough segments together.

Then insert hairpins or paper clips in the back if you want to hang the shapes up or make them react to a magnet.

Place the shapes on a cookie sheet and bake in a preheated oven at 350°F for 30 minutes to 1 hour.

The shapes may then be painted in bright colors with tempera or acrylic paints. Protect this finish with a coat of varnish after drying.

Hardened-flour shapes can be used for:

making geometric shapes
making animal shapes
making circles with numbers
  embedded in them
measuring activities
counting
weighing activities
symmetry lessons
classifying and sorting
observation activities
inferring activities

teaching numbers, a number
  line, and ordering numbers
teaching shapes, closed
  figures, straight and
  curved lines
animal or farm activities
storytelling
tactile number experiences
making tracks and traces
making leaf shapes

You can add three more to make twenty!

Related activities include bis 10, 21, 35, 54; and ss 15.

□

kiting is exciting

March winds are usually associated with kites, but that isn't necessarily so. Kiting is a year-round sport. The joy of kite flying is greatly increased when you make your own kite and experience the satisfaction of seeing it rise gracefully on the lightest breeze or soar rapidly to great heights on a stronger wind.

The kite is a modified "sled" that utilizes the same aerodynamic principle as an airplane wing, creating a vacuum above the kite surface for lift. Building kites is fun, easy, and comparatively inexpensive. Most people do not make their own kites for fear they will not fly. It is difficult to build a kite that will not fly. Follow a few basic instructions and it is "up, up, and away!"

Kites can be constructed in any size; however, a length of 20–40 inches should be more than satisfactory. Kites come in various shapes. Some kites are planar (one plane surface); some are not planar because they have a surface or surfaces not in the same plane; and still other kites are combinations of these two kinds. Only planar kites must have a tail.

Materials and necessary tools for kite construction are usually easily obtainable. Wooden fruit crates, especially orange and lemon crates that are made of sawed boards, make excellent kite sticks. Three-eighth-inch boards split easily lengthwise from these crates under the pressure of a pocket knife.

be careful in the splitting process

Split the wood in a direction away from you and other people nearby. These three-eighth-inch boards usually are trimmed down (using a knife, sandpaper, or a small plane) to a width of one-quarter inch.

For ordinary kite flying, plain tissue paper works best. If heavier duty is expected of the kite in the performance of aerial acrobatics, smooth (or even glazed) paper is recommended. Crepe paper can be used successfully when quiet flying conditions are anticipated. In the construction of box kites, thin wrapping paper is recommended. As an alternative to paper, you can construct fine kites using plastic sheets or plastic bags that have been cut to the desired measurements.

Liquid glue and string for joining the wooden sticks is recommended. Use the string to wrap intersecting cross members together. Some kite makers use a brad or two to fasten these joints. However, good, snugly tied, string saturated in liquid glue works extremely well. (Follow the recommended drying time for the glue.)

Each of the stick ends must be prepared to accommodate the string frame.

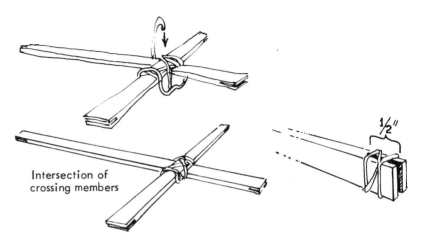

Intersection of crossing members

Mark the edges of the sticks half an inch from each end. Saw a narrow slit down to the half-inch mark. If you do not have a saw, simply notch the ends and proceed with the string frame wrappings. Do not pull too hard on the string when wrapping or you may snap the wooden sticks. Start at one stick end, wrap, and proceed to the next stick end. Continue until the entire kite is framed with string and each stick end is wrapped and glued.

Place the kite frame on a flat table top, with the lowest stick of the center intersection down. Cut the paper larger than the kite, allowing for a three-quarter-inch hem to be turned in over the framing string. Crease the paper so that it will fold over readily without pulling the framing string out of the notches. Paste the hem in place. Do not paste the hem to the string. Let the paste dry thoroughly.

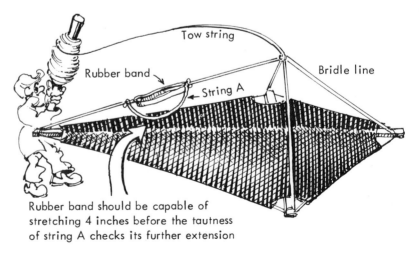

Tow string

Rubber band

String A

Bridle line

Rubber band should be capable of stretching 4 inches before the tautness of string A checks its further extension

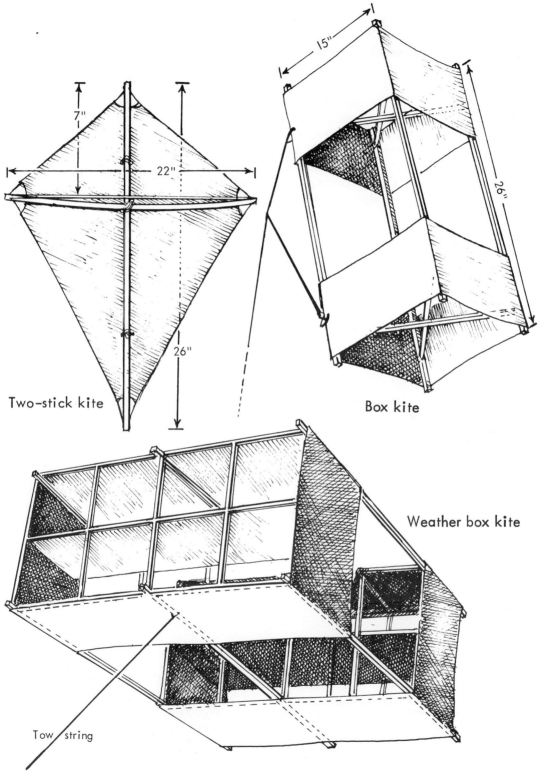

7"

22"

26"

Two-stick kite

15"

26"

Box kite

Weather box kite

Tow string

page 279

What is needed now is a bridle line. The purpose of the bridle line is to prevent sudden gusts of wind from tearing the kite or making it dart violently.

Techniques for flying kites

Do not run with a kite. Tug it, tug it, and tug it some more. When the kite is aloft, tug on the string if the kite head is pointed up, letting out the string slowly as you feel the wind pull against the kite face. If the kite head is pointed down, relax your pull on the string. This will bring the kite head back up. Then, tug again. Tug on the string when it is doing what you want. When it does not do what you want, relax on the string.

observe safety precautions while kite flying!

Never fly a kite near electric power lines. If your kite gets snagged in overhead wires, leave it. Rescuing it is risky and may cost you your life.

Never fly a kite in wet or stormy weather.

Stay away from highways and streets — always stick to parks and open fields. The beach is an excellent place to fly kites.

build, tug, and soar!

Related activities include bis 20, 30, 45, 80, 86, 114, 117, and 118.

□

building a Foucault pendulum

120
SS

One of the most convincing proofs of the earth's rotation was first demonstrated in 1851 by the French physicist Jean Bernard Leon Foucault. Foucault hung a cannonball on a 219-foot wire attached to the dome of the Pantheon building in Paris. The cannonball hung suspended almost to the floor. The cannonball, thus suspended, made a giant pendulum, free to swing in any direction. A pointer was attached to the cannonball. The pointer reached down into sand on the floor. When Foucault's pendulum was set in motion, the pointer traced a path in the sand below.

A pendulum set in motion in one direction will continue to move in the same direction. Foucault set the giant pendulum in motion in a north-south direction. As time passed, the pendulum appeared to shift the course of its motion in a clockwise direction. Actually, the pendulum continued to move in the original north-south direction. It was the earth beneath the pendulum that was turning on its axis in a counterclockwise direction causing the pointer on the cannonball to form clockwise tracings in the sand. This was a convincing proof of the earth's rotation.

To build a Foucault pendulum, you will need a phonograph, a pencil, a jar, some string, and a weight (lead fishing sinker). See the illustration.

Set up the apparatus as shown. Start the weight swinging. Turn the phonograph turntable on at its slowest speed. What do you observe? Does this verify Foucault's experiment?

Related activities include bis 51, 94; and ss 4.

□

weather or not

Weather is a topic of universal concern and interest. Children of all ages are aware of and affected by the weather. At the elementary level, interest is in the immediate condition of weather and is usually of short duration. At the middle and intermediate levels, interest spans greater periods of time allowing for a more in-depth study of weather. At these levels, weather stations may be constructed and maintained, data recorded, and inferences and predictions made. At the high school level, detailed studies of the causes of weather phenomena may be undertaken.

Generally, a study of weather involves the observation and recording of temperatures, humidity, and wind speeds and directions.

MEASURING TEMPERATURE

Temperature is measured with a thermometer. It measures the boiling point of water at 100°C or 212°F, and the freezing point of water at 0°C or 32°F. Commercial thermometers are relatively inexpensive and readily available. Introduction to reading thermometers by young children can be facilitated by attaching a zipper to a piece of cardboard that has graduations from 0°C to 100°C marked on it. The child moves the zipper up or down to correspond to various temperatures you specify. The child should realize "up" means warmer temperatures and "down" means cooler temperatures.

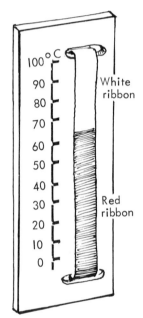

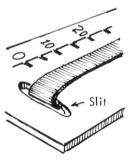

If a zipper is not available, mark a calibrated scale from 0°C to 100°C on a piece of cardboard. Cut two parallel slits in the cardboard, one just below 0° and one just above 100°. Join two ribbons — one white, one red — each slightly longer than the length of the scale. Thread the ribbon through the slits with the white portion above the red and join the ends together. This endless strip is now free and movable. The red ribbon represents the red portion of a thermometer. Position the top of the red ribbon at the current temperature. As changes in temperature occur, move the top of the red ribbon to show the changes. Children should note and record the temperature daily and compare it to the temperature of the previous day.

MEASURING WIND SPEED

Wind speed is measured by an anemometer. To make one, you need an upright stick attached to a base which should be fairly heavy or permanently fastened down, for a strong wind can whip the anemometer around. If it is not securely anchored, it will topple. At the top of the upright stick, attach two 50 cm wooden sticks or dowels at right angles to each other. At the ends of these sticks or dowels, attach plastic cups (paper cups go limp in rain, dew, and so forth) to catch the wind. Attachment of these sticks or dowels to the upright stick is critical. Reduced friction becomes an important factor. See the diagram.

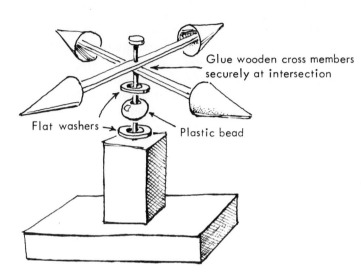

Glue wooden cross members securely at intersection

Flat washers

Plastic bead

One of the plastic cups or lids should be painted a different color, enabling you to keep track more easily of one full revolution of the anemometer.

An anemometer suitable for the primary grades may also be constructed, as shown in the diagram.

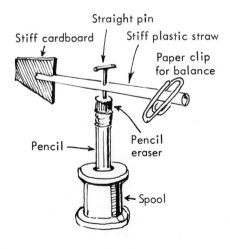

Straight pin

Stiff cardboard

Stiff plastic straw

Paper clip for balance

Pencil

Pencil eraser

Spool

FINDING WIND DIRECTION AND STRENGTH

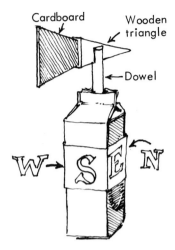

Cardboard

Wooden triangle

←Dowel

W · S · E · N

A weather vane can be constructed using an empty quart milk carton, plaster of paris, a dowel, and a small block of wood. Fill the empty milk carton with plaster of paris. When pouring the mixture into the container, add some small field stones. This will save on the amount of plaster of paris needed and also provide ballast for the carton. Before the plaster of paris hardens, insert a wooden dowel into the mixture. Center the dowel, making sure it is perpendicular. *This is extremely important.* Allow this mixture to harden completely. Staple the top of the milk carton closed. Fashion a triangular piece of wood approximately 1 by 3 inches. Drill a hole three-fourths of the way into the block of wood. The hole should be large enough for the dowel to fit into. Glue a triangle cut from stiff cardboard to the top of the dowel. Mark each side of the milk carton "north," "south," "east," or "west." Spray the entire vane with shellac or silicone to protect it from the weather. Place the weather vane outdoors, orienting north on the milk carton in the direction of geographic north.

A wind-strength gauge should add interest to the study of weather. You will need a short dowel and several scraps of wood. Dimensions are not critical. The diagram shows how to construct the gauge.

Strong

Moderate

Light breeze

MEASURING HUMIDITY

A hair hygrometer will enable you to observe changes in humidity. To build a hygrometer, obtain a few strands of human hair. Wash these in detergent to remove oils. Attach one hair to the upper end of a stand and stretch it by attaching it to a 50 gm weight. Use a rubber band to affix a toothpick to the weight so that it can serve as a pointer. Position a scale marked with a zero point and graduations above and below zero. Be sure that the pointer points exactly to zero. Changes in humidity will either

page 284

shorten or lengthen the strand of hair. The changes will be reflected in readings above and below zero. Checking with your local
weather station and correlating your measurements with theirs
will permit you to adjust your scale so that it gives more accurate
readings. Why does hair get the frizzies on rainy days?

A wet- and dry-bulb thermometer is useful in determining the
relative humidity. Two thermometers, similar in that they coinci-
dentally record the same temperature under identical conditions,
are needed. Attach both to a board. One thermometer remains as
is. This is the dry-bulb thermometer. Wrap the second thermometer in a sock or sleeve of muslin that fits snugly over the bulbous
portion of the thermometer, and suspend it in an adjacent small
jar or test tube kept filled with water. The bottle or test tube must
be fastened to the board so that the top of the bottle or test tube
is at the same level or slightly lower than the top of the thermometer bulb. Through capillary action this bulb remains wet; hence,
it is dubbed the "wet" bulb. Evaporation is a cooling process. The
wet-bulb thermometer should read lower than the dry-bulb thermometer. In order to determine the relative humidity consult a
relative humidity table. Two readings are necessary, one from the
dry and one from the wet thermometer.

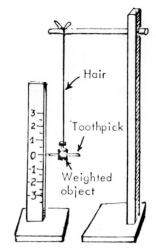

MEASURING RAINFALL

A rain gauge is a necessary weather instrument. A simple rain
gauge may be made from a funnel and a bottle. A steep funnel is
preferred because the steep sides prevent raindrops from bouncing
out. Bury the bottle in a hole so that the funnel is just above the
ground. This prevents the bottle from tipping over and makes it
easy to remove. After a rain, pour the contents of the bottle into
a graduated cylinder to determine the exact volume of rainwater
collected. Measure the diameter of the top of the funnel. Also
determine the surface area of the top of the funnel (Surface
Area $= \pi r^2$). Knowing these and the amount of collected rain, you
can determine the amount of rain per unit of area. If you have
recorded the time period of the rainfall, you can calculate the rainfall per unit of area, per unit of time.

With these weather instruments much data can be collected and
plotted on graphs providing opportunities for many interpretations
as well as correlations among various weather factors.

Related activities include bis 46, 58, 80, and 116.

building a simple kaleidoscope

A kaleidoscope is a wonderful child's toy. It also makes for a terrific science lesson.

Kaleidoscopes make use of multiple images seen in several mirrors. You can make a simple one. Using clay, balance two flat mirrors in an upright position with their reflective sides facing at right angles to each other and at right angles to a table top. Place a coin or any other object midpoint between the two mirrors. Look down on the object with your eyes close to the mirrors. Describe your observations.

Now adjust the mirrors to a 60° angle. Repeat your observations of the object. Describe your observations. Are they the same? Different? Continue to reduce the angle. What changes do you observe?

Increase the number of mirrors by placing the two upright mirrors on another mirror lying flat on a table top. How does this affect your observations?

In order to build a simple kaleidoscope you will need a small, plastic, food-storage container. The lid should be transparent and the container portion clear plastic. These items are available at local grocery stores. Other containers, even small plastic vials (providing they have the same properties described for the food-storage container), work equally well. Completely cover the bottom of the container with colored plastic shards. (Local hobby shops sell them.) Cap the container. Now cut a piece of cardboard about two inches long and to a width of about twice the diameter of the lid of the container you have elected to use. Cover this piece of cardboard with reflective aluminum. If you prefer, thin sheets of shiny metal can be purchased from local hardware companies. The metal works very well but

***care must be exercised when cutting the strip
and after cutting, all edges must be filed down
to remove sharp corners and burrs***

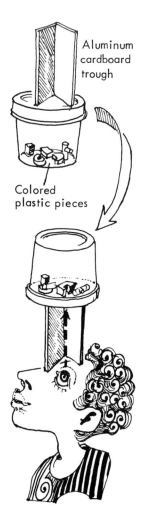

Aluminum cardboard trough

Colored plastic pieces

This aluminum-covered cardboard (or the metal) can be made to serve as reflective mirrors. Crease the aluminum-covered cardboard (or the metal) to form a 15° trough, and place it upright on top of the cover. Invert the entire apparatus, hold it directly over your head, and point it at a bright overhead light. While focusing your eyes on the vertex of the 15° angle, rotate the plastic container. Try changing the angle of the aluminum-covered cardboard (or the metal) trough. What happens when you increase the angle? Decrease the angle?

Related activities include ss 25, and 32.

□

make a metric wheel

Trace the pie-shaped wedge in the illustration on page 288 on three separate sheets of white paper. Be sure to include the black mark in the angle at the bottom right. Then trace the centimeter marks along the edge. Cut out the wedge in the book and all three tracings. You should have four forms that combine to make a circle.

Glue the forms in a circle onto a piece of cardboard. Trim the cardboard to the *exact size* of the circle. Now you have a metric wheel with a black dot at its center.

Draw a big arrow from the middle of the wheel down one seam to the edge. Begin numbering each centimeter mark starting with the one directly to the left of the arrow. You should have numbered to 100.

Nail your wheel through the black dot at the center to a dowel rod long enough to serve as a handle. Nail it loosely or use washers so that it will rotate easily.

1. Always start to measure with the arrow pointing down.
2. As you walk forward, count the number of times the arrow goes around. For every complete revolution, you have measured 1 meter. Then measure to the nearest centimeter.
3. When measuring from a wall, start with the wheel in the position indicated and measure as usual. When you have your complete measure, add 16 cm for the starting loss and 16 cm if you end at a wall.

Related activities include bis ss 24.

□

metric wheel -

make a liter container

Using the directions for making a cubic model in sst 13, construct a 10 cm cube from cardboard (corrugated cardboard works best).

Line the completed cube with a large plastic bag. The bag should lie on the bottom and sides of the container and overlap the edges, making the container leakproof. You now have a liter container to measure liquids.

Related activities include bis 49, 54, and 69.

a moon phase box

To observe the phases of the moon, suspend a golf ball (or Ping-Pong ball) from the middle of the top of a shoe box, using a string and brass fastener or similar items. Cut an opening in one end of the box so that a light source (flashlight, slide projector) can shine into the box. Cut small viewing holes (about 3 cm in diameter) in all four sides of the box. While the light is illuminating the golf ball from the front, observe the golf ball from each of the four sides of the box. You will observe the phases of the moon. Think of the golf ball as the moon, yourself as the observer on earth, and the flashlight as the sun. Under what conditions do we observe the full moon, half moon, or new moon? Using the moon phase box, set up those conditions to check your responses.

Related activities include bis 22 and 32.

a food-tray wave tank

Obtain a plastic cafeteria tray (one that is completely flat) and use a saber saw to cut out the center leaving a 6 cm border around the edge.

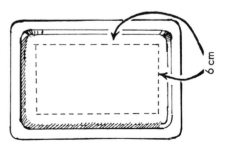

Obtain a piece of Plexiglas that is the same size as the entire tray, and glue it to the bottom of the tray using a waterproof sealant such as silicone.

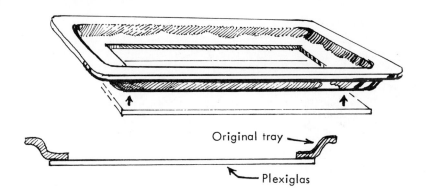

Original tray

Plexiglas

Place your completed wave tank on an overhead projector, add water, and your entire class can experience the excitement of learning about wave action.

You can use a pencil point as a wave generator and blocks of wood or paraffin as barriers.

Related activities include bis 17, 84, 99, 113, and 122.

☐

make a constellation finder

Cut out the constellation wheel on the next page and glue it to a piece of cardboard or heavy duty paper of the same diameter. Glue the constellation frame to a piece of cardboard or heavy duty paper and cut it out, following the solid lines and also cutting out the shaded areas.

Punch out the hole in the center of the wheel. Place the frame over the wheel until they line up. Then, using a brass paper fastener or similar device, fasten the frame and wheel together, allowing room for the wheel to turn.

CONSTELLATION WHEEL

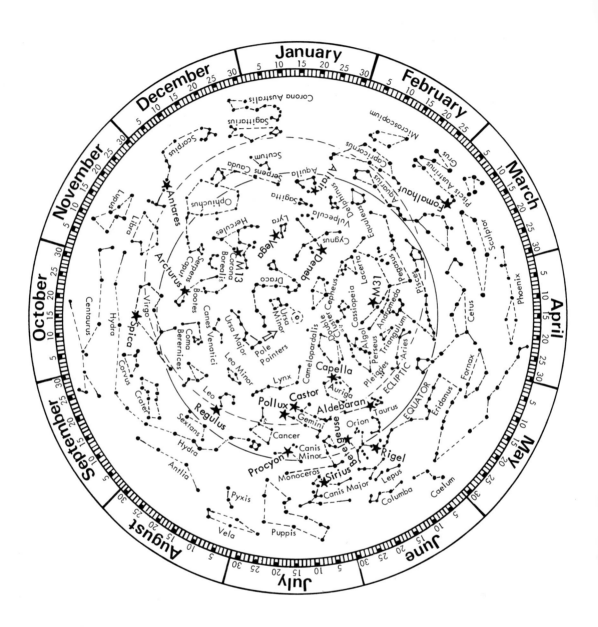

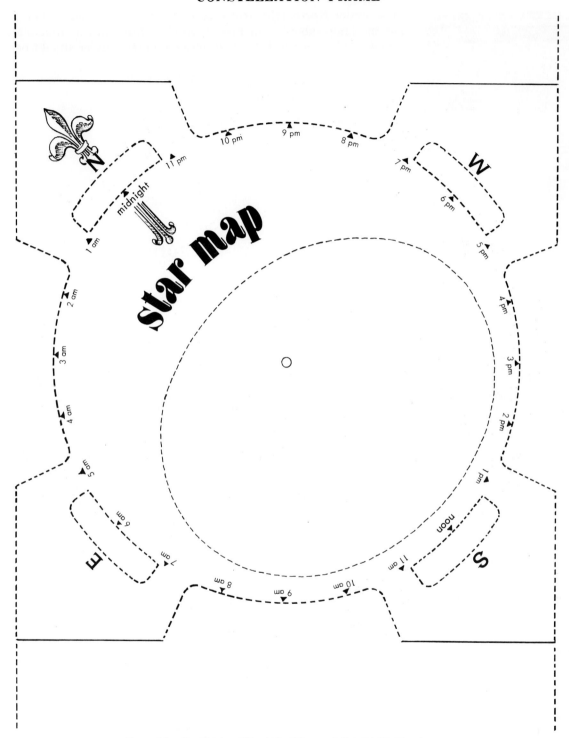

To use your constellation finder, line up the date — month and day — under North (the arrow above midnight). Go outside and hold the finder above your head with N pointing in the direction of geographical north. What you observe on the finder should be the same as what you observe in the sky.

Related activities include bis 19, 67, 74, and 125.

□

a milk-carton computer

You will need a quart-size milk carton, a cardboard strip, and some blank cards to build a milk-carton computer.

1. Carefully open up the top of the milk carton to gain access to the inside.

2. Cut a rectangular "input" opening about 3 inches below the triangle top and an "output" opening about 3 inches above the

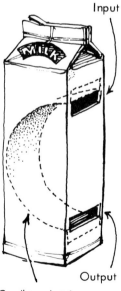

Input

Output

Cardboard strip

page 294

bottom. Make the openings large enough for the cards to go in and out easily.

3. Cut the cardboard strip to the width of the input and output openings on the milk carton.

4. Tape or glue the strip inside the carton, as shown.

5. Close the top of the milk carton and make your cards. Write a question on one side of each card and the answer on the other side (upside down). See the example. You might want to try sets of cards on shapes, colors, formulas, rock identification, weather symbols, constellations, and so forth.

6. Have students place the cards (question side up) into the input opening of the computer. The cards will come out the output opening, answer side up. Pretty neat!

7. Challenge your students to make their own individual milk-carton computers and input/output cards.

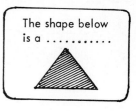

The shape below is a . . . .

Triangle

testing for acids or bases

To test for acids or bases, you will need:

raw red cabbage	liquid soap
small sauce pan	salt
large jar	lemon juice
strainer	orange juice
small jars or glasses	carrot
baking soda	soda pop
vinegar	tomato
hot plate	milk

1. Make your own litmus (indicator) solution by tearing up the leaves of a head of raw cabbage and putting them into a small sauce pan. Pour water over the leaves. Place the pan on the hot plate, and let it simmer for about fifteen minutes.

2. Using a strainer, pour the cabbage water into a large jar.

3. Now test different substances to see if they are acids or bases.

4. Begin by putting a teaspoon of baking soda into a small jar or glass and some vinegar in another jar or glass. Add a small amount of cabbage water to each jar. In the glass with the baking soda (a base), the water should turn green; and in the jar with the vinegar (an acid), the water should turn red.

5. Next, try the cabbage water on other materials, observing the color. Use such things as liquid soap, salt, fruit juices, and vegetables to decide if they are acids (red) or bases (green).

This activity may lead to the use of litmus paper. Litmus paper is rather expensive and is used up readily. To save money, use newspaper strips (from the borders where there is no print) which have been soaked in cabbage water. You can use the strips to test things just as you would use litmus paper. The strips will turn either red (acid) or green (base) just as the cabbage water did.

Related activities include bis 11, 19, 40, 43, 47, 82, 88, and 101.

□

preserving with plastic

caution: the resin and hardener used in this activity are dangerous. Thus, this activity is recommended only for upper grades and is to be done under the direct supervision of the teacher; make sure that all the safety precautions on all containers are read and followed

To embed and preserve objects in plastic, you will need:

    plastic resin with hardener (a catalyst available at auto supply
        or hobby stores)
    mineral oil
    wooden stirrers
    paper containers
    plastic measuring cup
    plastic molds (small or large ones can be used)
    tweezers

fan for adequate ventilation. All windows should be open in the classroom or the activity should be conducted outside.
newspapers

follow all directions carefully

1. Assemble the equipment and materials. Make sure the plastic mold is at least 65°F or warmer.

2. In a paper container, add hardener (catalyst) to the resin, using the proportional amounts indicated in the directions on the label.

3. Coat the plastic mold with a very light layer of mineral oil.

4. Decide on what you want to embed in the plastic. Almost anything will work — mealworms in stages from larvae to adult beetle, biological specimens, minerals, and so forth. However, remember that the result is *permanent*.

5. Pour the resin into the cavities of the mold until the bottom is covered (about $\frac{1}{8}$ inch deep). Allow it to stand until the plastic has gelled (about 15–20 minutes). Check for solidity with a toothpick.

6. After the first layer has gelled, pour a second layer ($\frac{1}{8}''$–$\frac{1}{4}''$ thick), using slightly less hardener.

7. Using tweezers, dip the object to be embedded into the paper container of catalyzed resin. Then place the embedded object into the liquid resin in the mold. Remember, the *first pour* was the *top layer* of the finished item, thus, you should position your object upside down.

8. Allow the second layer to cure until gelled — usually 4–5 hours.

9. When hardened completely, remove the casting from the mold.

do not pry the casting out;
damage may result

10. Sand or file the back of the casting until smooth. Allow to dry completely — 24 hours — before using.

For other projects, you can:

> add color to the resin.
> add glitter or sequins to the resin.
> add a jewelry fitting to the casting and wear it as jewelry.
> make a paperweight.
> apply a wax coating to the casting for protection and make it glow.

Related activities include bis 4 and 78.

making current weather maps

Several morning national television programs display professionally prepared weather maps, often showing them three or four times while the programs are on.

Obtain a piece of clear plastic food wrap and place it directly on the television screen before turning one of these programs on. Masking tape can be used to hold the wrap securely in place.

When the weather map is televised, trace the outline of the United States on the plastic wrap with a permanent marking pen. Quickly trace the highs, lows, and weather fronts within the outline. Add enough front symbols so that the map can be filled in later. Add the details, such as precipitation, last. After the tracing has been completed, peel the plastic wrap off the screen. Mount the wrap on a light background or use the overhead projector to display it.

Think of some other ways to obtain a copy of the television weather map. Why not try an instant camera?

Related activities include bis 67, 74, 75; and ss 33.

scope it out

You can make a simple telescope from two lenses (from an old camera or magnifying glass) and two cardboard tubes. Remember, your telescope, like that of an astronomer, will make objects appear upside down.

1. For the body of the telescope, use mailing tubes or make your own from stiff cardboard.

2. Fit one tube snugly inside the other tube.

3. Attach the lenses to the open ends with tape or glue.

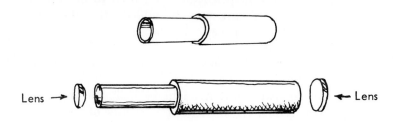

Lens → ← Lens

4. Now you're ready to look through the telescope. Slide the tubes in and out until the object you are viewing comes into focus.

remember: do not point your telescope at the sun!
looking at the sun can damage your eyes

Related activities include ss 22 and 25.

salt and flour relief maps

To make a relief map, you will need:

salt	watercolor paints
flour	brush
piece of heavy cardboard	water container
or wood	map (optional)

1. Combine three parts salt, one part flour, and enough water to bring the solution to the consistency of dough. This will create a mass suitable for sculptural modeling. The thickness may be modified for individual needs or desired methods of application by varying the quantity of water. Other recipes that can be used for this activity appear in csr 10, 11, and 12.

2. Draw a map outline on the cardboard or wood. Then, cover the cardboard or wood with a thin film of the salt and flour mixture.

3. Depending on the map features you wish to include, additional salt and flour mixture may be added after the first application has dried. Colors can also be added to show rivers, mountains, and so forth.

4. Objects such as train tracks and footprints can be pressed into the wet mixture.

5. Among other features that might be included are counties, countries, lakes, rivers, cities, highways, points of interest, and the like.

6. Students may want to construct maps of their own communities using the salt and flour mixture.

Related activities include bis 67, 74, 75; ss 7 and 31.

☐

a shoe-box slide projector

For this activity, you will need:

1 shoe box with lid
1 old camera lens
1 flashlight
a mat knife
scissors
3 strips of corrugated cardboard (each 45 x 10 cm)

1. Cut a hole in the center of both ends of the shoe box. (The easiest way to do this is to cut a star [★] with the mat knife and then fold back the edges and snip them off with scissors.) The holes should be just large enough for the lens to fit into one and the flashlight into the other.

2. Put the lens and the flashlight into the holes. (You may need a cardboard flashlight support to hold the back end up and keep the light focused through the lens.)

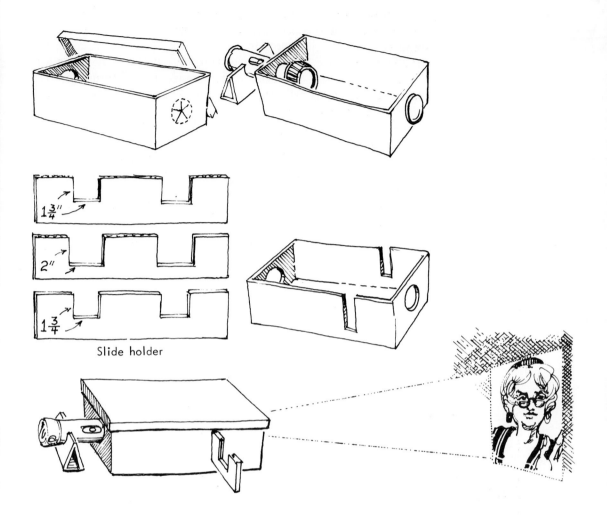

Slide holder

3. Now, point the projector (shoe box) toward a blank wall about five feet away. Put the lid on; turn the lights out and the flashlight on. Move the projector backward and forward until the image on the wall is in focus (as clear as you can get it). What are you seeing? Put your hand inside, leaving as much of the lid on as possible. Are you starting to get an idea of how a projector works?

4. To make a slide carrier that will hold your slides in place inside the projector, cut openings in the three strips of corrugated cardboard (see diagram 3). Glue the strips together. Your 35-mm slides should fit easily in the pockets.

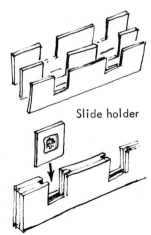

Slide holder

Hold a slide in the box and move it around with your hand until it projects on the wall as clearly as possible. Make a line across the bottom of the box to show where you are holding the slide. This is where you will put your slide carrier.

page 301

5. To allow the slide carrier to pass easily in and out, cut slots on both sides of the box where you drew the line (diagram 4). (You may have to cut slots in the cover as well to make room for the slide carrier.)

6. Cover the box, put a slide in the carrier, and project it. (If the slide is too high, trim the bottom of the carrier until the entire slide is visible on the wall.)

Related activities include ss 14.

☐

science skills and techniques □ sst

let me do it

Martha: John, have you bought my Christmas present yet?

John: No, Martha, I don't know what to get you. You've got everything. Can you give me any hints?

Martha: I thought you'd never ask me. I want:

a jigsaw

an electric drill with drill bits

two C-clamps

three files

two soldering irons with flux and solder

a level and T-square

two handsaws

three claw hammers

six flathead and Phillips-head screwdrivers in assorted sizes

one hacksaw

two wire cutters

two needlenose pliers

two adjustable wrenches

one 12 ft tape measure

one pair of safety glasses

and of course, a tool box to put everything in!

John: Are you crazy, Martha! What would you do with all that stuff? Build a house?

Martha: I'm going to have my students involved in science activities this fall and they are going to make things with me.

John: Martha, that sounds great, but you don't know how to use a jigsaw or an electric drill.

Martha: I don't, but I'll learn in *Creative Sciencing*, and then if I have to, I'll borrow a saw and drill from our school custodian. I know I'll love sawing and drilling!

The story you have just read is true, only the names were changed to protect the husband (from embarrassment — now he can't use a drill or saw as well as Martha can).

To get your creative sciencing program going, you will need some skills and techniques. "Science Skills and Techniques" is designed to help you get those. Once you have mastered the skills and techniques presented here, you will find that new areas for doing, manipulating, constructing, and experimenting will open, letting you supplant the chalk and chalkboard with solder and a soldering iron. It will provide you with the skills and techniques for soldering that piece of wire for your own circuit board, drilling the right hole for your own buzz box, boring your own cork for a collection tank, and identifying the basic tools you need. You will find that this division is a good reference section. When you are making an animal home

page 304

and need to solder, look it up in sst. By the way, Martha's "want list" should give you a good start, just in case you decide to build your own home.

And remember, if there is one guarantee that we can give you, it is that you will be

out of your seat
and onto your feet!

creative sciencing safety

When you conduct creative sciencing activities, proper planning and preparation will assure you of a happy ending. Make sure that you:

1. Label all bottles and containers of materials unless the contents are visible and recognizable to all (like nuts and bolts). List on the label the contents and precautions to follow.

2. Try all equipment and materials yourself before children begin using them.
3. Whenever the least danger of damaging eyes is apparent, such as breaking rocks with a rock hammer or heating liquids, wear approved safety glasses.

4. Have a satisfactory location and humane home for animals.
5. Arrange for proper care by responsible persons (such as the principal, school nurse, or parent) for burns, cuts, scrapes, and scratches.

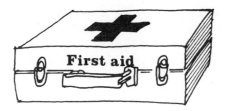

6. Send a note home to parents informing them of the precautions to follow when they work at home with their children in a creative sciencing endeavor.

remember the 3 p's:
planning
preparation
precaution
and a safe creative sciencing experience will be yours!

sst

have tools will travel
(in science plus)

Wing nut

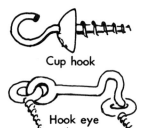

Cup hook

Hook eye
and screw

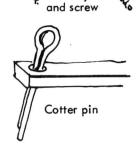

Cotter pin

Wood screw

Metal screw

If you believe that science is active involvement, that science is doing, and that science is fun, then science curriculums must move out of the realm of total exposition and into exposition plus physical participation. Talking and reading about pulleys is okay, but coupled with making pulleys and designing uses for pulleys, as in an elevator, and then building a miniature elevator, is a far superior teaching and learning technique. This transition from a spectator in science to a participant means that teachers (and children) need some familiarity with the tools of the trade. These tools can aid and abet your teaching in other areas, such as mathematics, art, and social studies.

This introduction to tools does not encompass every kind of tool, but it does cover the essentials. After this introduction, you will undoubtedly add many other tools to your collection to handle jobs that interest you.

Let's first examine things that join things together. Even the most common constructions usually have you joining wood to wood or wood to metal. You should have a hammer and an assortment of nails. The hammer should be a carpenter's claw hammer of a weight suitable for you and your students. Nails come in many sizes and materials, such as six penny (6d), and 8 penny. The penny reference has to do with the diameter of the shank of the nail. You must choose a shank to fit the job. A nail too large will split the wood. Nails are made of aluminum, iron coated with zinc, and other materials. Common nails, in most cases, will suffice.

Aluminum nails are fragile but sometimes are required where excessive rusting must be avoided. Zinc-coated nails are rust resistant and are used mainly in roofing. If the nails in an object are countersunk (driven in below the surface leaving a hole, which is then filled in with some filler) and painted upon completion, ordinary common nails will almost always do.

Screws are useful for joining wood to wood and metal to wood. For binding metal to metal, use sheet metal screws. Screws come in countless sizes (diameter and length) and head styles. When purchasing them, tell the supplier what you plan to do if you want suitable recommendations. Screws form strong, permanent joints that will not work loose even under repeated vibration and heavy stress. The two types of screws are wood screws and metal screws. All wood screws have three parts: a head, slotted so that the screw can be driven into the wood with a screwdriver; an unthreaded portion (immediately below the head); and a threaded body tapered to a point at the tip. Sheet metal screws have threads extending all the way up to the head, giving full holding power when you join thin sheet metal to sheet metal.

Screwdrivers are used for driving and loosening screws. The blade of the screwdriver should mate with the screw head in both thickness and width. A mismate will damage the screw head or the screwdriver, also making a very frustrating job either to finish driving or to back out a chewed-up screw. Two or three sizes of screwdrivers, from 9 to 18 cm in length, will handle most common jobs.

Among the multitude of screw heads, two are common, the Phillips or crosshead and the slotted head. Each takes only a proper mating screwdriver.

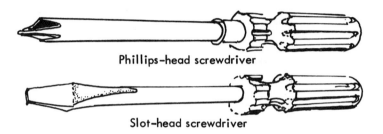

Phillips-head screwdriver

Slot-head screwdriver

Wood joiners are corrugated fasteners that you hammer into soft wood to join two pieces of wood together. The tapered edge is hammered into the wood.

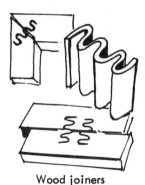

Wood joiners

Nuts and bolts also hold wood and metal together. The threads on bolts are not cutting threads, but are matched to a nut that rides on the thread. Therefore, a hole of suitable size must first be drilled to receive the bolt. Flat washers used with the nut increase the holding power. A spring or lock washer may be used if the nut must be held under tension to resist vibration. Bolts and the corresponding nuts come in many lengths and shank diameters.

Bolts have slotted, hexagonal, or recessed (Allen) heads. Tightening takes a variety of wrenches in two general classes — fixed and adjustable. Fixed or open-end wrenches cannot be varied in size. They are convenient because the opening is always fixed for one size of nut, as marked on the wrench. Adjustable wrenches can

Lock or spring washer

be opened or closed to fit nuts and bolts of many sizes. Allen wrenches are hexagonally formed to fit inside a recessed hexagonal hole in the bolt.

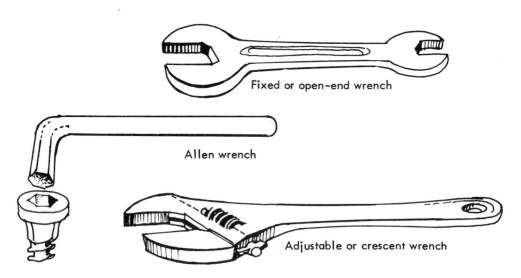

Fixed or open-end wrench

Allen wrench

Adjustable or crescent wrench

Pliers are sometimes used to tighten nuts and bolts, a wasteful practice for it damages both. Pliers come in all shapes and sizes. They are used to cut wire, bend and twist wire, and to hold things together while drilling, soldering, or what have you. Every teacher should have a pair of common pliers. Needlenose pliers are also worth acquiring. In the same category are tin snips or cutting shears for cutting screening and light metal sheet.

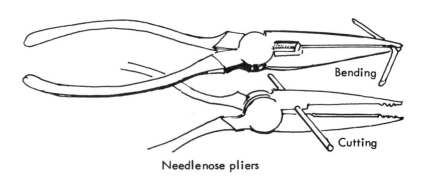

Bending

Cutting

Needlenose pliers

Files of all sorts are essential for smoothing rough areas and removing excess wood or metal. They are of two general kinds — files for use with wood and files for use with metal. When you purchase files, ask to be sure you will get files made for the purpose you intended.

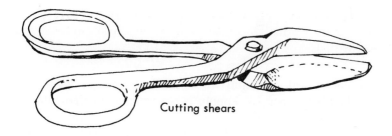

Cutting shears

Triangular files are necessary for filing notches, scratching glass tubing, and general filing. When using a triangular file to scratch glass tubing, place the pointed edge of the triangle on the glass tubing, which should rest on a smooth, flat surface. Bear down on the forward stroke only. On the return stroke, lift the file clear of the surface to avoid dulling its teeth.

Triangular file

Another invaluable tool is the adjustable combination square and level. The square is used for drawing perpendicular lines on material for accurate cutting. It also can be used in checking a right angle, a 45° angle, depth of a recess, and to check whether or not a surface is horizontal. If the surface is level, the bubble will balance between the two lines.

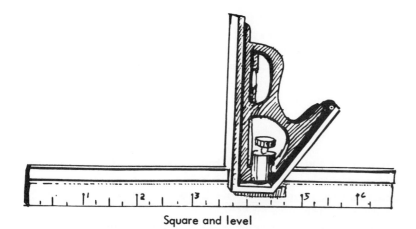

Square and level

sst

how to ignite a propane tank

A propane tank assembly (see the drawing) is useful in the classroom whenever a gas supply is not available or portability is desired.

First examine the parts of a propane torch and then look over the procedure for igniting it. Using the drawing and the real propane torch, identify the nozzle, gas valve, propane gas tank, and the wire stand or holder.

Before beginning, remember this precaution:

keep long hair tied in back of your head,
wear safety glasses,
and work in a safe place!

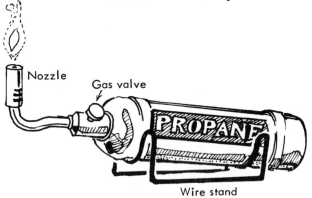

Nozzle

Gas valve

PROPANE

Wire stand

Turn the gas valve on and off *quickly* to get the feel of it. A *counterclockwise* turn opens the valve.

Light a match and hold it beside the gas nozzle.

Slowly turn the gas valve in a counterclockwise direction.

Place the flame of the match in the gas stream until the burner is lit.

Adjust the gas with the valve until the flame is as blue as you can make it.

To shut off the burner, turn the valve in a clockwise direction until no gas is released.

Practice this several times, but be careful *not* to let escaped gas build up in the room.

Propane tanks and nozzles may be purchased at hardware and discount stores. Notice that the valve-nozzle part screws into the top of the tank, making it easy to replace the tank.

working with glass tubing

Glass tubing, used in many creative sciencing activities, is easy to work with if you handle it properly. This activity is designed to acquaint you with the skills and safety precautions needed in manipulating the tubing.

For this activity you will need these supplies:

> glass tubing (5 mm or less in outside diameter), about 90 cm long
> Bunsen burner or propane torch (with wing top or flame spreader, if possible)
> a cloth
> rubber stopper with a hole appropriate for the tubing used
> triangular file
> heat-resistant pad (or other mat to put hot items on)
> matches
> glycerine (in dropper bottle) or any type of similar lubricant, like mineral oil

We will consider five steps in using glass tubing: cutting, fire-polishing, bending, preparing an eyedropper, and inserting glass tubing into a rubber stopper.

How to cut glass tubing

Use your thumb and forefinger to hold the edge of a triangular file against the glass. Rotate the glass about a quarter turn to make a short scratch on the glass. It is essential to distinctly etch the glass or it may shatter.

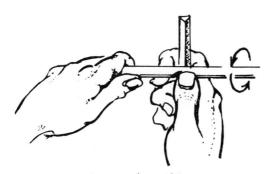

Cutting glass tubing

Grasp the tubing so that the file mark is away from you and each thumb is beside the mark.

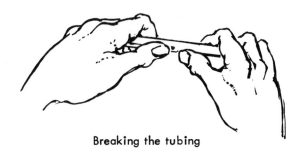

Breaking the tubing

Push your thumbs against the tubing and use your fingers to bend and pull apart the tubing. For safety's sake, wrap the glass tubing in a towel to protect your hands.

remember: this procedure does not require great force!

How to fire-polish glass tubing

The sharp edges of the tubing may be smoothed or rounded by following this procedure:

Place the end of the tubing at the tip of the inner (blue) portion of the burner flame. Use a fairly small, sharp flame (with too large a flame, the glass will sag because too much of it will be heated).

Rotate the tubing until its edges begin to soften and appear to be smoothed.

Cool the tubing by placing it on a heatproof pad.

caution: hot glass looks like cool glass

Wait five minutes before handling the fire-polished glass.

After waiting those five minutes, fire-polish the other end of the tubing.

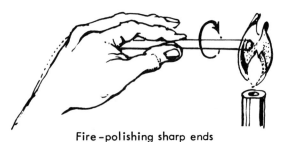

Fire-polishing sharp ends

How to bend glass tubing

For best results use the wing top attachment for the Bunsen burner or propane torch.

page 314

Rotate the tubing continuously in the flame.

For a 90° bend, let go of one end when the tubing just starts to sag. This end will fall to form the bend. Remove quickly from the flame and cool on a heatproof pad.

For smaller angles, heat tubing until it just begins to sag. Remove tubing quickly from flame and bend it to the desired angle on a heatproof pad.

You may need to practice this procedure several times to become a good glass bender. Also try angles of 45°, 60°, 120°.

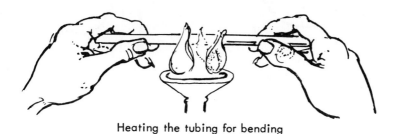

Heating the tubing for bending

How to make an eyedropper

Place glass tubing in the flame. Rotate the tubing until it is quite soft and thick.

Remove tubing from flame. Pull your hands apart quickly until the desired tip is formed. The pull should be straight and horizontal.

Cool on the heatproof pad five minutes.

Cut the glass in the middle of the drawn-out ends and polish the sharp ends with a file.

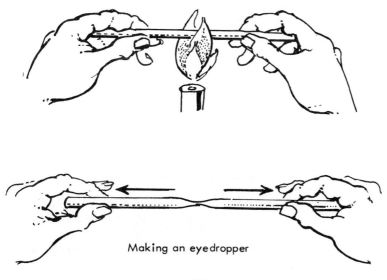

Making an eyedropper

If you wish to make a thick end for a dropper, heat the end of the tubing until it is red hot. Press this end on the heatproof pad. Cool the dropper before handling.

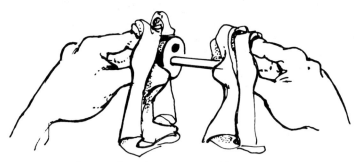

Easing the tubing into a rubber stopper

How to insert glass tubing into a rubber stopper

The hole in the stopper should be appropriate for the size of tubing.

Place a drop of glycerine or mineral oil in the stopper hole *or* moisten the stopper hole and the end of the tubing with water.

Protect your hands by wrapping the glass with a cloth or paper toweling.

Hold onto the part of the tubing near the stopper.

Insert tubing into the stopper with a gentle twisting motion.

do not force the tubing into the stopper — be careful!

how to bore a cork

Corks are necessary for many creative sciencing activities and projects. This activity will enable you to work with a cork borer and bore a perpendicular hole through a cork.

Corks can be purchased in assorted sizes or by the diameter of the top, bottom, or length from top to bottom.

Cork borers are usually made of brass or steel tubing and have wing handles for gripping. Sets containing borers graduated in diameter are available from scientific supply houses. Each borer is numbered on the handle according to size and each set also includes a ramrod for cleaning the cork from the borer (see the drawing).

To bore a hole in a cork, use a wooden board for your work surface and follow this procedure:

Select the borer by the diameter of the hole you wish to make.

Place the cork with the small diameter end up on the board and grasp the borer by the handle.

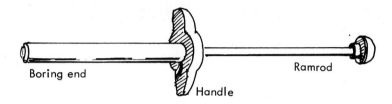

Boring end   Ramrod   Handle

Hold the cork tightly and with the other hand press the borer into the cork.

Press and turn the borer, keeping it perpendicular to the board.

When the borer has reached the bottom of the cork, pull and turn the borer back out of the cork.

Push the ramrod through the inside of the borer to remove the cork waste.

Replace the borer and ramrod in the proper position in the set and clean the table of any cork dust.

soldering

sst

Electrical and metal equipment is often used in the creative sciencing classroom. Soldering is needed to repair, use, or build equipment. It is a technique for permanently joining metal together. "Soft" solder is a mixture of lead and tin in varying proportions. Each mixture is labeled with suitable recommendations.

Look for the mixture suited for the job you propose to do. Solder is an alloy that, when heated to its melting point, flows into and around a preheated joint. As the alloy cools, it bonds the metal surfaces.

The entire art of soldering will not fit into these few pages, but we can hope, briefly, to whet your appetite for more information. Soldering is fun and useful. As the kingdom was lost for the want of a horse, so many a creative sciencing program has waned because some simple skill was not mastered. When you control some basic techniques, you will be able to go on to grander things. Soldering has many uses, but the greatest is to join wire together or to solder wire to a terminal. With proficiency in this skill alone, you can construct circuit boards, buzz boxes, jewelry, art forms.

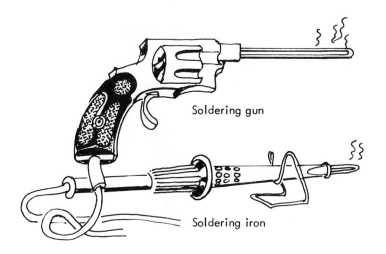

Soldering gun

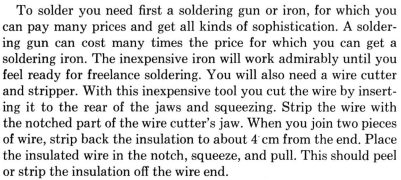

Soldering iron

To solder you need first a soldering gun or iron, for which you can pay many prices and get all kinds of sophistication. A soldering gun can cost many times the price for which you can get a soldering iron. The inexpensive iron will work admirably until you feel ready for freelance soldering. You will also need a wire cutter and stripper. With this inexpensive tool you cut the wire by inserting it to the rear of the jaws and squeezing. Strip the wire with the notched part of the wire cutter's jaw. When you join two pieces of wire, strip back the insulation to about 4 cm from the end. Place the insulated wire in the notch, squeeze, and pull. This should peel or strip the insulation off the wire end.

You will also need copper wire (such as ordinary household bell wire), fine sandpaper, soft solder, rosin flux, a brush, plus an area to work in. This work area should be able to take the dropping bits of hot lead and melting rosin flux.

Now we are ready to practice soldering. Cut and strip two pieces

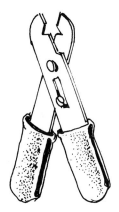

Wire cutter and stripper

of copper bell wire. Plug in the iron. Let it get hot. All surfaces of metal to be joined by solder must be clean and bright metal, free from dirt or oxidation. If your copper wire is dull, sand it lightly before attempting to solder. Dirt keeps the hot solder from flowing. Take the two bare ends of the wire and join them together, twisting as shown.

Overlap joint   Pigtail joint

Brush a light coat of flux onto the area being soldered to let the melted solder flow smoothly. Flux also removes tarnish and oxides, and prevents them from forming. Hold the point of the soldering iron on the twisted wire. Don't press; let the iron work for you. The contact of the iron with the copper wire will cause the flux to melt, bubble, and flow. When the flux has melted, place the solder on the copper wire next to the tip of the iron. When the solder melts, slide the solder and soldering iron along the bare twisted copper wire until all the wire is covered with solder. A little solder well distributed is better than isolated globs. Move the tip of the iron back along the soldered portion to remove such lumps. Do not move the copper wire after soldering until the solder is cold and hard.

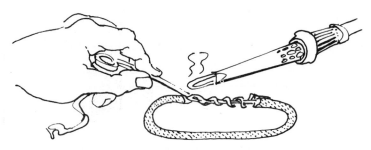

Putting solder on the heated wire

Periodically, a soldering iron must be retinned. Clean the tip with steel wool or sandpaper, coat it with rosin flux, and then coat the iron tip with solder. It is now ready to go again.

☐

how to use a portable electric drill

For this activity, you will need a portable electric drill with key and drill bit and a block of wood that can be clamped into place with either a vise or C-clamps.

The basic parts of an electric drill are shown in the figure. Bits are selected for the diameter and length of the hole needed and for the material being drilled. The drill bit fits into the chuck and is tightened with a chuck key. The most popular drill is the ¼ inch drill, so called because a drill of that diameter is the largest the chuck will hold. A one-speed drill is adequate for most uses.

here are safety precautions you should take when using an electric drill:

Ground the connection that gives the portable electric drill its power, to avoid getting a shock. Use a three-pronged outlet and plug. Double-insulated drills are recommended.

Disconnect the plug from the electric power outlet before you insert or change bits.

Do not use larger bits than the manufacturer recommends.

Fasten the bit *firmly* in the chuck before using it.

Keep the air-cooling vents on the drill housing free of dirt.

Tie *long* hair at the *back* of your head to avoid getting it tangled in the rotating drill bit.

Wear safety glasses or eyeglasses with plastic or hardened lenses.

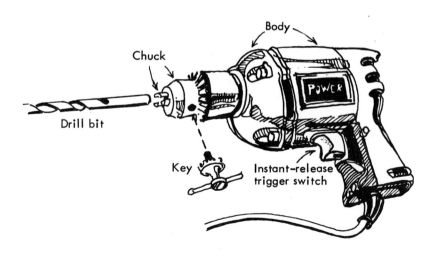

To drill a hole in wood, place your material to be drilled in a vise or clamp it to a table with C-clamps. If you cannot use a vise, put another board underneath your material so that you won't damage your work table. You will need to steady the material with your free hand.

Mark the center point for the hole with an awl or a nail to keep the bit from slipping. Connect the drill to an electrical outlet.

Put the bit point in this starting hole before you start the motor.

Make sure the bit is perpendicular to the material. Turn on the trigger switch and drill the hole.

Withdraw the bit from the hole with the motor running, then turn the drill off.

Place the drill on the table with the bit away from you.

Unplug the drill.

Notice: Drills make useful Christmas, anniversary, birthday, and wedding presents.

cutting wood with a jigsaw

For this activity, you will need a portable electric jigsaw with blade, C-clamps, and a sheet of wood.

A one- or two-speed jigsaw is adequate for most purposes. Jigsaw blades are made in tooth sizes and number of teeth per inch that are needed for specific cutting jobs in materials such as wood, metal, plastics, fiberglass, Formica, slate, or cardboard.

The basic parts of a jigsaw are shown in the illustration.

safety precautions for using a jigsaw include:

1. Make sure that you use a three-pronged outlet to ground the tool and keep from getting a shock. If you use an extension cord, make sure that it too is the three-pronged, grounded kind.
2. Disconnect the plug from the electric power outlet *before* you insert or change blades.

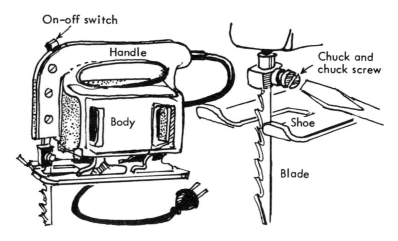

Parts of the jigsaw   Attaching the blade

3. Use the right blade for the job you are doing. The appropriate use is usually described on the package the blades come in.
4. Fasten the blade firmly in the chuck before starting the saw.
5. Keep the air-cooling vents on the saw housing free of dirt.
6. Tie long hair at the back of your head.
7. Wear safety glasses or eyeglasses with plastic or hardened lenses.

Before attaching the jigsaw blade, make sure that the saw is disconnected from the wall receptacle. Loosen the chuck screw or bolt with a screwdriver or wrench. Insert the blade into the chuck as far as it will go (usually about 1.5 cm). Tighten the screw or bolt until it is *firm* against the blade, as in the illustration.

To cut a piece of wood sheeting, such as plywood, be sure the board is firmly positioned and held to the table by the C-clamps. Hold the jigsaw by the handle and with the switch turn the saw on. *Don't* attempt to turn on the jigsaw when the blade is against the material to be cut; that might stall the motor. Place the front of the jigsaw shoe on the material to be cut and hold the shoe down firmly against the wood while cutting.

Remember *not to force* the tool; let the blade cut at its own speed. It is helpful to clamp or support the wood close to the line of cut. When you have finished cutting the wood, shut off the power and set the saw aside *before* loosening the work.

Notice: For the man or woman who has everything, a jigsaw may be just the right remembrance.

how to set up parallel and
series circuits

For this activity you will need at least two batteries (either 1½ volt dry cells or size D batteries), a wire cutter and stripper tool, about 120 cm of bell wire or similar electrical wire, at least two flashlight battery bulbs (numbers 41 and 48), and two bulb holders.

First let's go through the procedure of getting the light bulb to light. Place the bulb in the bulb holder (any type will do). Make sure that the bulb is screwed securely into the holder, with the bottom of the bulb touching the metal strip.

Cut wires 30 cm long and strip off 3 cm of insulation from both ends. Attach the wires as illustrated in the circuit diagram.

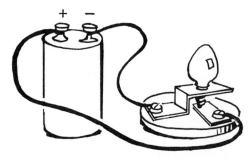

A complete circuit

If the bulb does *not* light, finding the explanation can be turned into an activity:

Investigate the variables in this system, including: the battery, wire, bulb, and bulb holder. What is the source of the problem?

Next, using two bulbs, two bulb holders, a dry cell, and wires, connect the circuit as shown on the next page.

Do both bulbs light?
Do they have equal brightness?
Unscrew bulb 1. What do you observe?
Screw back bulb 1. Unscrew bulb 2. Do you have any new observations?
Screw back bulb 2. Remove wire A. What do you observe?

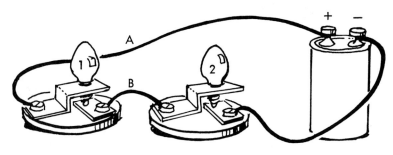

Bulbs in series

Connect wire A. What do you predict will happen if you remove wire B? Try it. Were you correct?

What conditions do you infer are necessary for all the bulbs to light?

To connect the bulbs in parallel, follow the circuit diagram.

Do both bulbs light?

Compare the observed brightness of the bulbs in the parallel circuit with the observed brightness of those in the series circuit.

Unscrew bulb 1. What do you observe?

Screw back bulb 1. Unscrew bulb 2. What additional observations can you make?

Screw back bulb 2. Remove wire A. What do you observe?

Replace wire A. Remove wire B. What do you observe after wire B has been removed?

What conditions do you infer are necessary for both bulbs to light?

When buying Christmas tree lights, do you prefer those hooked up in parallel or in series? Can you explain why you chose one over the other?

Should the lights in your home be connected in parallel or series?

What advantages would there be if your home were wired in series? Disadvantages?

Should the city streetlights be connected in parallel or series? Why?

Now, let's set up a parallel circuit with two dry cells or batteries and one light bulb.

Compare the brightness of the bulb in this circuit with that of other bulbs. What similarities and differences do you observe?

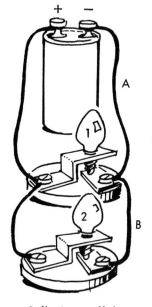

Bulbs in parallel

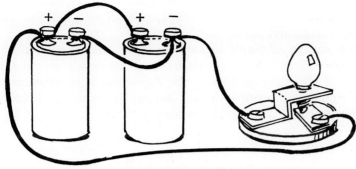
Batteries in parallel

To arrange the two batteries into a series circuit, follow this diagram:

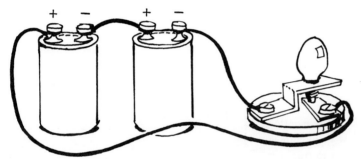
Batteries in series

Compare the brightness of the bulb in this circuit with bulbs in a series. Do you observe any similarities or differences?

Would you want the cells in your car battery connected in parallel or series? What would the advantages be? Disadvantages?

Check with an automotive store or garage to find out how car battery cells are connected.

Some cars run on batteries — are those connected in parallel or in series?

Spacecraft run on batteries and fuel cells. Would you predict that they are connected in series or parallel? Can you cite several advantages and disadvantages to support your choice?

more...

page 325

Try other combinations to satisfy your curiosity, such as: cells in series with bulbs in series; cells in parallel with bulbs in series; alternate cells and bulbs.

It is always advisable to have sufficient science equipment (if possible sufficient for each child), and inasmuch as individual pieces of electrical equipment are expensive, it is recommended that simple cardboard switches, battery holders, and light bulb holders be constructed by the children.

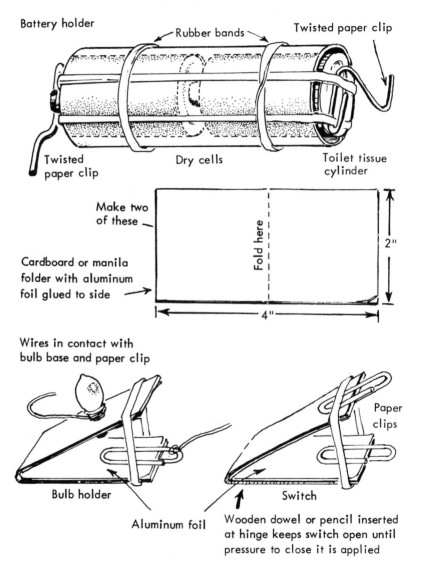

Related activities include bis 61, 68, 72.

science in a jar, or
a world of my own

Among all these interesting and thought-provoking science activities, few encompass as much sciencing as you will find in a terrarium. When you have assembled and sealed a terrarium, you have created a miniature world that illustrates the same laws as those of the world we live in.

The terrarium activity has unique advantages. It is individualized, each child having a miniature world that he or she has created and in which he or she controls the amount of light, heat, and water the terrarium receives. The child can elect to build a terrarium mimicking one of many ecosystems. Will it be a desert, a bog, a forest? Each captures a bit of the outside world and brings it into the classroom. Its existence, however, depends on its creator. How carefully were the plants selected? Is a cactus planted beside a violet plant? Does the soil and watering procedure suit the assemblage of plants? Children at first gather plants from field and woods randomly, trying to grow plants with very different requirements for light and water together. Some plants in the terrarium die but others flourish. This activity is best attempted in early fall or late spring, when plants and mosses are readily available outdoors.

To make your own terrarium, start with a large glass pickle or mayonnaise jar. With small children this much glass can be a problem, what with moving the container from place to place and eventually, as most children do, taking it home. Large plastic containers are sometimes available but are not as good because they usually are not clear. Also, plastic containers are not very rigid; they can, however, be used. Cut away a portion of the plastic container and glue or tape some clear plastic wrapping to the cutout portion. Be sure not to cut away too much material or you may weaken the support that the container offers.

A miniature terrarium can be assembled in a small, clear plastic lunch bag. To make this a successful substitute for a rigid container, it should be placed inside a small box. Roots of growing plants need to be firmly anchored in soil. Once growth has started, the pliable bag cannot be flexed or soil will be dislodged from the roots of the plants and stunt their growth.

Once you have a suitable jar, clean it thoroughly. It may rest horizontally or vertically. Put 3 cm of sand, crushed clay, pieces of broken flowerpots, vermiculite, or loose gravel in the bottom of the container to allow for drainage. Throughout the drainage material scatter bits of charcoal to sweeten the soil. Add good topsoil to fill the jar deep enough for the variety and the expected height of the plants you are planting in the terrarium. Place your plants deep enough in the soil for a good start. Do not overcrowd your plants. Later on, as necessary, thin them out or prune them. Sprinkle the soil with water but do not saturate your garden. For aesthetic value, add brightly colored stones. Complete the microcosm with a small piece of rotten log, which may add small insect inhabitants to your world. Some may want to sink a bottle cap or a clamshell into the soil and fill it with water. Cover the terrarium's opening with a clinging clear plastic wrap. You may need a rubber band to more effectively seal the wrap around the container. In one week, the plants should take hold and the sealed terrarium should maintain itself. Carbon dioxide for the plants comes from decaying organic matter in the soil. Oxygen given off by the plants may be used by small insects or be reabsorbed by the vegetable matter to continue decomposition. Water is cycled in much the same way. The plants take it from the soil and transpire it back into the air. It collects on the glass, running down and back into the soil. Everything recycles. If the balance is precise enough, the terrarium should survive even though sealed. Sometimes a little assistance, opening the seal once a day or once every two or three days, will help compensate for imbalances in water and air.

Plant several types of terraria. Contrast the growth and the different amounts of water, light, and heat the different ecosystems require.

Have the children place insects such as ants or worms in their terraria. Do they flourish equally well in all varieties?

Can the children identify the science concepts of balance or equilibrium, cycling and recycling of water and gases, as found in the terraria?

If the container is sealed and remains sealed, do the growing plants increase the mass of the complete terrarium?

Relate the variety of terraria to the social studies ideas of a community, environment, or habitat.

Related activities include bis 2, 26, 31, 55; ss 12; and sst 12.

☐

specific gravity and density

A characteristic property:

$$\frac{\text{Mass}}{\text{Volume}} = \text{Ratio}$$

A substance's characteristic property is determined by all the qualities of that substance, but not by the *quantity* of the substance examined.

In this activity you will measure the mass and volume of a substance and prepare a data table. You will need to use about ten volumes and masses for the data table.

A good substance to begin with is clay, because you can make different quantities, sizes, and shapes from the same substance. Prepare ten clay shapes of various sizes so that each can fit into a graduated cylinder.

First weigh each clay sample (number them to keep track) on a balance. Immerse the clay in a graduated cylinder that contains a *known* amount of water. Read the volume of the cylinder with the clay in it. The difference between the two readings is the volume of the clay.

Now prepare a data table like this:

DATA TABLE

Sample number	Mass, g	Volume, ml
1		
2		
3		
4		
5		
6		
7		
8		
9		
10		

After you have collected the data and completed the data table, prepare a graph of the data. Use the volume as the manipulated (independent) variable on the x axis and the mass as the responding (dependent) variable on the y axis.

Calculate the slope of the best line or curve drawn through your experimental points by using the change in y over the change in x, as shown on the next page.

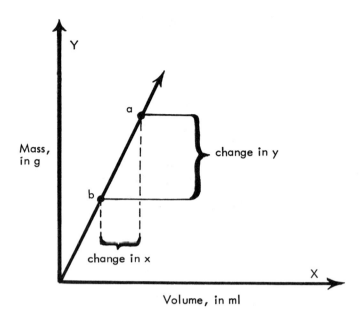

Volume, in ml

Your units will be in grams per milliliter, or g/ml. You have found the density for clay (drop the units and you can call it specific gravity). The accepted density for clay is 1.9 to 2.4 g/ml. How well did you do? You may wish to repeat this activity and see if you can improve your results.

What are your sources of error: accuracy in weighing, volume measurements, graphing data, or the size of clay spheres?

Other substances you may wish to try using this procedure are copper tubing (cut different sizes with a tube cutter), aluminum foil, tinfoil, nails, metal washers of different sizes, glass, limestone, and sandstone.

Another method to try is weighing the object in air and then weighing it immersed in water.

Subtract the mass of the object in water from its air mass; then divide the difference by the air mass. A piece of copper weighs 880 g in air and 780 g in water. Its loss of weight is then 100 g, and this is the weight of the water displaced. The specific gravity of copper then is $880/100 = 8.8$.

remember: specific gravity has no units but density does — g/ml

Try finding the density or specific gravity of objects that *float* in water, such as cork, paraffin, balsa wood, and ice.

Try liquids such as milk, alcohol, olive oil, and glycerine.

Related activities include bis 29, 41, and 48.

preserving flowers by dehydration

Preserving flowers has many uses. Preserved, flowers can be collected as representative of their species in a herbarium. They can be used to polish children's skill at observing and classifying. They are useful too as an art project that could grow into a take-home gift for Mother's Day. Dehydration can be related to food processing and to human existence.

Live flowers preserved retain their natural color, shape, and softness. To do it you need very fine, sifted, sterilized sand, preferably white sand from local pet shops. Freshwater beach sand should be sifted well and placed in an oven for a half hour at 375°F to sterilize it. Allow the sand to cool before using it.

In selecting flowers to preserve, pick them at the peak of their blooming, before they begin to show signs of wilting. Then be sure they are thoroughly dry before starting to dehydrate them. Cut the flowers so that you have at least two or three inches of stem.

Place the flowers on a 2 cm layer of sand in a container. Be sure the petals touch neither the side of the container nor each other. Sift or slowly pour sand over the flowers until they are completely covered. Add a little more sand to be sure the flowers are insulated all over so that no direct heat can come in contact with them. Place the sand-covered flowers in the oven of a gas range with only the heat from the pilot light for twelve hours. If a gas range is not available, put them in a dry place for two weeks at room temperature: a closet or a shelf in an unused room. Another way is to bring the container outdoors in the sun, where two sunny days should dry them. Avoid getting them wet.

After applying heat, cool the container slowly at room temperature for four to six hours. When cooled, pour off the sand slowly and remove the flowers. The stems should be stiff and sturdy, and the flowers vivid and soft with a windblown look. The flowers thus preserved may be used indefinitely for reference. They will store well in boxes with lids. Drying them is fun and gives a good finished product.

Related activities include bis 2, 26, 55; ss 12; and sst 10.

☐

making crystal models

The idea of symmetry is introduced in primary grades and is used through much of a student's years in school. It is useful in mathematics, science, art, and many other subjects. A study of crystals is a natural introduction to symmetry. Crystals are classified by their symmetry into six "crystal systems." Six outlines are provided for your use, to be cut out and traced on manila folders. The short dashed lines are the folds for the tabs, which form a surface onto which you can later glue the corresponding sides. The long dashed lines are fold lines necessary for constructing the three-dimensional figures. Cut out your manila folder tracings. Crease and fold at both the short dashed and the long dashed lines; then tape or glue your model together.

These models give you something to point to when you discuss planes, surface area, volume, axes of symmetry, planes of symmetry, and angles. If each or several members of the class makes similar models, you can try stacking similar (and dissimilar) crystals to get at the idea of bonding, cleavage planes, or simply to discuss stacking, surface area, and how the new configuration increases or decreases volume. These models also make fine mobiles.

Here are some brief descriptions of the six crystal systems.

Cubic

In cubic crystals all sides are equal and all angles are right angles. All three axes are of equal lengths.

Tetragonal

The tetragonal crystal has two sides of different lengths and all right angles. The three axes intersect at 90° angles. The two horizontal axes are of unequal lengths. The vertical axis is not equal to the horizontal axis.

Orthorhombic

Orthorhombic crystals have three sides of different lengths and all right angles. The three axes are of different lengths, all intersecting at 90° angles.

Hexagonal

A hexagonal solid has right angles only between its vertical sides and its top and basal (bottom) faces. The hexagonal system has four axes. The three horizontal axes intersect, forming 60° angles. The vertical axis intersects these three horizontal axes at 90° angles and is not equal in length to the horizontal axis.

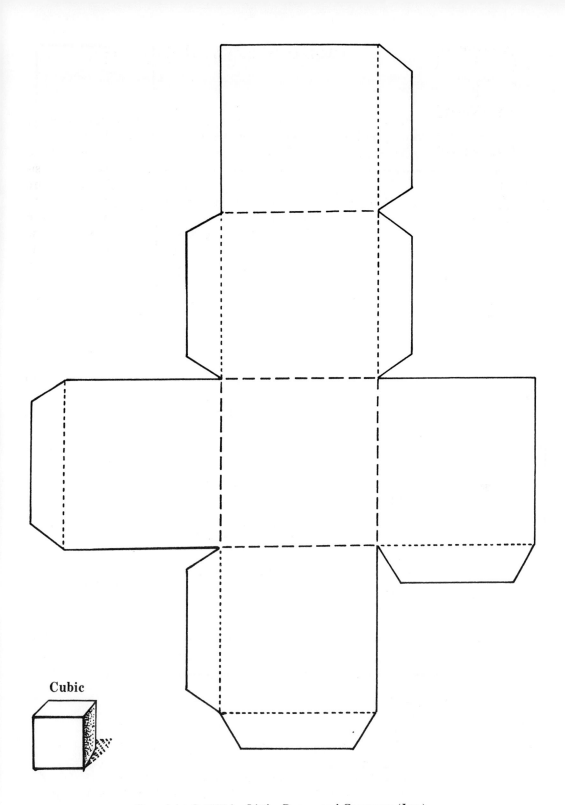

Cubic

Tetragonal

Orthorhombic

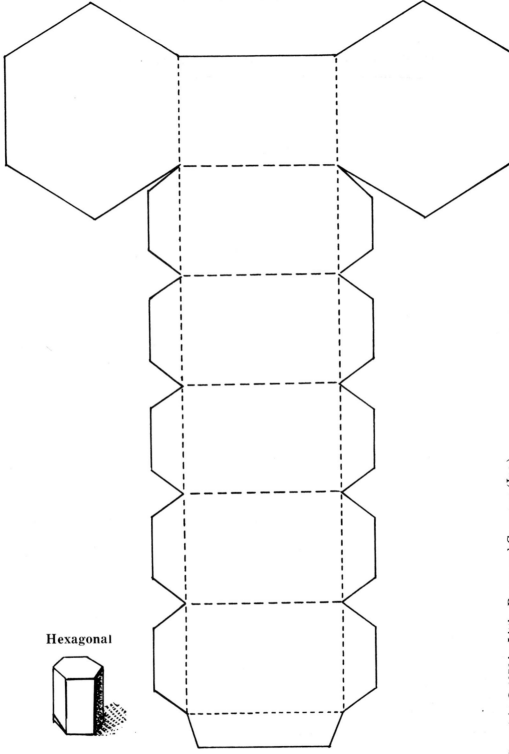

Hexagonal

Monoclinic

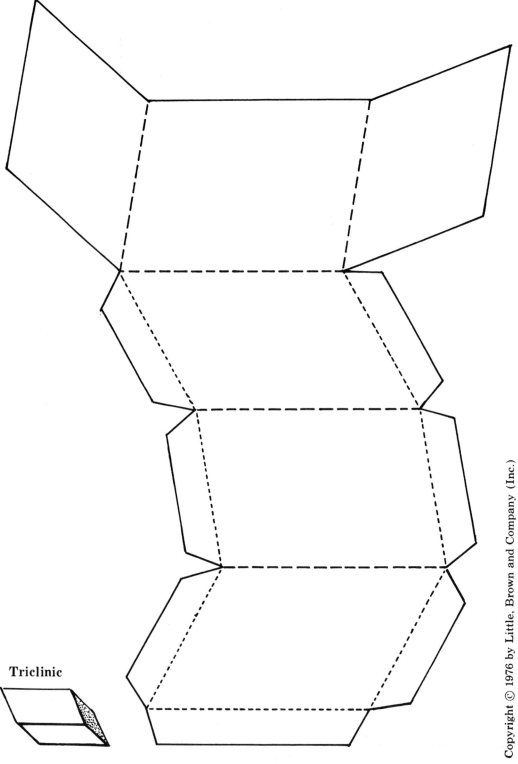

Triclinic

Monoclinic

Think of an orthorhombic solid distorted so that eight of its angles are no longer right angles (three different lengths of sides), and you have a monoclinic model. The system has three axes, two of them intersecting at 90° angles and the third oblique to these.

Triclinic

The best way of representing this crystal is to think of a monoclinic solid distorted so that all three axes are oblique to one another at the point of intersection and are of unequal length.

Related activities include bis 4, 26, 66; ss 3, 6, and 14.

☐

paper making

Elaborate equipment is not necessary for paper making, but a little patience is. You will need these materials: starch, a basin, tissue paper, water, an electric iron, blotting paper, some aluminum or copper screen, pans, a measuring cup, tablespoon, rolling pin, eggbeater, some food coloring, and several samples of paper.

Tear thirty white facial tissue papers into small pieces. Place this material in a basin. Pour in starch and additional water to make about two quarts (you will want to experiment with the amount of starch). Beat this mixture until thoroughly mixed. Then pour the mixture into a flat, shallow pan with wire screen cut to fit on the bottom of the pan. Fold up the screen at both ends of the pan so that it can be lifted out of the pan. Paddle the mixture in the pan back and forth over the screen. Avoid letting the solid material collect in one spot. Slowly lift out the screen on which the pulp has collected, and holding it over the pan, clean off the excess pulp; you want uniformity. Allow the liquid to drip back into the pan. Dry the screen and wet sheet of pulp between two pieces of blotting paper. The pulp will adhere to the blotter sheet. Remove the screen and replace the blotter. Press out excess water with a rolling pin. Finally, iron-dry (not too hot) the pulp sheet between the blotters. Trim the edges with scissors. Peel off the blotters. You now have a sheet of handmade paper.

Which tissue paper works best? What other materials might successfully be used in place of tissue? Paper is made from small fibers bonded together. The starch acts as a glue in bonding together the fibers. How could you make the paper stronger? Would warm water improve the end product?

Can you make various thicknesses of pulp?

Can you make colored paper from colored paper tissues?

What effect does food coloring have on the finished product?

Is flour a glue? Will it work as well as starch?

Why are paper-making factories located where they are?

How can one recycle paper?

Related activities include ss 16.

☐

creative sciencing recipes □ csr

every recipe you've always wanted but couldn't locate

Creative sciencing recipes are designed to provide you with sources of basic materials such as paints, inks, dyes, pastes, clays, papier-mâché, modeling materials, and nature recipes; and with instructions for manufacturing gases, making a stethoscope, constructing a manometer, preparing a bubble solution, and making your own slides. The recipes are not technical; they are easy to prepare and call for inexpensive ingredients that are readily obtained. We have purposely avoided lengthy applications statements, since all these recipes have a variety of uses. The limitations for their use will be dictated by your individual needs. Most of the recipes can be prepared by children, but a few should be made only by the teacher as indicated by the cautions.

We now present the recipes for creative sciencing!

powder paint

5 tablespoons powder paint
5 tablespoons water

Put powder paint and water in an empty and washed school milk carton. Press the lid down firmly and shake the carton until the paint is thoroughly mixed. To make the paint keep better and go on more smoothly, add enough liquid starch or detergent to give it the consistency of cream or of poster paints.

For larger quantities

8 tablespoons powder paint
1 teaspoon white library paste
2 tablespoons liquid starch

Add enough water to give the mixture a consistency of cream or of poster paints. To prevent a sour smell, add a little oil of cloves, wintergreen, or peppermint.

WATERCOLOR

For a transparent watercolor, add sufficient water to the powder paint to obtain a runny consistency. For an opaque watercolor, add enough water or liquid starch to the powder paint to make a creamy consistency.

COLORED INK

Mix enough water with the powder paint to allow it to flow easily from a lettering pen or mechanical drawing tool.

OIL PAINT

Mix 2 tablespoons of powder paint with water to allow it to flow easily from a brush, lettering pen or mechanical drawing tool.

Add a few drops of glycerine and powder paint to raw linseed oil to make a thick cream consistency. Use zinc oxide with linseed oil for a white oil paint.

Add boiled linseed oil to powder paint and stir well.

Add powder paint to liquid paste. Use a stiff brush.

ENAMEL

Add clear shellac, lacquer, or varnish to the powder paint until a desired brushing consistency is reached.

WOOD STAIN

Mix powder paint with linseed oil or turpentine until a brushing consistency is reached. To make a waterproof lacquer, mix powder paint with a gloss oil. Rub crayons on the wood to be stained with the grain. Then rub the wood vigorously with a cloth saturated in linseed oil.

finger paints

CORNSTARCH FINGER PAINT

½ cup cornstarch
1 quart boiling water

Dissolve the starch in a small amount of cold water and gradually add the hot water. Cook until clear. To keep the paint made in this and other recipes from drying, add 2 tablespoonfuls of glycerine. Add oil of cloves or wintergreen to keep the paint from souring. For color, use poster paint, India ink, or powdered tempera mixed with water to the consistency of a smooth paste.

LIQUID STARCH FINGER PAINT

Pour a tablespoon of liquid starch in the center of a sheet of dampened paper. Add a small amount of colored powder paint. Shaker cans or saltshakers are convenient to use. Work the powder paint and starch together. Spread the combination over the paper with your hand.

LAUNDRY STARCH FINGER PAINT

2 quarts boiling water
1 cup soap flakes
1 cup laundry starch
½ cup talcum powder

Dilute the starch in a cupful of cold water. Add the boiling water slowly, stirring constantly to avoid lumping. Stir in the soap flakes and talcum powder. This will make about 5 pints. The soap flakes added to the paint act as a binder. The paint made from this recipe can be used to finger paint on glass or over a heavy coat of crayons.

FLOUR FINGER PAINT

2 cups flour
1 cup sugar
1 cup cornstarch

Mix the ingredients in cold water to a thick, heavy paste. Pour on enough boiling water to make a thick, heavy starch, stirring constantly until clear.

CHALK FINGER PAINT

colored chalk
water
school paste
oil of cloves

Use finely ground colored chalk. Leftover ends of chalk are good, mixed with water, school paste, and 2 drops of oil of cloves. The result will be a paint with an interesting texture.

printing inks

OIL BASE PRINTING INK

2 quarts powder paint
1 part linseed oil
1 part varnish

Mix the ingredients to the consistency of a smooth paste. This paint spreads on evenly but will not dry quickly. It is good for a paper with a rough-textured surface.

VARNISH BASE PRINTING INK

3 parts powder paint
1 part varnish

Mix the powder paint and varnish with a palette knife on glass. Use a brayer, or printing roller, to roll the mixture back and forth until it is tacky before applying it to the block to be printed. This ink will dry more quickly than the oil base ink and is suitable to use on nonabsorbent, smooth finish paper. (The ink can be thinned with denatured alcohol.)

bleaching and dyeing

BLEACHING FLOUR AND SUGAR SACKS

chloride of lime
water
5% sulfuric acid
carbonate of soda

Make a strong solution of water and chloride of lime (bleaching powder). Allow it to settle, and draw off the clear liquid. Rinse the sacks to be bleached in clean water mixed with the 5% sulfuric acid, and then pull the sacks slowly through the bleaching solution.

*acid should be added to water;
never add water to acid!*

Rinse them well in water containing a little carbonate of soda. If any color remains, allow the fabric to stay a short time in the sulfuric acid solution. Be sure to rinse well.

Soak the sacks in tepid water. Wash them well with naphtha soap, roll them tightly, and dampen them with kerosene. Allow them to stand overnight. Then wash out and boil the sacks with a bleaching powder or naphtha soap. If the color remains, the process should be repeated.

Use a commercial bleach, following directions carefully.

MAKING NATURAL DYES

Collect plants, moss, herbs, roots, nuts, berries, and so on. Chop a quantity of one of these materials, and put it through a meat grinder. Cover the ground material with water, and allow it to stand overnight. Drain off the water the next morning and save it. Add a little more water to the pulp and simmer for 30 minutes.

After allowing the pulp to simmer 30 minutes, drain off the water and add it to the water drained from the ground material. Add more water to cover the fabric if necessary.

DYEING THE MATERIAL

Rinse the dried fabric in hot water, wring it well, and then place it in the dye, making sure it is well covered.

Bring the dye to a simmering stage and cook until the fabric is as deep in color as you wish. Rinse the fabric in lukewarm water. Squeeze lightly, but do not wring. Avoid direct rays of sunlight while drying.

□

silk screen paints

TEMPERA SILK SCREEN PAINT

tempera paint
soap flakes
water

Add a small quantity of soap flakes to the tempera to give it viscosity and to deter drying. Add water only if necessary. If the paint is too thick, it will clog the screen. If too thin, it will run. Finger paint of a creamy consistency can be used instead of tempera.

LIQUID STARCH SILK SCREEN PAINT

liquid starch
powder paint

Add liquid starch to powder paint and mix until it is the consistency of light paste.

☐

pastes

BOILED FLOUR PASTE

½ cup flour
water

Add enough water to the flour to make a thin paste. Boil the paste for 5 minutes over a slow fire, stirring constantly. Cool and thin with water. Add a few drops of wintergreen or peppermint to keep the paste from spoiling. Keep it in a covered jar, and use it in any projects requiring large quantities of paste.

CORNSTARCH PASTE

2 tablespoons cornstarch
water

Add enough cold water to the cornstarch to make a smooth paste. Add boiling water until the mixture turns clear. Cook until it thickens, and then remove it from the fire. This paste becomes thicker as it cools. It may be thinned with water. Use cornstarch paste on tissue paper or thin cloth, since it is less likely to show than flour paste.

WALLPAPER PASTE

1 cup wallpaper paste
water

Mix the wallpaper paste with water until the desired consistency is reached. Add a few drops of wintergreen, peppermint, or salicylic acid to keep the paste from souring. Store it in a jar.

BOOKMAKER'S PASTE

1 teaspoon flour
2 teaspoons cornstarch
$\frac{1}{4}$ teaspoon powdered alum
water

Mix the first three ingredients together. Add 6 tablespoons of water slowly, stirring until smooth. Cook the mixture over a low flame, preferably in a double boiler. Stir constantly until the paste is thickened. Keep it in airtight jars, and thin with water when necessary. Use this paste to make notebooks and in bookmaking projects.

BOOK PASTE

library paste
water

Thin ordinary library paste with hot water to the consistency of very thick cream. This paste is excellent for mending books.

ADHESIVE PASTE

Mix equal parts of paste and glue. Use the adhesive paste when pasting objects too heavy to be held securely with regular paste on thick cardboard.

LAMINATING PASTE

Mix equal parts of glue and water. Use this paste to brush between the sheets when laminating paper with cellophane or other shiny surfaces.

□

adhesion tips

For mounting	Paper or cloth on paper	Use rubber cement, school paste, flour paste, glue stick or dispenser
	Paper on glass	Use rubber cement
For hanging	Paper on painted walls, brick or cement, wood, wallpaper, chalkboard	Use adhesive circles, double-faced tape, masking tape, adhesive dough
For cementing	Cardboard to cardboard	Use rubber cement
	Ceramic pieces	Use white glue, colorless cement
	Metal to metal	Use household cement, solder

clay

SELF-HARDENING CLAY

This clay hardens in drying and requires no baking. It can be bought commercially in craft stores or supply houses. It is practical to use when you have no kiln or where you do not wish to fire young children's work. To make your own, add 1 part dextrin to 19 parts clay flour.

Dextrin added to clay will harden the pieces so they will be substantial enough to last without firing. Be sure to use dextrin made from yellow corn. (The white dextrin is not satisfactory.)

Dextrin may also be worked into wet clay. Use a teaspoonful of dextrin to a pound of wet clay. Objects made from this clay may be painted when dry.

Inexpensive substitutes for clay:

CREPE CLAY

1 sheet crepe paper (any color)
1 tablespoon salt
1 cup flour
water

Mix the salt and flour. Cut the crepe paper into tiny pieces (confetti size). Place the pieces in a large bowl, and add only enough water to cover the paper. Allow the mixture to soak for 15 minutes and pour off the excess water. Add enough of the flour-salt mixture to make a stiff dough. Knead it well until it is blended with the crepe paper.

FLOUR CLAY

1 cup flour
1 cup salt
1 rounded teaspoon powdered alum

CORNSTARCH CLAY

½ cup cornstarch
1 cup salt
1 cup boiling water

Add water slowly to the ingredients for *flour clay* and knead until a claylike consistency is reached. Boil the ingredients for the *cornstarch clay* to a soft-ball stage and knead on wax paper until malleable.

Wrap the clay you mixed in a wet cloth and keep for a few days. Either clay may be handled exactly like regular clay. The substitute clay may be pressed on maps to show relief, and when dry, it can be painted. It retains its shape without crumbling. For color, add powder paint to the water when mixing.

MAGNESITE MODELING CLAY

Mix magnesite, a building material, with enough magnesium chloride to produce a doughlike consistency. Use a rolling pin to flatten it like clay. Work with the magnesite dough on wax paper and leave it there to dry. Use it like clay to make beads and tiles. If the dough gets too sticky, dip the modeling tool you're using into water. (Tongue depressors and old table knives make good modeling tools.) Color with powder paint; varnish or rub with linseed oil when dry.

papier mâché

BASIC PULP

Tear newspapers, paper plates, or egg cartons into fine bits. Cover the paper bits with water and soak for 24 hours in a non-rusting container. Put the mixture in a cloth bag, and squeeze it to get rid of excess water. Work on a wax paper surface so water will not damage the table or desk. Add *one* of the following for each quart of pulp:

6 tablespoons flour
6 tablespoons of dry laundry starch or 1 cup of cooked (starch paste will not sour as readily as flour paste)
1 cup liquid starch
1 cup thin library paste
1 cup wheat (wallpaper) paste mixed to consistency of cream
1 cup boiled flour paste (see csr 6)

A few drops of wintergreen or oil of cloves will help to keep the pulp from souring. A little salt added to the mixture will prevent fermentation. Knead the pulp to the consistency of soft modeling clay. Drying may take as long as a week.

QUICK-DRYING AND MODELING PULP

4 cups papier mâché pulp
1 cup plaster of paris
½ teaspoon commercial glue

Combine the ingredients and knead to the consistency of heavy dough. It will dry in from 3 to 6 hours.

For greater tensile strength, make modeling pulp by adding one cup of plaster of paris to one gallon of any papier mâché pulp. Mix thoroughly. This pulp is suitable for modeling fruits, vegetables, toys, animals, and so on.

☐

sawdust modeling

SAWDUST 1

2 cups sawdust (clean and fine)
1 cup flour
1 tablespoon glue
hot water or liquid starch

Mix the sawdust, flour, and glue, and moisten with water or starch until a modeling consistency is reached. If this sawdust mix is used to make ornaments, strings or wires should be put in place while they are being modeled. After drying, the ornaments may be painted.

SAWDUST 2

sawdust
wallpaper paste
water

Mix equal parts of the ingredients. If the mixture is sticky, add more sawdust.

SAWDUST 3

3 cups sawdust
1 cup wheat paste
water

Add enough water to mix the ingredients. Do not make the mixture too stiff.

SAWDUST 4

1 cup sawdust
1 cup plaster of paris
thin glue

Mix the ingredients. Add enough glue to hold the mixture together.

SAWDUST 5

2 cups sawdust
1 cup plaster of paris
½ cup wheat (or wallpaper) paste
2 cups water

Mix the ingredients. Add water gradually until a modeling consistency is reached. This sawdust mix is excellent for making puppet heads, fruits, vegetables, masks, figures, and animals.

SAWDUST 6

1 cup sawdust
water

Add enough water to mix the sawdust into a pliable pulp. The mixture will appear pebbled.

SAWDUST 7

1 cup flour
1 quart water
1 teaspoon alum
1 teaspoon oil of cloves
sawdust

Cook the flour and water until a creamy stage is reached. Add alum. Remove the liquid from the stove and add cloves. Stir in enough sawdust to make a modeling consistency. Sawdust 7 may be painted with powder paints or other coloring media when dry.

TEXTURE SAWDUST

sawdust
powder paint
water

Mix powder paint with water to a thin, creamy consistency. Pour the liquid over sawdust, stir well, and spread on a newspaper to dry. Use this sawdust mix to sprinkle on a glued surface for a textured effect.

SAWDUST MIX FOR RELIEF MAPS

Add a teaspoon of commercial glue to any of the sawdust recipes to increase the adhesive quality of the sawdust mix when applying it to a wooden surface.

dough modeling

DOUGH 1

2 cups flour
2 cups salt
water

Mix the flour and salt. Add enough water to make a creamy consistency. Powder paint or other coloring may be added, or the dough may be painted after it is dry. This dough is excellent for relief maps. Build the elevations in layers, allowing each to dry before adding another.

DOUGH 2

½ cup soft breadcrumbs
½ cup flour
½ teaspoon powdered alum
beaten egg white

Mix all the ingredients together and color with powder paint or watercolors.

DOUGH 3

1 cup flour
½ cup salt
3 teaspoons powdered alum
water

Add enough water to the other ingredients to make a proper consistency.

DOUGH 4

½ cup table salt
½ cup cornstarch
¼ cup water

Mix the ingredients thoroughly and cook the mixture over low heat, stirring constantly until it stiffens into a lump. Use the dough as soon as it is cool enough to handle.

DOUGH 5

1 cup cornstarch
1 cup salt
1 cup cold water

Mix the ingredients, and cook the mixture over low heat. Cool it and allow it to set until it does not stick to the fingers. A few drops of food coloring or powder paint may be added to the mixture for color.

This dough may be cut with cookie cutters or pressed into a butter mold. Holes for hanging may be punched with a toothpick before the material is dry. Glitter, sequins, or feathers may be pressed into the damp dough.

□

plaster and paraffin modeling

PLASTER

Any container may be used for mixing plaster of paris. Wax cartons are preferable, as they may be discarded. Plastic bowls and enamelware are quite easy to clean, but aluminumware should not be used.

do not mix plaster in the sink;
the plaster will lodge in the drain pipes
and clog the drain

Pour the amount of water needed into the container. A mold full of water is a good measurement. Use about half that amount of plaster (with powder paint added if you wish to tint it). Add plaster without stirring, as long as it continues to sink. When a mound of plaster forms and remains above the water, enough has been added. Stir it with the hands and press out any lumps. Use the plaster immediately.

It is safer to test a small amount of plaster for drying before beginning a project. It may dry fast, slow, or, if old, it may not dry at all. There are three grades of plaster. One will dry within 20 minutes, one within 40 minutes, and one within an hour and a half. If a plaster of paris mold doesn't dry as fast as it should, sprinkle it with cornstarch or talcum powder. This will facilitate drying.

PLASTER OF PARIS

Pour the approximate amount of water needed for a mold into a container (1 quart of water to 4 cups of plaster of paris is a good proportion to use). Add plaster of paris until a small mound stays on the surface of the water, and then stir until it thickens. Pour the thickened plaster into a mold, form, or box of the size desired for carving. Use forms or molds of cardboard, heavy paper, clay, or any other medium which will hold the plaster firm until it sets. The form or box should be a little larger than the size of the finished carving. After the plaster has set, it can be removed from the form. Even though still wet, it is ready for carving. It will stay damp for several days or can be resoaked in water and then carved or shaped with tools.

PLASTER AND PACKING EXCELSIOR

Mix 1 part plaster with 1 part excelsior. Gradually add enough water to achieve a modeling consistency. This mixture may be used for modeling directly on an armature. Suggestion: Make distinctive Easter baskets.

PLASTER AND CLEANSING TISSUE

If the tissues used are two-ply, separate them into single sheets. Tear the sheets into small pieces (about the size of a dime). Mix them with spackle plaster for a direct modeling medium.

PLASTER AND COFFEE GROUNDS

Gradually mix 1 part plaster with 1 part coffee grounds. Add water until the mixture acquires the consistency of heavy gravy. The mixture is quite porous.

PARAFFIN

Melt paraffin in a pan placed in very hot water —

never directly over the fire!

Pour the melted paraffin into another container. When it has solidified somewhat but is still soft, model it as you would any other plastic material. The warmth of your hands will keep it soft, especially if you dip your hands in warm water from time to time. If color is wanted, shave a little wax crayon into the paraffin while it is melting. A marbleized effect is brought about by adding the wax crayon shavings after the paraffin is melted. Crushed colored chalk may also be added. When the object is molded, dip it in cold water to harden. Polish the paraffin by rubbing it with a cotton cloth.

zonalite, magnesite, and gesso

ZONALITE MIXTURE 1

4 parts coarse zonalite (a building material)
2 parts sand

2 parts cement
water

Mix the ingredients and pour the mixture into a wax carton. Allow three days for drying. Peel the carton away and carve the zonalite mixture with a coping saw, nail, or tongue depressor. Paint it with varnish or shellac.

ZONALITE MIXTURE 2

1 part dry zonalite
3 parts vermiculite
water

Add water gradually until the mixture looks like a cooked cereal. Pour the mixture into a box or form, and allow it to dry for one week. Then carve.

page 358

MAGNESITE MATERIAL

1 part magnesite (a building material)
1 part magnesium chloride

Mix the ingredients to a consistency of dough. Use a rolling pin and work the dough like clay. Dry it on wax paper. Use wire or nails for carving tools.

GESSO 1

10 teaspoons whiting (precipi-
tated chalk)
6 teaspoons glue

4 teaspoons boiled linseed oil
water to make a thick cream
1 teaspoon varnish

The whiting can be purchased at most hardware stores. Mix the ingredients, and

caution! for teachers only

boil the mixture for 10 minutes in a double boiler until it looks like thick cream. Color the gesso by adding powder paint.

GESSO 2

3 envelopes Knox gelatine
3 or more handfuls whiting
16 ounces cold water

Combine the gelatine and water in the top of a double boiler, and let them soak for 10 minutes. Place the top pan over the bottom of the double boiler, and heat until the mixture becomes liquid. Add whiting. Mix with a brush and strain through cheesecloth.

Gesso is especially good for making relief designs. Powder paint or metallic powder will color it. Gesso can also be molded and, when dry, carved with the fingernail or a pencil.

□

nature recipes

DRYING PLANTS FOR WINTER BOUQUETS

Strip the leaves from fresh flowers immediately. Tie the flowers by their stems with string, and hang them with the heads down in a cool, dry place away from the light. Darkness is essential for preserving their color. Thorough drying takes about two weeks.

PRESERVING FALL LEAVES

Place alternate layers of powdered borax and leaves in a box. The leaves must be completely covered. Allow them to stand for four days. Shake off the borax and wipe each leaf with liquid floor wax. Rub a warm iron over a cake of paraffin. Then press the iron over front and back of the leaves.

PRESERVING MAGNOLIA LEAVES

Mix two parts of water with one part of glycerine. Place stems with the magnolia leaves in the mixture, and let them stand for several days. The leaves will turn brown and will last many years. Their surfaces may be painted or sprayed with silver or gold paint.

CATTAILS

Use cattails in their natural color or tint them by shaking metallic powders over them. Handle them carefully. Cattails are dry and fall apart easily.

TREATING GOURDS

Soak some gourds in water for two hours. Scrape them clean with a knife. Rub them with fine sandpaper, and cut an opening to remove the seeds while the gourds are still damp.

PRESSING WILD FLOWERS

When gathering plant specimens, include the roots, leaves, flowers, and seed pods. Place them between newspapers, laying two blotters under the newspaper and two blotters on top to absorb the moisture. Place all the layers between two sheets of corrugated cardboard and press. Change the newspapers three times during the week. It usually takes seven to ten days to press plant specimens. Cardboard covered with cotton batting makes a good mounting base. Lay each specimen on the cotton and cover with cellophane or plastic wrap to preserve the color.

WAX MIXTURE

4 pounds paraffin
4 ounces spermaceti
half a plumber's candle
flowers

Melt the ingredients over slow heat in a deep container (a two-pound coffee can, for instance) to a temperature of 130°F. To determine the temperature, use a candy thermometer, or dip a piece of crepe paper in the liquid, removing it immediately. If the paper shrivels, the wax is too hot; if it is covered with a thin coating of wax, the temperature is just right.

for safety's sake,
the teacher should handle this procedure

Also, the teacher must insist that children dip their flowers in the wax only when an adult is standing by to supervise.

INDIAN COLOR DYES

Seed pods, bark, leaves, and roots contain coloring that can be made into attractive dyes. Collect and process them, following the directions under the headings "Making Natural Dyes" and "Dyeing the Material" in csr 4. You can get the following colors by processing one of the materials listed below. With some experimenting, you may be able to process other natural materials to get colors or combine some for new and unusual effects.

brown — walnut shells
red brown — onion leaves, bark
purple — blueberries, elderberries, grapes
yellow — mustard, sumac, peach leaves, moss
red — root and berry of the cactus
black — oak bark, gum of the piñon tree

☐

manufacturing oxygen (O₂)

Pour an inch of hydrogen peroxide in a test tube, and add a small amount of manganese dioxide. Shake slightly and notice the reaction taking place. Insert a glowing splint and observe what happens. Notice that, here, no attempt is made to collect the oxygen. How would you modify this procedure if you wanted to collect some oxygen? See bis 47.

□

manufacturing carbon dioxide (CO₂)

See bis 47 before reading on. Afterwards, fill a collecting bottle with water and place it in a pan. Pour baking soda in the flask, and when all preparations are made, add vinegar. The tube should be inserted into the water-filled collecting bottle. When the CO_2 has been collected, place a glass plate over the mouth of the bottle and remove it from the pan.

be careful! remember any gas built up
in a closed system is a potential danger

Should the bottle be placed on the table right side up or upside down? Why? How do you know you have collected carbon dioxide? How would you go about proving it?

□

make a stethoscope

small funnel
T-tube or Y-tube
rubber tubing

Slip a piece of rubber tubing 7 or 8 cm long over the tip of the funnel. Insert the T-tube (or Y-tube) into the other end of a short piece of the rubber tubing. Attach longer pieces of tubing to

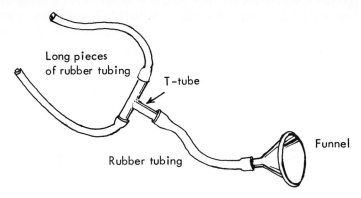

Long pieces
of rubber tubing

T-tube

Rubber tubing

Funnel

both arms of the T-tube. To use the stethoscope, have one student hold the funnel firmly over his or her heart, while another listens to the heartbeat through the long tube.

an instrument
to observe heartbeats

manometer tube	thistle tube
colored water	wooden base
plastic tube	masking tape

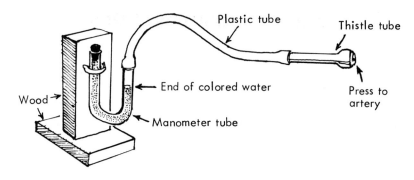

Plastic tube

Thistle tube

End of colored water

Wood

Press to artery

Manometer tube

Attach the manometer tube to the wooden base by using masking or other heavy tape. Fill the tube half-full with colored water. Attach one end of a plastic tube to the manometer. Attach the other end of a plastic tube to the thistle tube. See the diagram. Find the carotid artery in the neck, alongside the windpipe. Press the thistle tube against the region of the carotid artery. The column of water in the manometer tube should pulsate with each heartbeat.

make a bubble solution

4 liters tap water
240 milliliters liquid soap detergent
1 4-liter container
wire bubble blowers
container for each student

Pour the soap into the water and stir gently to mix the two ingredients. Then invite the students to make bubbles.

make your own slides

Select a picture from a magazine.

Cut out the viewfinder, place it on the image selected, and draw a pencil line around the image.

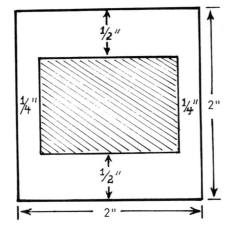

Viewfinder

Using scissors, cut out the image just outside the guidelines. You should have a 2 x 2 inch square.

Take a piece of clear contact paper and peel off the paper backing. Keep the backing for burnishing purposes.

Press the printed surface of your picture onto the sticky side of the contact paper.

Burnish the photograph carefully, image side up. For added protection, place the paper backing on the photograph before you rub.

Soak in water for 2 minutes. Then peel away the paper that the image was printed on.

Sponge away the milky residue and rinse the film well.

Center the image, and press the sticky side of the wet film onto a slide mount.

Dry the mounted image and trim off the excess plastic.

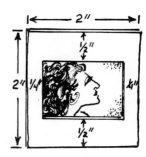

Viewfinder

Area	Reading and language arts		Math		Social studies		Art		Music	
Total number of bis activities	28		37		22		16		2	
Activity number	5	73	2	79	12	71	32	114	99	105
	6	81	10	82	33	73	37	115		
	24	83	11	83	38	88	38	117		
	25	85	22	86	53	89	73	118		
	28	88	29	87	56	98	83	119		
	35	92	37	94	57	101	105	124		
	44	98	39	97	63	110	112	126		
	46	101	40	100	64	116	113	127		
	52	110	43	101	67	120				
	53	113	53	103	69	123				
	57	116	54	104	70	128				
	63	124	55	105						
	69	126	57	106						
	71	127	58	109						
			61	118						
			62	121						
			67	123						
			71	128						
			77							

TABLE 1 □ CELSIUS TO FAHRENHEIT CONVERSION TABLE

°C	°F	°C	°F	°C	°F	°C	°F
0	32						
1	34	26	79	51	124	76	169
2	36	27	81	52	126	77	171
3	37	28	82	53	127	78	172
4	39	29	84	54	129	79	174
5	41	30	86	55	131	80	176
6	43	31	88	56	133	81	178
7	45	32	90	57	135	82	180
8	46	33	91	58	136	83	181
9	48	34	93	59	138	84	183
10	50	35	95	60	140	85	185
11	52	36	97	61	142	86	187
12	54	37	99	62	144	87	189
13	55	38	100	63	145	88	190
14	57	39	102	64	147	89	192
15	59	40	104	65	149	90	194
16	61	41	106	66	151	91	196
17	63	42	108	67	153	92	198
18	64	43	109	68	154	93	199
19	66	44	111	69	156	94	201
20	68	45	113	70	158	95	203
21	70	46	115	71	160	96	205
22	72	47	117	72	162	97	207
23	73	48	118	73	163	98	208
24	75	49	120	74	165	99	210
25	77	50	122	75	167	100	212

TABLE 2 □ THE METRIC SYSTEM

Measures of length	10 millimeters (mm) = 1 centimeter (cm) 10 centimeters = 1 decimeter (dm) 10 decimeters = 1 meter (m) 1,000 meters = 1 kilometer (km)
Measures of area	100 square millimeters (mm^2) = 1 square centimeter (cm^2) 100 square centimeters = 1 square decimeter (dm^2) 100 square decimeters = 1 square meter (m^2)
Measures of volume	1,000 cubic millimeters (mm^3) = 1 cubic centimeter (cm^3 or cc) 1,000 cubic centimeters = 1 cubic decimeter (dm^3) 1,000 cubic decimeters = 1 cubic meter (m^3)
Measures of liquid volume	1,000 milliliters (ml) = 1 liter (l) Note that 1 cubic centimeter of volume is approximately equal to 1 ml of liquid volume; 1 ml of water weighs approximately 1 gram (g).
Measures of mass	1,000 milligrams (mg) = 1 gram 1,000 grams = 1 kilogram (kg) 1,000 kilograms = 1 metric ton

TABLE 3 □ BASIC METRIC UNITS, THEIR ABBREVIATIONS, AND EQUIVALENTS IN IMPERIAL UNITS

Measure	Metric unit	Abbreviation	Equivalent in Imperial measure
Length	Meter	m	39.37 inches
Volume	Liter	l	1.06 quarts
Mass	Gram	g	0.035 ounce
Weight or force	Newton	n	0.224 pound
Temperature	Degree Celsius	°C	1.8 degrees Fahrenheit
Heat	Calorie	c or cal	0.004 British Thermal Unit (BTU)

APPENDIX C

where do we go from here?

sources for more ideas and activities

SOURCES FOR COURSE AND CURRICULUM IMPROVEMENT PROJECTS

Biological Sciences Curriculum Study Company, Box 930, Boulder, CO 80302

HUMAN SCIENCES PROGRAM (HSP) 1971. William V. Mayer.

Center for Educational Research, 51 Press Building, New York University, 32 Washington Place, New York, NY 10003

CONCEPTUALLY ORIENTED PROGRAM IN ELEMENTARY SCIENCE (COPES) 1967–1973. Morris H. Shamos, Department of Physics, New York University, 4 Washington Place, New York, NY 10003

Curriculum Development Associates, Inc., 1211 Connecticut Avenue NW, Washington, DC 20036

MAN: A COURSE OF STUDY (MACOS) 1963–1970. Peter B. Dow, Education Development Center, Inc., 15 Mifflin Place, Cambridge, MA 02138

Curriculum Laboratory, University of Illinois, 1210 Springfield Avenue, Urbana, IL 61801

MADISON MATHEMATICS PROJECT (MADM) 1961–1973. Robert B. Davis.

Education Development Center, 55 Chapel Street, Newton, MA 02160

THE ARITHMETIC PROJECT 1965–1970. David A. Page, Mathematics Department, University of Illinois at Chicago Circle, Box 4348, Chicago, IL 60680

EARLY CHILDHOOD EDUCATION STUDY

Building a Playground, 1970.

Building with Tires, 1971.

Building with Tubes, 1970.

Moments in Learning, 1968.

A Useful List of Classroom Items That Can Be Scrounged or Purchased, 1971.

UNIFIED SCIENCE AND MATHEMATICS IN THE ELEMENTARY SCHOOL (USMES)

The Complete USMES School Library, 1975.

The USMES Design Lab, 1974.

The USMES Guide, 1974.

Teacher resource books, 1974: *Burglar Alarm Designs, Consumer Research Product Testing, Describing People, Designing for Human Proportions, Dice Design, Electromagnetic Device Design, Lunch Lines, Pedestrian Crossings, Play Area Design and Use, Soft Drink Design, Traffic Flow,* and *Weather Predictions.*

Arranging the Informal Classroom, 1973, by Brenda S. Engel.

A Bibliography of Open Education, 1971, by Roland S. Barth and Charles H. Rathbone.

Children's Literature: A Bibliography, 1972.

A Classroom for Young Children: Approximation No. 1, 1966, by Allan Leitman and Edith H. F. Churchill.

Infant School, 1969, by Courtney B. Cazden.

An Interview with Bruce Whitmore, 1969.

An Interview with Dorothy Welch, 1969.

An Interview with Pat Hourihan, 1971.

Environmental Studies for Urban Youth, Evergreen State College, Olympia, WA 98505

ENVIRONMENTAL STUDIES FOR URBAN YOUTH (ES) 1970. Richard R. Sluss.

Ginn and Company, Xerox Education Group Distribution Center, 555 Gotham Parkway, Carlstadt, NJ 07072

SCIENCE — A PROCESS APPROACH (SAPA) Commission on Science Education, 1962–1971.

Harper and Row, Inc., Elementary and High School Division, 2500 Crawford Avenue, Evanston, IL 60201

ELEMENTARY SCHOOL SCIENCE PROJECT (ESSP) 1960–1969. J. Myron Atkin, College of Education, and Stanley P. Wyatt, Department of Astronomy, University of Illinois, Urbana, IL 61801.

D. C. Heath and Company, 285 Columbus Avenue, Boston, MA 02116

UNIVERSITY OF ILLINOIS COMMITTEE ON SCHOOL MATHEMATICS (UICSM) 1962–1971. Russell E. Zwoyer, University of Illinois Curriculum Laboratory, 1210 West Springfield, Urbana, IL 61801

Houghton Mifflin Company, One Beacon Street, Boston, MA 02108

INVESTIGATING THE EARTH: EARTH SCIENCE CURRICULUM PROJECT (ESCP) 1963–1973. William D. Romey, Box 1559, Boulder, CO 80302

Hubbard Scientific Company, PO Box 105, Northbrook, IL 60002

BIOLOGICAL SCIENCES CURRICULUM STUDY (BSCS) 1972–1976.

Life sciences for the educable mentally handicapped.

Imperial International Learning, Kankakee, IL 60901

INDIVIDUALIZED SCIENCE 1968–1972. Leo Klopfer et al. University of Pittsburgh, College of Education, Pittsburgh, PA

Institute for Mathematical Studies in the Social Sciences, Stanford University, Stanford, CA 94305

EXPERIMENTAL TEACHING OF MATHEMATICS IN THE ELEMENTARY SCHOOL 1959–1971. Patrick Suppes.

ISIS Headquarters, 415 North Monroe Street, Tallahassee, FL 32301

INDIVIDUALIZED SCIENCE INSTRUCTIONAL SYSTEM (ISIS) 1972–. Ernest Burkman, Florida State University, Tallahassee, FL 32306

J. B. Lippincott Company, East Washington Square, Philadelphia, PA 19105

BSCS ELEMENTARY SCHOOL SCIENCE PROGRAM 1975 (grades 4–6); 1978 (grades K–3).

Lawrence Hall of Science, University of California, Berkeley, CA 94720

OUTDOOR BIOLOGY INSTRUCTIONAL STRATEGIES (OBIS) 1972–. Watson M. Laetsch.

OBIS Trial Editions; Outdoor Biology Instructional Strategies.

SCIENCE CURRICULUM IMPROVEMENT STUDY (SCIS)

SCIS Evaluation Supplements for *Communities, Ecosystems, Electric and Magnetic Interactions, Energy Sources, Environments, Interaction and Systems, Life Cycles, Material Objects,*

Populations, Relative Position and Motion, Organisms, and *Subsystems and Variables*.

SCIS Omnibus (a collection of Readings from 1962–1973 related to SCIS), 1973.

SCIS Teacher's Handbook, 1974.

Teacher's Guide for Science for Kindergarten, 1974.

McGraw-Hill Book Company, Webster Division, 1221 Avenue of the Americas, New York, NY 10020

ELEMENTARY SCIENCE STUDY (ESS) 1962–1973. Joseph Griffith, Education Development Center, 55 Chapel Street, Newton, MA 02160

The ESS Reader, 1970.

A Materials Book for the Elementary Science Study, 1972.

TIME, SPACE, AND MATTER: SECONDARY SCHOOL SCIENCE PROJECT (TSM) 1963–1972. George J. Pallrand, Science Education Center, Rutgers, The State University, New Brunswick, NJ 08903.

McGraw-Hill-Ryerson Ltd., Toronto, Canada

ELEMENTARY SCIENCE CURRICULUM STUDY (ESCS). Robert K. Crocker.

ESCS Teaching Guide, Volume 1 (grades 1–3), 1973.

ESCS Teaching Guide, Volume 2 (grades 4–6), 1973.

Bicycles to Beaches, 1972, by W. Gillespie et al.

Broadway to Boot Hill, 1974, by W. Gillespie et al.

National Association of Geology Teachers, Department of Earth Sciences, Southeast Missouri State University, Cape Girardeau, MO 63701

CRUSTAL EVOLUTION EDUCATION PROJECT 1976–80. Edward C. Stoever, Jr.

Prentice-Hall, Inc., Englewood Cliffs, NJ 07632

INTRODUCTORY PHYSICAL SCIENCE (IPS) 1963–1969. Uri Haber-Schaim, Education Development Center, Inc., 55 Chapel Street, Newton, MA 02160

Project on Elementary School Mathematics and Science, c/o Peter B. Shoreman, College of Education, University of Illinois, Urbana, IL 61801

PROJECT ON ELEMENTARY SCHOOL MATHEMATICS AND SCIENCE (PESMS) 1969–1973.

Rand-McNally and Company, Box 7600, Chicago, IL 60680

SCIENCE CURRICULUM IMPROVEMENT STUDY (SCIS)

Teacher's guides for 12 booklets; pupil activity books.

W. B. Saunders Company, West Washington Square, Philadelphia, PA 19105

MINNESOTA SCHOOL OF MATHEMATICS AND SCIENCE PROJECT (MINNEMAST) 1961–1970. James H. Werntz, Jr., University of Minnesota, Minnesota School of Mathematics and Science Center, 720 Washington Avenue SE, Minneapolis, MN 55455

School Mathematics Study Group, c/o E. G. Begle, School of Education, Stanford University, Stanford, CA 94305

SCHOOL MATHEMATICS STUDY GROUP (SMSG) 1958–1972.

Silver Burdett Company, Morristown, NJ 07960

NATIONAL ENVIRONMENTAL EDUCATION DEVELOPMENT PROGRAM

(NEED), Educational Challenges, Inc., Silver Burdett General Learning Corporation.

PROBING THE NATURAL WORLD: INTERMEDIATE SCIENCE CURRICULUM STUDY (ISCS) 1969–. David Redfield and William R. Snyder, Florida State University, Tallahassee, FL 32306

Level III minicourses for the middle grades (6 and up) including a teacher's edition, a student record book, and a master set of equipment: *Crusty Problems, Environmental Science, Investigating Variation, In Orbit, Well-Being, What's Up? Why You're You,* and *Winds and Weather.*

SOURCES FOR LEARNING CENTER IDEAS

Addison-Wesley Publishing Company, Inc., Sand Hill Road, Menlo Park, CA 95025
Developmental math cards.

Allyn and Bacon, Inc., 470 Atlantic Avenue, Boston, MA 02210
Investigate and Discover: Elementary Science Lessons, 1975, by Robert B. Sund, Bill W. Tillery, and Leslie W. Trowbridge.
Involving Students in Questioning, 1976, by Francis P. Hunkins.

Tunis Baker, 650 Concord Drive, Holland, MI 49423
Baker Science Packets.

Contemporary Ideas, Box 1703, Los Gatos, CA 95030
Math activities, books, and assorted math game packets.

Creative Publications, Box 328, Palo Alto, CA 94320
Creative math activities.

CTM Publishing Company, Box 1513, Sunnyvale, CA 95088
Learning Center Guide, 1972, by Barbara Guiske and Bernard T. Cote.

Dell Publishing Company, 750 Third Avenue, New York, NY 10017
Big Rock Candy Mountain, 1971, edited by Samuel Yanes and Cia Holdorf.

Educational Resources Information Center (ERIC) for Science, Mathematics, and Environmental Education, 1800 Cannon Drive, 400 Lincoln Tower, Ohio State University, Columbus, OH 43210
100 Teaching Activities on Environmental Education, 1974, by John H. Wheatley and Herbert L. Coon.

ERIC Clearinghouse on Early Childhood Education, 805 West Pennsylvania Avenue, Urbana, IL 61801
Opening up the Classroom: A Walk Around the School, 1971, by Sylvia Hucklesby.

Educational Service, Inc., Box 219, Stevensville, MI 49127
Nine elementary teacher's aid books with excellent ideas.

Fearon Publishers, 6 Davis Drive, Palo Alto, CA 94002
Preparing Instructional Objectives, 1962, by Robert F. Mager.

Follett Publishing Company, 1010 West Washington Boulevard, Chicago, IL 60607
Individualizing Instruction and Keeping Your Sanity, 1973, by William M. Bechtol.
Junior activity books.

page 373

Garrard Publishing Company, 1607 North Market Street, Champaign, IL 61920

Reading games and language arts activities.

Harcourt Brace Jovanovich, Inc., 757 Third Avenue, New York, NY 10017

Teaching Elementary Science Through Investigation and Colloquium, 1971, by Brenda Landsdown, Paul E. Blackwood, and Paul F. Brandwein.

Harper and Row, Inc., 10 East 53rd Street, New York, NY 10022

Classroom Questions: What Kinds? 1966, by Norris M. Sanders.

Highlights for Children, 2300 West Fifth Avenue, Columbus, OH 43216

Fun/do packs containing a variety of activities.

Holt, Rinehart, and Winston, Inc., 383 Madison Avenue, New York, NY 10017

Environmental Education in the Elementary School, 1972, by Larry L. Sale and Ernest W. Lee.

Teachers, Children, and Things: Materials-Centered Science, 1971, by Clifford J. Anastasion.

Ideal School Supply Company, 11002 South Lavergne Avenue, Oak Lawn, IL 60453

Laminated crossword puzzles, magic cards, and number puzzles.

Incentive Publishing Company, Box 12522, Nashville, TN 37212

Center Stuff for Nooks, Crannies, and Corners: Complete Learning Centers for the Elementary Classroom, 1973, by Imogene Forte et al.

Cornering Creative Writing: Learning Centers, Games, Activities, and Ideas for the Elementary Classroom, 1973, by Imogene Forte et al.

Creative Math Experiences for the Young Child, 1973, by Imogene Forte and Joy MacKenzie.

Creative Science Experiences for the Young Child, 1973, by Imogene Forte and Joy MacKenzie.

Nooks, Crannies, and Corners: Learning Centers for Creative Classrooms, 1972, by Imogene Forte et al.

Individualized Books Publishing Company, Box 591, Menlo Park, CA 94025

Individualize with Learning Station Themes, 1973, by Lorraine Godfrey.

Individualizing Through Learning Stations, 1972, by Lorraine Godfrey.

Instructor Publications, Inc., Dansville, NY 14437

Metric Measurement Activities and Bulletin Boards, 1973, by Cecil R. Trueblood.

Marie's Educational Materials, 195 South Murphy Avenue, Sunnyvale, CA 94086

Variety of reading and math aids.

Charles E. Merrill Publishing Company, 1300 Alum Creek Drive, Columbus, OH 43216

Behavioral Objectives and Evaluational Measures, Science and Mathematics, 1972, by Robert B. Sund and Anthony J. Picard.

Mind/Matter Corporation, Box 345, Danbury, CT 06810
Excellent manipulative and motivational materials.
National Aeronautics and Space Administration (NASA), Educational Publications, Washington, DC 20546
National Science Teachers Association, 1742 Connecticut Avenue NW, Washington, DC 20009
"Outstanding Science Trade Books for Children," *Science and Children.*
Metric Exercises: Lively Activities on Length, Weight, Volume, and Temperature, 1973. Stock #471–14664.
Elementary Science Packets on the following topics: Drug Education; Environmental Education — I. Environmental Education — II. Measurement and the Metric System; Multidisciplines.
Parker Publishing Company, West Nyack, NY 10994
Individualized Techniques for Teaching Earth Sciences, 1975, by Joseph D. Exline.
Outdoor Science for the Elementary Grades, 1972, by John H. Rosengren.
Pawnee Publishing Company, 1 Pondfield Road, Bronxville, NY 10708
Investigating Air, Land, and Water Pollution, 1971, by Diane Storin.
Prentice-Hall, Inc., Englewood Cliffs, NJ 07632
Classroom Instructional Tactics, 1973, by W. James Popham and Eva L. Baker.
Developing Teacher Competencies, 1971, edited by James E. Weigand.
Evaluating Instruction, 1973, by W. James Popham.
Teachers College Press, Columbia University, 1234 Amsterdam Avenue, New York, NY 10027
The Experience of Science: A New Perspective for Laboratory Teaching, 1976, by O. Roger Anderson.
Teachers Exchange of San Francisco, 600 35th Avenue, San Francisco, CA 94121
Excellent math task cards and a variety of other materials.
U.S. Department of the Interior, Bureau of Land Management, Washington, DC 20240
All Around You: An Environmental Study Guide, 1971, Superintendent of Documents, Stock #2411–0043.

PERIODICALS

Learning. 1255 Portland Place, Boulder, CO 80302
School Science and Mathematics. School Science and Mathematics Association, Lewis House, PO Box 1614, Indiana University of Pennsylvania, Indiana, PA 15701
Science Activities. 400 Albemarle Street NW, Washington, DC
Science and Children. National Science Teachers Association, 1742 Connecticut Avenue NW, Washington, DC 20009
Science Education. John Wiley and Sons, 605 Third Avenue, New York, NY 10016

Science Teacher. National Science Teachers Association, 1742 Connecticut Avenue, NW, Washington, DC 20009

BOOKS

A Child's Garden: A Guide for Parents and Teachers, 1972, Chevron Chemical Company, Public Relations, 200 Bush Street, San Francisco, CA 94120

Children and Science, 1975, by David P. Butts, and Gene E. Hall. Prentice-Hall, Inc., Englewood Cliffs, NJ 07632

City Planning: The Games of Human Settlement, 1975, by Forrest Wilson. Van Nostrand Reinhold Company, 450 West 33rd Street, New York, NY 10001

Creative Activities Resource Book for Elementary School Teachers, 1978, by Thomas Turner. Reston Publishing Company, Reston, VA 22090

Early Childhood Curriculum: A Piaget Program, 1970, by Celia Stendler Lavatelli. American Science and Engineering, Inc., 20 Overland Street, Boston, MA 02215

Energy Environment Source Book, 1975, by John M. Fowler. National Science Teachers Association, 1742 Connecticut Avenue NW, Washington, DC 20009

Energy: Historical Development of the Concepts, 1975, by R. Bruce Lindsay. Dowden, Hutchinson and Ross, Box 699, Stroudsburg, PA 18360

Energy: Resource, Slave, Pollutant, 1975, by Robert Rouse and Robert O. Smith. Macmillan, Inc., 866 Third Ave., New York, NY 10022

Energy: The Continuing Crisis, 1977, by Norman Metzger. Crowell Press, New York, NY

Energy: The Solar Prospect, 1977, by Denis Hayes. Worldwatch Institute, 1776 Massachusetts Avenue NW, Washington, DC

Errors in Experimentation, 1977, by Carl W. Hall. Matrix Publishers, Champaign, IL 61820

Evolutionary Ecology, 1978, by Erik R. Pianka. Harper and Row, Inc., 10 East 53rd Street, New York, NY 10022

Games for the Science Classroom, 1977, by Paul B. Hounshell and Ira Trollinger. National Science Teachers Association, 1742 Connecticut Avenue NW, Washington, DC 20009

How Children Learn Science: Conceptual Development and Implications for Teaching, 1977, by Ronald G. Good. Macmillan, Inc., 866 Third Avenue, New York, NY 10022

Living: An Attitude of Imagination, 1976, by Pam Early. Kendall/Hunt Publishing Company, Dubuque, Iowa 52001

Living with Energy, 1978, by Robert Alves. Viking Press, 625 Madison Avenue, New York, NY 10022

Magic, Science and Civilization, 1978, by Jacob Bronowski. Columbia University Press, 562 West 113th Street, New York, NY 10025

Making Scientific Toys, 1975, by Carson Ritchie. Nelson Publishing Company, Nashville, TN 37203

On Aesthetics in Science, 1978, by Judith Wechsler. MIT Press, 28
  Carleton Street, Cambridge, MA 02142
New UNESCO Source Book for Science Teaching, 1973. UNIPUB,
  Inc., 650 First Avenue, New York, NY 10017
Principles of Three-Dimensional Design, 1977, by Wucius Wong. Van
  Nostrand Reinhold Co., 450 West 33rd St., New York, NY 10001
Progress and Its Problems: Toward a Theory of Scientific Growth,
  1977, by Larry Laudan. University of California Press, 2223 Fulton Street, Berkeley, CA 94720
Quasar, Quasar, Burning Bright, 1978, by Isaac Asimov. Doubleday
  Publishing Company, 245 Park Avenue, New York, NY 10017
Readings in Science Education for the Elementary School, 1975, by
  Edward Victor and Marjorie S. Lerner. Macmillan, Inc., 866
  Third Avenue, New York, NY 10022
Science and Building, 1978, by Henry J. Cowan. Wiley Interscience
  Publications, 605 Third Avenue, New York, NY 10016
Science and Creation in the Middle Ages, 1976, by Nicholas Steneck.
  University of Notre Dame Press, Notre Dame, IN
Science and Immortality, 1977, by William Osler. Arno Press, 330
  Madison Avenue, New York, NY 10017
Science and Its Critics, 1978, by John Arthur Passmore. Rutgers University Press, New Brunswick, NJ 08901
Science and Its Public: The Changing Relationship, 1976, edited by
  Gerald Holton and William A. Blanpied. D. Reidel Publishing
  Company, 306 Dartmouth Street, Boston, MA 02116
Science and Society: Past, Present and Future, 1975, by Nicholas
  Steneck. University of Michigan Press, Ann Arbor, MI 48106
Science as a Human Endeavor, 1978, by George F. Kneller. Columbia
  University Press, 562 West 113th Street, New York, NY 10025
Science Development: Toward the Building of Science in Less Developed Countries, 1975, by Michael J. Morovesik. Indiana University Press, Bloomington, IN 47401
Science Experiences for Young Children, 1975, by Rosemary Althouse
  and Cecil Main. Teachers College Press, 1234 Amsterdam Avenue, New York, NY 10027
Science Experiences for Young Children, 1975, by Viola Carmichael.
  Southern California Association for the Education of Young Children Press, Los Angeles, CA
Science Fair Project Index, 1960–72, 1975, edited by Janet Y. Stoffer.
  Scarecrow Press, 52 Liberty Street, Metuchen, NJ 08840
Science for the Elementary School, 1975, by Edward Victor. Macmillan Inc., 866 Third Avenue, New York, NY 10022
Science Since Babylon, 1975, by Derek De Solla Price. Yale University Press, New Haven, CT 06511
Science, Technology and the Environment, 1975, by John T. Hardy.
  W. B. Saunders Company, West Washington Square, Philadelphia, PA 19105
Science: Who Needs It? 1975, by Ben Bova. Westminster Press, Witherspoon Building, Philadelphia, PA 19107
Sourcebook for Biological Sciences, 1972, by Donald L. Troyer, Maurice G. Kellogg, and Hans O. Andersen. Macmillan, Inc., 866
  Third Avenue, New York, NY 10022

Sourcebook for Earth Sciences and Astronomy, 1972, by Russell O. Utgard, George T. Ladd, and Hans O. Andersen. Macmillan, Inc., 866 Third Avenue, New York, NY 10022

The Ecology of Man: An Ecosystem Approach, 1976, by Robert Leo Smith. Harper and Row, Inc., 10 East 53rd Street, New York, NY 10022

The Game of Science, 3rd ed., 1977, by Garvin McCain and Erwin M. Segal. Wadsworth Publishing Company, Belmont, CA 94002

The Great Perpetual Learning Machine, 1976, by Jim Blake and Barbara Ernst. Little, Brown and Company, 34 Beacon Street, Boston, MA 02106

The Science of Ethics of Equality, 1977, by David Hawkins. Basic Books, 10 East 53rd Street, New York, NY 10022

The Spheres of Life: An Introduction to World Ecology, 1975, by Joseph W. Meeker. Charles Scribner's Sons, 597 Fifth Avenue, New York, NY 10017

Toward One Science: The Convergence of Traditions, 1978, by Paul Snyder. St. Martin's Press, 175 Fifth Avenue, New York, NY 10010

Water Mix Experiments Teacher's Guide: Conceptually Oriented Program in Elementary Science (COPES), 1971. American Science and Engineering, Inc., 20 Overland Street, Boston, MA 02215

Weather Study: An Approach to Scientific Inquiry, 1972, by J. W. Bainbridge and R. W. Stockdale. Methuen Educational Ltd., 11 New Fetter Lane, London EC 4, England.

Will the Real Teacher Please Stand Up? 1972, by Mary Greer and Bonnie Rubenstein. Goodyear Publishing Company, 15115 Sunset Boulevard, Pacific Palisades, CA 90272

for teachers and children

BOOKS

Addison-Wesley Publishing Company, Inc., Reading, MA 01867

Investigating Science with Coins, 1969, by Laurence B. White, Jr.

Investigating Science with Nails, 1969, by Laurence B. White, Jr.

Investigating Science with Paper, 1969, by Laurence B. White, Jr.

Investigating Science with Rubber Bands, 1969, by Laurence B. White, Jr.

Science Games, 1975, by Laurence B. White, Jr.

Science Series for the Young, 1969, by Herbert H. Wong and Matthew F. Vessel. Including *Our Tree, My Ladybug, My Goldfish,* and *Our Terrariums.*

Science Toys, 1975, by Laurence B. White, Jr.

Science Tricks, 1975, by Laurence B. White, Jr.

The Riddle of the Stegosaurus, 1969, by D. C. Ipsen.

What Does a Bee See?, 1971, by D. C. Ipsen.

Animal Care From Protozoa to Small Mammals, 1977, by F. Barbara Orlans.

Science Puzzles, 1975, by Laurence B. White.

American Education Publications, 245 Long Hill Road, Middletown, CT 06457

Clowns, Colors, Corks, and Carrots, 1972, by John F. Mongillo.

Art Education, Inc., Blauvelt, NY 10913

100 Ways to Have Fun with an Alligator and 100 Other Involving Art Projects, 1969, by Norman Laliberte and Richey Kehl.

Atheneum Publishers, 122 East 42nd Street, New York, NY 10017

What Is It Really Like Out There? Objective Knowing, 1977, by Thomas Moorman.

Belwin-Mills Publishing Corporation, 250 Maple Avenue, Rockville Centre, NY 11570

The Sierra Club Survival Songbook, 1971, by Jim Morse and Nancy Mathews.

Marshall Cavendish Corporation, 110 East 54th Street, New York, NY 10022

The Illustrated Encyclopedia of Science and Technology: How It Works, 1977.

Creative Publications, Inc., Box 10328, Palo Alto, CA 94303

Georule Activities, 1971, by Ernest R. Ranucci.

Pattern Blocks Coloring Books, 1974, by Linda Silvey and Marion Pasternack.

Pic-a-Puzzle, 1970, by Reuben A. Schadler and Dale G. Seymour.

String Sculpture, 1972, by John Winter.

Thomas Y. Crowell Company, 10 East 53rd Street, New York, NY 10022

Curiosities of the Cube, 1977, by Ernest R. Ranucci and Wilma E. Rollins.

John Day Company, 666 Fifth Avenue, New York, NY 10019

Food, 1977, by Irving Adler.

Dodd, Mead and Company, 79 Madison Avenue, New York, NY 10016

How to Build a Better Mousetrap Car — And Other Experimental Science Fun, 1977, by Al G. Renner.

Doubleday and Company, 245 Park Avenue, New York, NY 10017

More Brain Boosters, 1975, by David Webster.

More Brain Boosters, with photos, 1975, by David Webster.

Dover Publications, 180 Varick Street, New York, NY 10014

Soap-Bubbles, 1959, by C. V. Boys.

M. Evans and Company, 216 East 49th Street, New York, NY 10017

The Good Drug and the Bad Drug, 1970, by John S. Mars, M.D.

Farallones Designs, Star Route, Point Reyes Station, CA 94956

Making Places, Changing Spaces in Schools, at Home, and Within Ourselves, 1971.

Garrard Publishing Company, 1607 North Market Street, Champaign, IL 61820

Exploring Fields and Lots: Easy Science Projects, 1978, by Seymour Simon.

Grosset and Dunlap, 51 Madison Avenue, New York, NY 10010

"Wonder Starters." Including *Bees, Clothes, Dinosaurs, Eggs, Fire, Hair, Homes, Milk, Rain, Sleep, Teeth,* and *Telephone.*

Houghton Mifflin Company, One Beacon Street, Boston, MA 02108

Recyclopedia: Games, Science Equipment, and Crafts from Recycled Materials, 1976, Robin Simons.

Kids Are Natural Cooks: Child-Tested Recipes for Home and School Using Natural Foods, 1972, by Parents' Nursery School.

Little, Brown and Company, 34 Beacon Street, Boston, MA 02106

I Saw a Purple Cow and 100 Other Recipes for Learning, 1972, by Ann Cole.

McDonald's Ecology Action Pack, 1973, PO Box 2344, Ketting, OH 45429

McGraw-Hill Book Company, 330 West 42nd Street, New York, NY 10036

Colourweeples, 1972, by D. Craig Gillespie.

Weeple People, 1972, by D. Craig Gillespie.

McGraw-Hill Dictionary of the Life Sciences, 1976, edited by Daniel Lapedes.

Mira Math Company, PO Box 625, Station B, Willowdale, Ontario, MZK 2PQ, Canada

Mira Math Activities for the Elementary School, 1973.

Mira Math Activities for High School, 1973.

C. V. Mosby Company, St. Louis, MO 63141

Earth in Crisis: An Introduction to the Earth Sciences, 1976, by Thomas L. Burns and Herbert J. Spiegel.

Jeffrey Norton Publishers, 145 East 49th Street, New York, NY 10017

Deal Me In! The Use of Playing Cards in Teaching and Learning, 1973, by Margie Golick.

Parker Publishing Company, West Nyack, NY 10994

Illustrated Treasury of General Science Activities, 1975, by Robert G. Hoehn.

Prentice-Hall, Inc., Englewood Cliffs, NJ 07632

The Centering Book — Awareness Activities for Children, Parents, and Teachers, 1975, by Gay Hendricks.

Experiments with Everyday Objects, 1978, by Kevin Goldstein-Jackson, Norman Rudnick, and Ronald Hyman.

Paper, Pencils and Pennies: Games for Learning and Having Fun, 1977, by Ronald T. Hyman.

Random House, 201 East 50th Street, New York, NY 10022

Charlie Brown's Second Super Book of Questions and Answers about the Earth and Space, 1977.

Scholastic Book Services, Four Winds Press, 50 West 44th Street, New York, NY 10036

Just a Box, 1973, by Goldie Taub Chernoff.

Music and Instruments for Children to Make, 1972, by John Hawkinson and Martha Faulhaker.

Pebbles and Pods, 1972, by Goldie Taub Chernoff.

Play with Paper, 1973, by Thea Bank-Jensen.

Sheed and Ward, Inc., 6700 Squibb Road, Mission, KS 66202

Sneaky Feats: The Art of Showing Off and 53 Ways to Do It, 1975, Tom Ferrell and Lee Eisenberg.

Simon and Schuster, Rockefeller Center, 630 Fifth Avenue, New York, NY 10020

The Great International Paper Airplane Book, 1967, by Jerry Mander et al.

Performing Plants, 1969, by Ware T. Budlong.

Troubador Press, 126 Folsom Street, San Francisco, CA 94105

Geometric Playthings to Color, Cut and Fold, 1973, by Jean J. Pedusen and Kent A. Pedusen.

University of California Press, 2223 Fulton Street, Berkeley, CA 94720

Great Scientists Speak Again, 1975, by Richard M. Eakin.

Van Nostrand Reinhold Company, 450 West 33rd Street, New York, NY 10001

The Collector's Guide to Rocks and Minerals, 1975, by James R. Tindall and Roger Thornhill.

Van Nostrand's Scientific Encyclopedia, 1976, edited by Douglas Considine.

Wayne County Intermediate School District, 1610 Kales Building, Detroit, MI 48226

Suggestions for Getting in Touch with Me and You and Us: For Elementary Teachers and Children, Drug Abuse Reduction Through Education, 1972.

Winston Press, Inc., 25 Groveland Terrace, Minneapolis, MN 55043

Examining Your Environment series, 1972–1974, by J. Kenneth Couchman, John C. MacBean, Adam Stecher, and Daniel F. Wentworth. Includes *Astronomy, Birds, The Dandelion, Ecology, Mapping Small Places, Miniclimates, Pollution, Running Water, Small Creatures, Snow and Ice, Trees,* and *Your Senses.*

for children

BOOKS

Abelard-Schuman, 666 Fifth Avenue, New York, NY 10019

The Continental Shelves, 1975, by John F. Waters.

Atheneum Publishers, 122 East 42nd Street, New York, NY 10017

More About What Plants Do, 1975, by Joan Elma Rahn.

Bantam Books, Inc., 666 Fifth Avenue, NY 10019

The Lives of a Cell: Notes of a Biology Watcher, 1975, by Lewis Thomas.

Bobbs-Merrill Company, 4300 West 62nd Street, Indianapolis, IN 46206

The Creation of the Universe, 1977, by David E. Fisher.

Children's Press, 1224 West Van Buren Street, Chicago, IL 60607

What Will It Be? 1976, Jane Belk Moncure.

Wind Is Air: A Concept Book, 1975, by Mary Brewer.

Coward, McCann and Geoghegan, 200 Madison Avenue, New York, NY 10016

Fitting In: Animals in Their Habitats, 1976, by Gilda and Melvin Berger.

Thomas Y. Crowell Company, 666 Fifth Avenue, New York, NY 10019

Think Metric, 1973, by Franklyn M. Branley.

Anno's Counting Book (The World of Numbers), 1977, by Mitsumasa Anno. Ages 4–10.

Black Holes, White Dwarfs and Superstars, 1976, by Franklin M. Branley.

Cancer, rev. ed., 1977, by Alvin and Virginia Silverstein. Ages 8 and up.

Caves, 1977, by Roma Gans. Ages 4–8.

Corals, 1976, by Lili Ronai.

Energy from the Sun, 1976, by Melvin Berger. Ages 4–8.

How Life Began, 1977, by Irving Adler. Ages 12 and up.

How Little and How Much: A Book About Scales, 1976, by Franklyn M. Branley.

Hunger on Planet Earth, 1977, by Jules Archer. Ages 12 and up.

Little Dinosaurs and Early Birds, 1977, by John Kaufmann. Ages 4–8.

Living Together in Tomorrow's World, 1976, by Jane Werner Watson.

The March of the Lemmings, 1976, by James Newton. Ages 4–8.

Medical Center Lab (Scientists at Work Series), 1976, by Melvin Berger. Ages 8 and up.

Shells Are Skeletons, 1977, by Joan Berg Victor. Ages 4–8.

The Sunlit Sea, 1976, by Augusta Goldin.

A Walk in the Forest — The Woodlands of North America, 1977, by Albert List, Jr., and Ilka List. Ages 10 and up.

Wild and Woolly Mammoths, 1977, by Aliki. Ages 4–8.

Crown Publishers, One Park Avenue, New York, NY 10016

A January Fog Will Freeze a Hog and Other Weather Folklore, 1977, edited by Hubert Davis.

John Day Company, 666 Fifth Avenue, NY 10019

Environment, 1976, by Irving Adler.

Petroleum: Gas, Oil and Asphalt, 1975, by Irving Adler.

Dodd, Mead and Company, 79 Madison Avenue, New York, NY 10016

Harness the Wind: The Story of Windmills, 1977, by Joseph E. Brown and Anne Ensign Brown.

What Does a Geologist Do? 1977, by R. V. Fodor.

The World of the Woodlot, 1975, by Thomas Fegely.

Drake Publishers, 801 Second Avenue, New York, NY 10017

The Weekend Fossil Hunter, 1977, by Jerry C. LaPlante.

Four Winds Press, 50 West 44th Street, New York, NY 10036

Death Is Natural, 1977, by Laurence Pringle.

Harper and Row, Inc., 10 East 53rd Street, New York, NY 10022

Elephant Seal Island, 1978, Evelyn Shaw.

A Nest of Wood Ducks, 1978, by Evelyn Shaw.

Holiday House Inc., 18 East 53rd Street, New York, NY 10022

The Cloud Book, 1975, by Tomie De Paola.

Living Together in Nature: How Symbiosis Works, 1977, by Jane E. Hartman.

The Quicksand Book, 1977, by Tomie De Paola.

J. B. Lippincott Company, East Washington Square, Philadelphia, PA 19105

Space Monsters: From Movies, TV and Books, 1977, by Seymour Simon.

Lothrop, Lee and Shepard Company, 105 Madison Avenue, New York, NY 10016

Alpha Centaur: The Nearest Star, 1976, by Isaac Asimov.

Macmillan, Inc., 866 Third Avenue, New York, NY 10022

The Air of Mars and Other Stories of Time and Place, 1976, edited by Mirra Ginsburg.

Evening Gray, Morning Red: A Handbook of American Weather Wisdom, 1976, by Barbara Wolff.

The Hidden World: Life under a Rock, 1977, by Laurence Pringle.

McGraw-Hill Book Company, 1221 Avenue of the Americas, New York, NY 10020

Science Fun for You in a Minute or Two, 1975, by Herman Schneider.

Science Fun with a Flashlight, 1975, by Herman and Nina Schneider.

William Morrow and Company, 105 Madison Avenue, New York, NY 10016

Valleys, 1976, by Della Geotz.

What Makes a Lemon Sour? 1977, by Gail Kay Haines.

Parents' Magazine Press, 52 Vanderbilt Avenue, New York, NY 10017

How Heredity Works, 1975, by Jeanne Bendick.

Penguin Books, Harmondsworth, England

The Penguin Book of the Physical World, 1976, edited by Sonia Larkin and Louis Bernbaum.

G. P. Putnam's Sons, 200 Madison Avenue, New York, NY 10016

Colonizing Space, 1978, by Erik Bergaust.

I Was Born in a Tree and Raised by Bees, 1977, by Jim Arnosky.

Random House, 201 East 50th Street, New York, NY 10022

The Berenstain Bears' Science Fair, 1977, by Stanley Berenstain.

Sterling Publishing Company, 419 Park Avenue South, New York, NY 10016

Discover the Trees, 1977, by Jerry Cowle.

Van Nostrand Reinhold Books, 120 Alexander Street, Princeton, NJ 08450

The Art of Light and Color, 1972, by Tom Douglas Jones.

Building with Balsa Wood, 1965, by John Lidstone.

Building with Cardboard, 1968, by John Lidstone.

Building with Wire, 1972, by John Lidstone.

How to Be a Scientist at Home, 1971, by John Tuey and David Wickers.

How to Find Out About Zoo Animals, 1972, by Barrington Barber and John Eason.

How to Make and Fly Kites, 1972, by Eve Barwell and Conrad Bailey.

How to Make Things Grow, 1972, by David Wickers and John Tuey.

How to Make Your Own Kinetics, 1972, by David Wickers and Sharon Finmark.

New Math Puzzle Book, 1969, by L. H. Longley-Cook.
Photography Without a Camera, 1972, by Patra Holter.
Small Motors You Can Make, 1963, by John Michel.
Teaching Film Animation, 1971, by Yvonne Anderson.
Walker Press, 720 Fifth Avenue, New York, NY 10019
The California Iceberg, 1975, by Harry Harrison.
Franklin Watts, Inc., 730 Fifth Avenue, New York, NY 10019
Coal, 1976, by Betsy Harvey Kraft.
Western Publishing Company, 1220 Mound Avenue, Racine, WI 53404
I Like to See (A Book About the Five Senses), 1973, by Jane Tymms.

index

See also the Alternate Table of Contents and Appendix A, which classify activities by skills and subject areas.